CW00394353

GCSE SOCIAL SCIENCE

Ann Cotterrell Anthony Russell

HEINEMANN EDUCATIONAL BOOKS

Heinemann Educational Books Ltd
Halley Court, Jordan Hill, Oxford OX2 8EJ

OXFORD LONDON EDINBURGH
MELBOURNE SYDNEY AUCKLAND
SINGAPORE MADRID
IBADAN NAIROBI GABORONE HARARE
KINGSTON PORTSMOUTH (NH)

ISBN 0 435 46199 0

© Ann Cotterrell and Anthony Russell 1988

First published 1988

British Library Cataloguing in Publication Data

Cotterrell, Ann
    GCSE social science.
    1. Social sciences – For schools
    I. Title II. Russell, Anthony, 1939-
    300
                                Jun 88
    ISBN 0-435-46199-0

Designed and produced by the
Pen and Ink Book Company Ltd, Huntingdon,
Cambridgeshire

Illustrated by DMD, Gecko Ltd, Maureen and Gordon
Gray and Sally Launder

Cartoons by Dave Parkins

Printed in Great Britain by Thomson Litho Ltd,
East Kilbride, Scotland

The authors and publishers would like to thank the following for
permission to reproduce photographs on the pages indicated:

Barnaby's Picture Library: pp. 30 (top) and 50; BBC Hulton Picture
Library: pp. 101 and 104; Camera Press/Snowdon: p. 17 (lower); John
Cole/Network: pp. 53 (upper left) and 122; The Commission of the
European Communities: p. 141; Mark Edwards/Panos Pictures: p. 86;
Ford Motor Co.: p. 89; Sheila Gray/Network: pp. 124 and 144 (top);
Greater London Photograph Library: p. 94 (top); Sally and Richard
Greenhill: pp. 6, 15, 19 (left and right), 22 (middle), 25, 32, 44, 46 (top),
50, 57, 64 (lower), 65, 74, 106 and 144 (lower); Tom Hanley: p. 128;
Roger Hutchings/Network: p. 115; Intermediate Technology: p. 142;
Roshini Kempadoo/Format: p. 36; Barry Lewis/Network: pp. 19
(middle) and 137; London Docklands Development Corporation: p.95;
Ian MacQuillin: pp. 112 and 149 (lower); Manor Bakeries Ltd: p. 8;
Jenny Matthews/Format: p. 43 (middle); Museum in Docklands Project:
p. 94 (middle); Nissan Motor Co. Ltd.: p. 143; Joanne O'Brien/Format:
pp. 43 (top); Raissa Page/Format: pp. 50 and 64 (middle); Picture Bank
Photo Library Ltd.: pp. 17 and 87; Popperfoto: pp. 22 (lower), 23 (top),
43 (lower), 53 (Figs. 2 and 3), 116 and 147; Port of London Authority:
p.94 (lower); Brenda Prince/Format: p. 28; Rex Features: p. 64 (top);
Carlos Reyes/Andes Press Agency: pp. 22 (top), 26, 38 (top), 50 and 145;
Laurie Sparham/Network: pp. 23 (lower) and 111; John Sturrock/
Network: pp. 77, 85, 98, 130 and 135; Topham Picture Library: pp. 50,
141 (right) and 149 (top); Janine Wiedel Photo Library: pp. 38 (lower), 46
(lower) and 50; Val Wilmer/Format: p. 30 (lower).

The authors and publishers also wish to thank the following for
permission to reproduce copyright material on the pages indicated:

Cambridge University Press for the table on p. 41; The *Daily Telegraph*
for the article on p. 111; Gower Publishing for the tables on pp. 9, 110
and 124; The *Guardian* for the article on p. 111; The Controller, Her
Majesty's Stationery Office, for Crown Copyright material on pp. 12, 13,
27, 37, 44, 48, 49, 58, 59, 60, 69, 73, 76, 79, 84, 85, 90, 91, 93, 97, 118,
135, 138, 151; *Lancashire Evening Telegraph* for the newspaper article on
p. 139; F. H. McClintock for the table on p. 148; *Mirror Group
Newspapers (1986) Ltd* for the diagram on p. 81; *New Society* for the table
on p. 39; Oxford University Press for material on pp. 36 and 150;
Penguin Books for the table on p. 62; Pergamon Press for material on
p. 125; Times Newspapers for the newspaper article on p. 12; *The
Washington Post* for the newspaper article on p. 79; *Yellow Advertiser* for
the newspaper article on p. 71.

Cover photographs (left to right) by: Sally and Richard Greenhill,
Barnaby's Picture Library and W.H. Smith & Sons Ltd.

ACKNOWLEDGEMENTS

Ann Cotterrell wishes to acknowledge the helpful comments on Section 9 made by Dr David Whitehead of the
University of London Institute of Education. She also
wishes to acknowledge the support and many useful
criticisms and comments on her sections provided by
Roger Cotterrell, and the support and advice of David and
Linda.

Both authors wish to thank Janice Brown of Heinemann
Educational Books for her encouragement and co-
ordination of this project.

CONTENTS

PREFACE

We began this book with the assumption that the new national criteria for social sciences had made all previous textbooks obsolete. The book was therefore designed from the beginning to meet the aims of the national criteria, which we saw as promoting in students an awareness, knowledge and understanding of society and its development. We thus aimed to provide the opportunity to analyse social issues and to promote a critical awareness of the social, economic and political arrangements which affect the way people live. We hope to foster an understanding of the methods used in the social sciences and to develop the ability of students to evaluate different types of information.

The contents have been chosen to cover the main areas of all of the syllabuses. They have been grouped under ten sections, each of which contains a number of units. Each unit is displayed as a double-page spread in order to give students an immediate presentation of the material on a particular topic. Cross-references are provided to link topics, methods and perspectives. A variety of formats has been used for the units. Some consist of long case studies, while others provide summaries of key topics. The overall purpose is to provide an attractive and accessible text.

A major feature of the book is the use of contemporary materials as sources for questions. These exercises are designed to enhance the understanding and appeal of the contents, while following the examination format used by the various examining groups. The questions are intended not only to assess knowledge but also to provide the opportunity for students to apply their knowledge to given material, to question the accuracy and relevance of data and to develop skills in writing and in analysing numerical and graphical data.

The questions based on stimulus material have been graded in two ways. They tend to start with the more straightforward questions such as how to extract data from the stimulus, and then get gradually more demanding, requiring an evaluation of the material itself. However, it should be possible for all students to attempt all the questions, because they have been designed so that they can be answered at different levels. Although in many questions one number has been given in square brackets for each question, this should be seen as indicating a range of marks. For example, where [4] is shown, 1 or 2 marks could be awarded for a descriptive answer and 3 or 4 for a more critical one. Reference should be made to the marking schemes of the examining groups to see how this operates.

We have anticipated that GCSE Social Science will be studied by students of differing abilities. The graded questions have been included to meet their needs. In addition, in the extension activities, we have provided a mechanism for students to extend their coverage of some of the areas. Some of the suggestions in the extension activities could serve as the basis of project work and assessed course work, although the detailed design of any project is left to the student.

Project work or extended course work is a major feature of all social-science syllabuses. We see this as arising naturally from the topics under consideration. Underlining all of these projects are research methods. The selection and application of appropriate research methods and the evaluation of data from a variety of sources are central to GCSE Social Science. Research methods are covered in Section 1, in order to serve as an introduction to social science and for ease of reference; it is anticipated that students will return to this section in order to complete the questions and extension activities. The research methods section has been written in such a way as both to be an introduction to the uses of each method and to provide practical exercises in their use.

The division of labour in writing this book is as follows: Sections 1 to 4 and Section 10 are by Tony Russell; Sections 5 to 9 are by Ann Cotterrell.

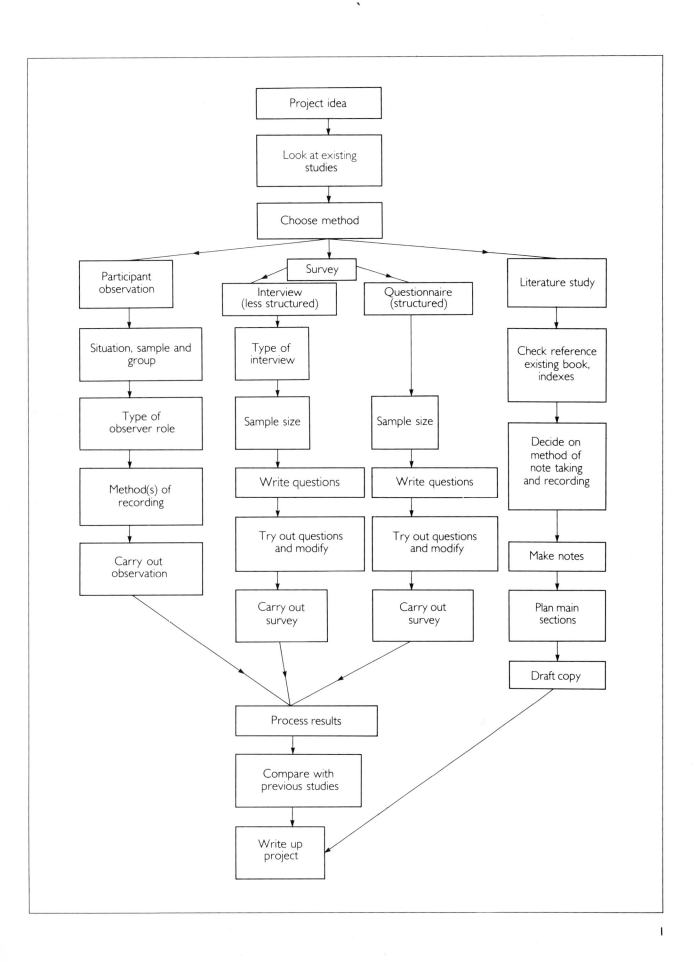

THE QUESTIONNAIRE

What is a questionnaire?

First date

1 It's your first date with the guy/girl of your dreams. Would you expect:

(a) to pay all the expenses? ☐
(b) to share the expenses? ☐
(c) your date to pay for everything? ☐

2 You've arranged to meet your date at 8 pm outside a local disco. It's now 8.30 pm and he/she hasn't arrived. Do you:

(a) go home? ☐
(b) find a phone box and ring him/her? ☐
(c) stand and fume? ☐

Fig. 1

I expect you have seen something like Fig. 1 in magazines before. It is used by the writers to find out what the reader thinks about something. Magazine editors aren't the only people who want to know what people think. Sociologists, advertisers and the government all need answers to questions. The questionnaire is one way of finding out. Usually the questions are written down, and we have to fill in the answers in the spaces provided.

If you look carefully at Fig. 2 you may notice that there are two types of question. For some, you have to choose which of the answers you agree with. These are called *structured questions*. But in number 2 you have to fill in your own answer. This type of question is called *open-ended*.

Each type of question has advantages and disadvantages. Structured questions are easy to fill in because you do not have to think so much about them. They also make it easy for the person asking the questions to work out the results. However, people may not always agree with the choices of answer they are given but they feel they have to tick one. The person asking the questions has to know the possible answers beforehand.

Unstructured questions are good for getting the answers people want to give, but it may be difficult to sort out exactly what they mean. They may be less willing to fill in this type of question because it involves more effort.

Problem questions

Answer the following:

1. Which is your favourite radio channel?
    Radio 1 ☐
    Radio 2 ☐
    Radio 3 ☐
    Commercial radio ☐

2. How much do you spend each week on clothes?

3. How much do you spend each week on records or tapes?
    £1–£3 ☐
    £3–£5 ☐
    £5–£6 ☐
    More than £6 ☐

4. Do you think that using animals for experiments is wrong?
    Yes ☐
    No ☐

Fig. 2

QUESTIONS

1 Give an example from the questionnaire (Fig. 2) of:

a) a structured question; [1]
b) an open question. [1]

2 Why are structured questions the most common type used in questionnaires? [2]

3 Choose two of the questions above and, using examples, explain clearly why each would cause problems if it were used in a questionnaire. [6]

Advantages and disadvantages of questionnaires

Advantages

Questionnaires can be a cheap way of finding things out, because they can be posted or given out. Questionnaires are very useful if you want opinions from people all over the country – you just post them. If structured questions are used, people find them easy to fill in; they can do it when they like and at their own speed. If people don't have to put their name on the paper, they may be more willing to answer embarrassing questions. Questionnaires give people time to look up the answers to questions or to ask someone. Researchers like questionnaires because the answers can be added up quickly and easily, especially on a computer.

Disadvantages

A major problem with this method of getting information is that we can never be sure that people have filled in the questionnaire truthfully. We can't even be sure who filled it in if we aren't there to check. Another disadvantage is that the questions have to be easy to understand, because you can't explain them. Obviously this is not a method suitable for blind people or people who can't read. Finally, although it is easy to send out questionnaires, it is not easy to get them back. In many cases less than 10 in every 100 are sent back, and researchers are unable to judge how typical the answers are.

For examples of questionnaires, see also Unit 4.8.

A researcher's reasons

'In asking the boys to answer a questionnaire I realised that I was doing something far from original. Yet there were sets of background information about the boys' experiences which could only really be gained by this method. I needed some information before I could use the more sensitive techniques of structured interview, observation and just plain chatting. So I administered a questionnaire myself to groups of boys in both schools.

I gave the questionnaires to the boys, preceded by a patter which I hoped would allay some of their fears. There were a variety of techniques used in the questionnaire, but in the pilot survey and throughout I realised the tremendous difficulty of collecting information from people whose thoughts are not expressed in the same way as the researcher's. Many of the boys found difficulty in writing at all, and a few of them just didn't write anything or answer any questions. All the time I stressed that I did not mind if they didn't write sentences and that one word would do in sentence completion.'

From P. Corrigan, *Schooling the Smash Street Kids* (Macmillan, 1979), pp. 14–17.

EXTENSION ACTIVITIES

1 **Explain** why someone who wanted to find out what people do in their spare time might use a questionnaire. Why would they choose this method and what would be its limitations in this case?

2 **Think about** how companies can find out about what people think of their products. Besides using questionnaires, what other way could they do this? What advantages and disadvantages would your suggestion have over the postal questionnaire? (See Unit 1.2 on interviews.)

3 **Make up a list** of ten questions to ask your friends about the music they like. Five questions should be structured, and five open-ended. Try them out on each other in pairs. Which were easiest to answer and which were most useful for providing information?

QUESTIONS

4 What did the author want from the questionnaire? [1]
5 Give two advantages of using a questionnaire in a study of this kind. [2]
6 What would you have done if you had been asked by Corrigan to fill in his questionnaire? Give reasons for your answer. [3]
7 What are three problems which the writer thought he might meet, and how did he hope to solve them? [6]
8 What other method could the writer have used to get the same information? Explain the advantages of your chosen method. [8]

ASKING QUESTIONS: INTERVIEWS

Problems of interviews

> The interview is a conversation between an interviewer and a respondent with the purpose of eliciting certain information.

From C. Moser and G. Galton, *Survey Methods in Social Investigation* (Heinemann Educational Books, 1971), p. 271.

Types of interview and their uses

Interviews are another way that social scientists gather information. If we know what we want to find out, we usually use *structured interviews*, where the person asking the questions reads out exactly what is written down and usually records the answer by ticking a box. This is similar to the structured questions used in questionnaires (see Unit 1.1).

If little is known about a subject, then we use what is called an *unstructured* or *focused interview*. In these cases the interviewer has a list of topics to discuss and lets the respondent (the person being interviewed) talk on about them. Sometimes it is difficult to write down the answers when carrying out an unstructured interview, and so a tape recorder may be used if the respondent agrees.

Fig. 1a

Fig. 1b

QUESTIONS

1 What problems for interviewers are illustrated by each of the dialogues in Fig. 1? [6]
2 If the dialogue in Fig. 1a was part of a structured interview you were carrying out, which of the following boxes would you tick? Give reasons for your choice.

Spend it on luxuries ☐
Save it ☐
Spend it on necessities ☐
Spend it on other people ☐ [4]

3 Make up two structured questions of your own to find out people's views on smoking.

Fig. 1c

Advantages and disadvantages of interviews

Advantages

In an interview you meet the respondent face to face so you can make sure the right person answers the question. You can also make sure the questions are answered without the help of others and see how seriously they are taken. The interview can be taken quickly or slowly to suit the person being questioned. Interviews can be conducted with blind people and with people who can't read. If a question isn't understood, then the interviewer can explain it. The results of structured interviews are easy to work out.

Disadvantages

Meeting people to ask them questions can cause as many problems as it solves. People may be worried at answering some questions and try to give the 'right' answer rather than what they really think. People sometimes lie. In a focused interview, people may be put off by the tape recorder; or the researcher may not be able to write down everything that is being said. Interviews may take a long time, and so people become tired and give shorter answers. They may also refuse to give an interview or refuse to answer embarrassing questions. The interviewer may not understand what an answer means or may write it down wrongly.

Fig. 2 Interviews are not always straightforward

QUESTIONS

4 Look at Fig. 2. What special problems might this particular sociologist face in conducting the interview? [3]

5 What sort of people might be best for conducting the following interviews? Give reasons for your choice.

   a) Interviewing teenage girls about their boy-friends. [3]
   b) Interviewing teenage boys about their girl-friends. [3]
   c) Interviewing black people about racial discrimination. [3]

6 Suggest how you could overcome the following problems of interviews:

   a) The respondent does not answer fully. [2]
   b) The respondent is lying. [2]
   c) The respondent is not willing to answer sensitive questions. [2]
   d) The respondent does not trust you. [2]

EXTENSION ACTIVITIES

1 **Compare** the unstructured interview with the questionnaire as a method of getting information.

2 **Describe** the problems that the researcher in Unit 1.1 may have had when he used a semi-structured interview to find out about a group of boys in the lower classes of a secondary school who messed around. What problems do you think he might have met in interviewing them? Could he have got his information in any other way? Explain your answer.

3 **Think** of some questions to ask a friend about his or her favourite food. Take it in turns to be the interviewer and the respondent. What did each role feel like? What problems did you meet in getting answers to your questions?

Interviews were used in studies mentioned in Units 3.3 and 3.5.

PARTICIPANT OBSERVATION

Observation

Observation is a method in which the researcher becomes involved in some way with the person or group being studied.

Fig. 1 Researcher at work

Observer roles

- Margaret Hammond wanted to study small children when they were playing, so she brought them into a special room at the university where there was a two-way mirror. She then watched and recorded what they did.
- Patrick 'Smith' joined a gang in Glasgow. His friend in the gang knew he was a teacher, but the rest of the gang didn't. He wrote up what he saw each night. When he published his research he kept his real name secret because he was frightened that the gang would come after him.
- David Hargreaves studied some fourth-year children in a secondary school by following them from class to class during the day and by interviewing them about what they did.

These are examples of three ways in which sociologists have got information by observation. The first method is called the *complete observer* or 'fly on the wall', because the researcher does not reveal him or herself. The second is known as the *complete participant*, because he or she takes part in the life of the group without them knowing who he or she is. The third is called *observer as participant* where the researcher watches and interviews the people being studied but doesn't join in as one of them.

The second and third approaches – complete participant and observer as participant – are together known as *participant observation*.

Methods used

When people gather information by observation they may use a number of methods. They watch what is happening. They go around with the group or follow them. Sometimes they ask questions, arrange group discussions or even use a formal interview. The information can be collected by writing it down later in a field notebook (like a diary) or by recording the interviews and discussions.

Advantages and disadvantages of participant observation

Advantages

The main advantage of participant observation is that we can take part in the group being studied. As things happen, they can be recorded. We do not have to rely on what other people say. If we stay with a group for a time, they will get used to being studied and act naturally. It is also possible to check that people do what they say they do.

For example, Alan may say he is a friend of Julie. By observing him it is possible to check this. This is an advantage over an interview or questionnaire, where you would have no way of telling whether this was true. Information can also be checked with different people in a group to see whether it is true. With participant observation the researcher can record his or her own feelings about a situation, and these might be useful.

Disadvantages

Some people think that participant observation is too *subjective*. By this they mean that it relies too much on the opinions of the person doing the observation; there is no way to check on what the researcher says he or she has seen. If the members of a group know they are being studied, they may behave differently. You can see an example of this when people know there is a television camera near them.

Researchers also have problems in recording what they see. If they write down what they are seeing at the time, people may become embarrassed. But if they wait till they are alone, they might have forgotten something. Another problem can arise when the researcher joins a group. He or she may in some way change how the people behave. It takes a long time to study a group, so not many are studied. This makes it difficult to know whether a group is typical or unusual.

An observation case study

Ken Pryce did some research on Afro-Caribbeans in St Pauls, an area of Bristol.

'My entrance into St Pauls and the surrounding area was gained at three separate points. The first point of entry was through Shanty Town – the scene of the hustler and teeny-bopper. My introduction to Shanty Town took place on my first night in Bristol while I was prowling around on my own in the city centre. As I was boarding a No. 11 bus going into the St Pauls district, a very friendly and talkative Jamaican – a man in his early thirties–saw me and asked me if I was new to Bristol. He had heard me ask the conductor if the bus would take me into the section of the city where the black people lived. Without revealing my true identity as a researcher, I told him I was a Jamaican like himself and that I was a student, but that I was new to Bristol and was interested in finding the Panorama Club. My concealment of my role as a researcher was not intended to deceive but merely to keep on good terms with the stranger.'

From K. Pryce, *Endless Pressure* (Penguin, 1979), pp. 279–82; quoted in M. O'Donnell, *New Introductory Reader in Sociology* (Harrap, 1983), p. 50.

QUESTIONS

1 What type of observer role was Ken Pryce using in the study? [1]
2 Why didn't Ken Pryce tell the man who he really was? [1]
3 Give two reasons why Ken Pryce was especially suited to carry out this research in this way. [2]
4 What three advantages would Ken Pryce have had in taking this type of observer role? [6]
5 What other method could Pryce have used to study the lives of black people in Bristol? What would be the advantages and disadvantages of your chosen method over participant observation? [10]

EXTENSION ACTIVITIES

1 **Explain** why sociologists studying gangs might prefer to use participant observation rather than a questionnaire.
2 **List** the methods that people use to record their information when they are doing participant observation. What are the advantages and disadvantages of each method?
3 **Discuss** how you and your friends would react if someone was studying your class by talking to you and going around with you. Would you behave naturally? Would you tell them everything you were asked?

Participant observation is used in the studies mentioned in Units 3.5 and 4.6.

SURVEYS AND SAMPLING

Surveys–a way of finding out

Fig. 1

If you look at the statements in Fig. 1, they are both clearly untrue. But how do we know whether something is true or not? Tony took himself as an example and thought everyone was the same as him. Linda and Karen believed that because they both had dark hair and were good at Art, then all dark-haired girls would be similarly talented.

To find out if something is generally true, we should really ask everyone – or at least a lot of people. This is what we mean by a survey. A survey is a method of getting information by asking people questions. This can be done by questionnaire or by interviews.

Advantages and disadvantages of surveys

Advantages

A *survey* is the cheapest method of finding out information from a large population. It can be used to find out facts about people, their opinions and their activities. The information gathered by a survey can often be processed with a computer, which can save time and produce accurate results.

The government carries out a lot of surveys all the time, and you may see some of them reported on television or in the newspaper. Every year it publishes *Social Trends*, which is a summary of the findings of some of its surveys. Did you see any of these headlines? They all came from government surveys.

If you want to find something out, you can be sure someone has done a survey on it!

Disadvantages

The problem with surveys is that you have to know what you want to find out before you begin. This may seem obvious, because you have to ask people questions to get an answer. So surveys are useful only for researching things we already know something about. Because they use either questionnaires or interviews, they have the disadvantages of these methods (see Units 1.1 and 1.2). There is also a limit on the type of questions that can be used. Generally the questions and possible answer have to be set out very clearly, although we do not always think so clearly.

Sampling

Fig.2

If you wanted to claim that cakes like the ones in Fig. 2 tasted good, how many would you have to eat to be sure? Well, to be absolutely sure you would have to eat them all.

Because even if you ate six of them and they were fine, you could not be sure that the last one was nice as well. However, in practice you assume that they are all the same; so if you eat say two and they are fine, you assume the rest are the same.

This is what we mean by a *sample*. A sample is where a small part of a population is carefully chosen to represent the whole. The advantages of sampling are that it saves time, money and effort. It can also produce better results sometimes, because researchers can afford to employ better interviewers if they use smaller numbers.

There are different types of sample which are useful in particular cases. The idea is always to get the most accurate results.

QUESTIONS

Types of sample

1 Try out the following ways of sampling your class or year group.

   a) Put each name onto a slip of paper. Then draw out the sample size you want – say, 30 per cent. This is called a *simple random sample*.

   b) Write out all the names in any order, then take every third name. This is called a *systematic random sample*.

   c) Divide the names into males and females. Then take a random sample from each group. This is called a *stratified sample*.

   d) Select from the group one tall person, one short person, one athletic person and one person who likes music. This is a *quota sample*.

2 On the basis of what you did in question 1, try to make up a definition of your own of a) a random sample, b) a systematic random sample, c) a stratified sample and d) a quota sample.

Panel or longitudinal methods

One special type of sampling is where researchers use the same sample many times. This method is very useful for studying how people change over a period of time, because you always have the same people. The BBC uses this to check on television-viewing habits. Commercial companies also use it to see how well an advertisement works. They ask a panel what washing-powder they use before some advertisements are shown on television. Then, after the advertisements have been shown, they ask the same group again and see whether the adverts have made them change their powder.

The problem with panel samples is that just being a member of the panel may lead people to change their habits. Imagine you were asked by your local commerical radio station to be on their panel and that every so often they were going to ask what you listened to. Then it might make you listen more. This is called *panel conditioning*.

Example of a panel/longitudinal study

A team of researchers have been following the progress of the same group of children since 1946 (Fig. 3).

Fig.3

Sources	Age of children when the information was collected
Interviews with mother	8 weeks, 4, 6, 8, 9, 11, 15 years
Schoolteachers' reports	7, 10, 13, 15 years
Questionnaire filled in by the researchers	13, 15 years
Medical examination	6, 7, 8, 15 years
Intelligence tests	8, 11, 15 years

From J. Douglas, J. Ross and H. Simpson, *All Our Future: A Longitudinal Study of Secondary Education* (Peter Davis, 1968), p. 198.

QUESTIONS

3 What type of sample was used in the research above (Fig. 3)? [1]

4 Over what period of time did the researchers collect their information? [2]

5 Give three types of information about the children which were collected in this study. [3]

6 What methods were used to check the children when they were 8 years old? [2]

7 If you were using this method, how would you overcome the following problems?

   a) Persuading people to take part in the first place. [3]

   b) Keeping in touch with the sample over time. [3]

   c) Panel conditioning. [4]

Studies using surveys and samples are mentioned in Units 4.7, 5.1, 5.5, 6.1, 6.10, 8.5, 9.3, 9.5 and 10.4.

SECONDARY SOURCES: DOCUMENTARY EVIDENCE

Surveys and participant observation are methods we use to gather new information. But there is a great deal of information already published which we can use without having to collect it ourselves. This is called *secondary source material* or *documentary evidence*. Many of the projects you will want to do for GCSE will involve using material which has already been published in books, reports and news-papers. Looking at this material and using it in a study is fully accepted as a method of research.

Reports and statistics

Government facts and figures

The government collects a great deal of information. Some of this is gathered together and published on a regular basis in government reports. If you go to a library and ask for information on almost any aspect of our society, there will be a government report of some sort on it. For example, you could find out how many people have videos, washing-machines or telephones, how many smoke in each age group or how many people die in sports accidents.

It is hard to think of any subject the government has *not* got figures on. This means that whenever we want to study a subject we can always get some basic information about it. The same will be true for your projects. If you want some facts and figures on something, then start by looking at government publications and reports. Some of the most common are given in Fig. 1.

Non-government sources

In addition to the government, almost every organisation produces reports on its work. If we want to research a topic then all we have to do is to find the name and address of an organisation connected with the topic and write to it for information. If the information is not confidential the organisation will usually send it. The police, television companies, charities, pressure groups, large companies and local councils all produce reports which you may be able to use, and many of them are available in local reference libraries.

The problem with reports and statistics

It is obviously convenient to get all this information from somebody else. It saves us a great deal of work and time. However, because we have not gathered the information ourselves, we cannot always be sure how it was collected or how reliable it is. It may not always be exactly what we want. For example, we may want to know about the spending habits of young people aged sixteen to eighteen, but the only official information is about people of eighteen and over. So this kind of secondary material has to be used with care.

Name of publication	Information provided
Annual Abstract of Statistics	Collection of many government figures on all aspects of the government's work.
Social Trends	An easily read summary of some government figures, covering all aspects of social life; published annually.
Economic Trends	Similar to Social Trends but dealing with economic aspects of Britain.
General Household Survey	An annual report on all aspects of people's everyday lives based on a sample of 15,000 households.
Monthly Digest of Statistics	Statistics on economic change.
Special reports	The government often sets up committees to look into different aspects of society; these surveys are published as special reports. Lists of these can be found in your local library or at HMSO bookshops.

Fig. 1 Some useful government publications and the type of information they provide.

Publishing and the media

Books and journals

Another place to begin research is to look at books on the same topic. These may give you general information about the subject and will often have a bibliography at the back listing all the books and articles the author has used. By looking at these lists you can get some suggestions for your own study.

There are also many journals published in the social sciences, such as the *British Journal of Sociology*. You may find these journals difficult to find and to read. However, *New Society* is much easier. It is published each week and is stocked by larger newsagents such as W. H. Smith. It contains short articles on a wide range of topics, and on its back page there is a useful *data base* – a summary of information on a particular topic. Your local library should have an index of *New Society* so that you can look up any topic you are interested in.

Newspapers and broadcasting

Information doesn't have to appear in official reports for it to be useful to social scientists. As you will see later in our suggestions for projects, newspapers and television are also suitable sources. But just as you have to be careful when you use official sources, so you must when you use these. One way of using material from newspapers and magazines is to make a content analysis of it. That is, you look at how much coverage is given to a topic over a period of time.

Novels, stories and TV 'soaps'

If you want to investigate everyday aspects of society, you can also look at novels and stories. These provide a different sort of information. It is more impressionistic than documents and reports, but it does give us an idea of what people do and how they think. The novels of Charles Dickens and Emily Brontë describe family life in Victorian England in the same way that *Eastenders* and *Coronation Street* do for today. Both novels and television are useful sources of information, provided you are aware that they are fiction, giving pictures rather than complete facts.

Combining methods

When social scientists carry out research, they are aware of the advantages and disadvantages of the different methods they use. To try to overcome the disadvantages they often combine methods. They may use a survey to get a broad idea and then participant observation for more detail. In your studies you may like to begin by looking at documentary sources and then try a small-scale research project.

EXTENSION ACTIVITIES

Crime and the press

1 **Carry out** a content analysis of any newspaper, to see how it deals with crime. Take any daily newspaper for one week – it can be a local or national paper – and cut out all the reports and articles about crime. At the end of the week, divide them into stories about male crime, those about female crime and those involving both sexes. You can then either add up the number of stories or measure the amount of space given to the stories in each category.

Compare the results of different newspapers and comment on them.

Fiction and real life

2 **Make a study** of a short story, a play, a film or TV 'soap'. Show how although it is a work of fiction it tells us about everyday life, how people behave and think. In what ways does it give a true picture, and in what ways is the picture untrue to real life?

PRESENTING THE INFORMATION

In your study of the social sciences you will come across information presented in many different ways. You may yourself have to display information as part of your course work. Graphs, charts and diagrams are all useful if they are used carefully. But the important thing to remember is that the method you use should make the information clear and attractive.

Tables

When we read a passage containing figures it is sometimes difficult to take in everything that is written down. Changing the numbers from words into a table can make the point clearer.

Sale of records suffers in wake of compact discs

By Teresa Poole

Demand for single and long-playing records has fallen sharply this year, with sales of records high in the pop charts suffering the most.

Deliveries of singles to retailers fell by 17 per cent to 15.2 million in the first three months of this year, compared with the same period last year. Deliveries of LPs fell by 8 per cent to 9 million, according to the British Phonographic Industry, the record company trade organization.

It is said the poor performance of singles' sales was partly due to the success of the Band Aid Christmas record, which sold more than one million copies early last year.

The BPI said that, by contrast, sales of cassettes and compact discs have continued to rise. Cassettes are increasingly being purchased in preference to LPs, with cassette deliveries showing a 13.6 percent improvement to 10.6 million units in the first quarter.

The burgeoning compact disc market showed the strongest growth with shipments more than doubling to 1.2 million discs. Annual sales by British manufacturers to the trade are forecast to reach 6 million units.

Fig. 1   From *The Times*, 1986.

Changing words into tables

1 Change the information in this newspaper report into a table as shown below.

	Music sales for January February and March
Singles	
LPs	
Cassettes	
Compact discs	

2 Make up three questions to go with the table.

Examples of tables can be seen in many Units including 3.3, 4.7, 5.3, 6.7, 7.8 and 8.3.

Line graphs

This is a way of presenting information which you will have met in mathematics. Line graphs are useful for showing changes over time or the relationship between two pieces of information. To make a graph attractive you can draw it over a picture which is related to the subject. For example, a graph showing how less and less people have been going to the cinema over the last ten years could be drawn over the top of a photograph of an old cinema.

Changing figures into a graph

3 Show this information as a graph and choose a suitable background picture:

Average attendance at football matches, England and Wales, Division 1 (from *Social Trends*, 1987, p. 169):

1980–1	24,660	1983–4	18,856
1981–2	22,556	1984–5	21,129
1982–3	20,120	1985–6	19,562

4 Write down three questions which could be asked about the graph.

5 Redraw the graph using a different scale to make it look as if there has been a great decline in attendances.

Example of line graphs can be seen in Units 5.4 and 5.5.

Bar graphs

Bar graphs, like line graphs, are used to show trends or relationships. But instead of showing a continuous trend they are used to provide 'snapshots' – the situation at particular points. Again they are more interesting if they are drawn with suitable pictures. Fig. 2 shows this.

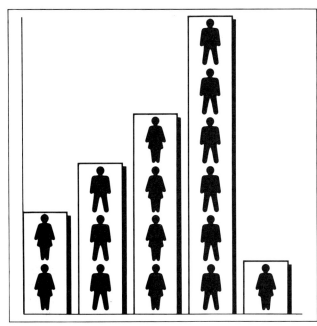

Fig. 2 An example of a bar graph

QUESTIONS

Making bar graphs
6   The following information shows the magazines that men and women read. Turn this information into a bar graph. Choose a suitable background or shape for the bars. One column will be percentages, and the other will show the magazines. Each bar will have two levels, one for males and one for females.

Percentage reading each magazine, 1984		
	Males	*Females*
TV Times	22	25
Reader's Digest	17	14
Smash Hits	4	6
Exchange & Mart	6	2
Woman's Own	4	20
Woman	3	16

7   Make up three questions which could be asked about your bar graph.

Examples of bar graphs can be seen in Units 2.8 and 4.8.

Pie charts

Pie charts can be used when we want to show how something is divided up. To make a pie chart you have to know the total size of something and then the size of each part. Usually this is given in percentages so that the total 'pie' represents 100 per cent. Pie charts don't have to be round. You can divide anything into parts, if it makes the point. Look at Fig. 3.

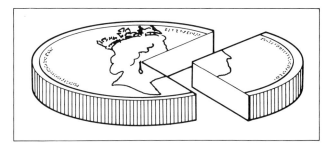

Fig. 3 An example of a pie chart

QUESTIONS

8   Turn the following information into a pie chart. Choose a suitable form of illustration.

Destination of holidays abroad, 1985 (adults only) (from *Social Trends*, 1987, p. 169, table 10.13):

France 13%	Spain 32%
W. Germany 4%	Other European countries 21%
Greece 9%	USA 3%
Italy 5%	Other countries 5%
Austria 4%	No country for more than one night 4%

Examples of pie charts can be seen in Unit 9.4.

Flow charts

Flow charts are used to display a set of features which are connected with each other. They are useful as a summary or as an aid for revision.

QUESTIONS

Making a flow chart
9   Make a flow chart using the following information. It should show how the parts are connected.
    The *self-fulfilling prophecy* (see Unit 3.5): the teacher thinks the student is clever; the teacher gives the student more attention; the student is encouraged and tries hard; the student gets good results; the teacher thinks he/she is right.

Examples of flow charts can be seen on page 1 and in Unit 3.5.

SOCIALISATION

Learning or instinct?

Is our behaviour taught or instinctive? Some people rub noses when they like someone; won't fight even when hit; have several wives or husbands at the same time. All these examples may seem unusual to us, but they are normal in some societies. Have you ever wondered which of the things you do are *natural* (you do them because you were born that way) and which are *learned* from people around you?

This is the key question in what is called the *nature/nurture debate*. Some writers think that much of our behaviour is 'natural' – we do it without thinking. Others think we are taught how to behave or we learn it from other people – it is how we are nurtured. Sociologists usually support the 'nurture' idea, while psychologists mostly agree with the 'nature' approach.

An example of the nature/nurture debate

The two points of view can be illustrated by how each would explain the behaviour of a boy. Imagine this boy is in a secondary school. Alan Dale is fifteen years old. He is in the lowest stream. He messes about in class and plays up the teachers. He often stays away from school without his parents knowing.

Psychologists would explain Alan's behaviour by describing his 'nature' – characteristics he was born with. Sociologists, on the other hand, would look at factors which have 'nurtured' (influenced) him. See Fig. 1.

Psychological Explanation:
- low intelligence
- agressive
- can't stick at things
- lacks motivation

Sociological Explanation:
- family doesn't believe in school
- goes around with other boys who don't like school
- the teachers pick on him

Fig. 1 The nature/nurture debate

Socialisation

In this section we are going to take a sociological view to explain people's behaviour. We shall look at how the family and the school can influence what we do and how we do it. The process of learning how to behave is called *socialisation*. Frederick Elkin, a United States sociologist, defined socialisation as 'the process by which someone learns the ways of a given society or social group so that they can function within it'.

We learn how to behave in a number of ways. People such as our family teach us some things. We teach ourselves by watching and thinking what to do. And we copy other people by a process known as *role-modelling*.

In a society everybody learns more or less the same ways of behaving, and this is why people are able to live together more or less peacefully. This is the importance of socialisation. If people in a group were taught different ways of behaving, then the group would always be quarrelling. For example, in your school or college you are perhaps asked to walk on the left-hand side of corridors. If a few people had been asked to walk on the right-hand side, then you can imagine what would happen at the end of classes or going upstairs.

People who have not been socialised

Most people are socialised to live in their group or society, but occasionally people are found who have not been taught how to behave. One famous case is that of Anna, an American girl who was locked in a room for six years and just kept alive. She was not taught anything. She is described below.

> Anna was an illegitimate child whose grandfather disapproved of the mother's behaviour and therefore caused the child to be kept in an upstairs room. As a result she received only enough care to keep her barely alive. She apparently had no instruction or friendly attention. When she was finally found at the age of six, Anna could not walk, talk or do anything that showed her intelligence. She didn't want to do anything, remaining immobile, expressionless and indifferent to everything. She could not feed herself or make any move on her own behalf.

Adapted from Kingsley Davis, *Human Society* (Macmillan, 1948), p. 204.

1 What could Anna not do that you would expect a normal six-year-old child to do? [3]
2 Explain how Anna's case supports the view of sociologists that we are taught most of our behaviour. [7]
3 When Anna was found, would you call her a human being or an animal? Give reasons for your answer. [10]

Agents of socialisation

In society there are many groups and organisations that teach us how to behave. They are called by sociologists the *agents of socialisation*. These agents are shown in Fig. 2.

The dotted lines in Fig. 2 are meant to show that the influence of these different groups is not just one-way. People can reject what they are told, or change it in some way.

1 **Find out** more about the agents of socialisation. Make notes on the part played in the socialisation process by the family, the school and the peer group. Frederick Elkins's book, *The Child and Society* (Random House, 1972), is very clear on this and easy to read. (See also Units 2.2 and 3.1.)
2 **Discuss** whether there is any behaviour which is 'natural' to girls or 'natural' to boys.
3 **Make a study** of people who have not been fully socialised. There have been a number of such people, like Anna in the example above. There was another little girl called Isabelle, and there is also said to have been a boy who was reared by wolves. You could start with Kingsley Davis's book, *Human Society* (Macmillan, 1948).
4 **Compare** two agents of socialisation. Compare how they teach people how to behave in our society. What do they teach us? How do they teach us? Use examples from your own life to show what they do.

Fig. 2 Agents of socialisation

THE FAMILY

Your family

1   Make a list of all the people in your family.
2   Draw a table like the one on the right and fill it in from your list.
3   Compare your answers with those of other students in the class:
   a) Do they have any different ideas about who is in their family?
   b) Are there any differences in the number of people they have seen recently?

Members of my family I have had contact with

In the last 24 hours

In the last 48 hours

In the last 7 days

In the last month

In the last 6 months

In the last year

Can we define 'the family'?

The questions above were meant to show you that it is not easy to say exactly who is in your family. Question 3 might also have revealed that people have different types of family. In the social sciences we mostly begin a topic by defining the terms we are using. But this is not always possible, because sometimes there is no definition that everyone accepts.

A well-known definition of the family is that by G. P. Murdock, an American who studied a number of simple societies. He defined the family as 'a social group characterised by common residence, economic cooperation and reproduction. It includes adults of both sexes, at least two of whom maintain a socially approved sexual relationship, and one or more children, own or adopted, of the socially cohabiting adults'.

More recently, we have come to accept that the *one-parent family*, where there is only one parental adult, also counts as a family. Also, a family may *not* share a common residence, as when husband and wife are separated or children have left home. And even two childless adults may sometimes be considered as making up a family.

Types of family

Your answers to the questions may have shown that there is a wide range of family structures. Some are very small, others large. Some families see each other a great deal, others rarely meet. Sociologists know about these variations, but they have tended to focus on two main types, which they call the nuclear family and the extended family.

The *nuclear family* is a family where there are just two generations, parents and children, living together. It is small in size. If there are two parents, they are more or less equal. They both do similar things about the home and with the children. The nuclear family tends to act without the help of other relatives and, if it wants to, it can easily move to another area.

The *extended family*, as its name suggests, is large in size. Three or more generations live together or near each other: parents, grandparents and children. They tend to rely on each other, which makes it harder for them to move about the country, say, to look for work. In this family the husband and wife often do different things. The wife may do the cooking and look after the children, while the husband is the main wage-earner. This is called having *separate roles*.

4   Which of the following characteristics of the family, given in Murdock's definition, are found in the group you said were your family in the questions at the start of this unit?

   a) They live in the same house.
   b) They support each other financially.
   c) They have children.
   d) Adults of both sexes.

5   Does Murdock's definition include an adopted child living with guardians or a child with foster-parents? Give reasons for your answer.

6   Are the people in Fig. 1 a nuclear family or an extended family?   [1]
7   How many generations are shown in Fig. 1?   [1]
8   If the people in Fig. 1 did not have any children, would they still be a family? Explain your view.   [4]
9   How would you decide whether the people in Fig. 2 were a family?   [6]
10   Describe the main differences between a nuclear and an extended family.   [7]

See also Unit 2.9 on single-parent families.

The part played by the family in society

When sociologists come to look at different aspects of society they often ask the question, 'What *function* does it perform in society?' There is some disagreement about the functions of the family, but there are four that many people agree on:

● To rear and take care of children until they can take care of themselves.
● To socialise children so that they know how to behave in society.
● To provide a place where all family members can relax and have a loving and caring relationship.
● To control and provide for sexual relationships.

Fig. 1 The process of socialisation

Fig. 2

EXTENSION ACTIVITIES

1 **Write** about the differences between a nuclear and an extended family. Why is the nuclear family the main type in modern Britain?
2 **Explain** what you understand by the term 'extended family'. Is it declining in importance?
3 **Make a study** of your own family. Draw your family tree going back at least four generations (if you can). Find out where your family has lived and w. at jobs each person has had. Work out whether your family has moved about the country (been *geographically mobile*) and whether they have become better off (have been *socially mobile*).

4 **Make a study** of family life in one other society and compare it with your own. We mention the kibbutz in Unit 2.6. It should be easy to find information on this way of organising families if you write to the Israeli Embassy. You might consider such things as family size, relationship between the adults, child-rearing practices and parent-child relationships.
5 **Discuss** the good and bad aspects of living in a family for people of your age.

THE FAMILY
AND
SOCIALISATION

QUESTIONS

		I was taught	I copied from someone	I taught myself
1	How do you know how to hold a knife and fork?			
2	How do you know how to use a calculator?			
3	How do you know how to ride a bike?			

Being shown what to do, copying something, learning for yourself – all these are methods of *socialisation*.

Agents of socialisation

In Unit 2.1 we described how socialisation was the way in which we are taught how to behave so that we can fit into the society we live in. The process of teaching people how to behave is carried out by a number of groups, the *agents of socialisation*. These include the peer group (people of your own age), the church or temple, the school, the mass media and the community, as well as the family. Some of these groups influence us all our life; others are important only at certain times.

For most of us, the family is the most important influence on our behaviour. It is the main group we come into contact with when we are very young. Because our ties to parents and other family members are usually very close, their influence on us is very strong.

QUESTIONS

4　Which is the only agency that has contact with the child for the first few years of life? [1]

5　In Fig. 1, which two agencies seem to influence the child for the longest period of time? [2]

6　Give one example of how your peer group has influenced your behaviour. [3]

7　Which of the agencies shown in Fig. 1 might have influenced you most in your choice of subjects for GCSE? Give reasons for your answer. [6]

8　The influence of the family is shown as getting less when people reach their twenties. Can you think of four reasons for this? [8]

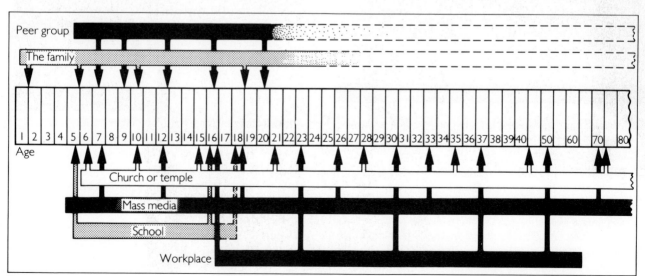

Fig. 1

Functions of the family

Learning what to do and how to behave is not a simple thing. The family, the school and the community all keep trying to teach the child the same thing. Sometimes all of them fail! However, we are going to describe some of the things the family does in this process we call socialisation. These are called the *functions of the family*.

The first thing the family does is teach children how to live within the family. This involves teaching them about different members of the family and what their position is. From this children learn about their own role and status. *Role* is the behaviour which is expected of someone, and *status* is the position in a group – how important any person is. The family teaches patterns of male and female behaviour. The family also passes on to the child its own values, its views of what is right and what is wrong.

Secondly, the family prepares the child for the wider society. Much of what is taught in the family is preparation for the world outside. The family is part of society, but it tends to be easier with the child than other people are. Gradually the parents get stricter as the child becomes old enough to go out of the family circle. For example, parents may dress children and tie their shoelaces for them at home, but children must be taught to do both before they start school. To some extent parents control when their children meet other people outside the family. They decide who their children play with, how long they stay out and when they can go to the cinema or to a party.

The family also provides a place where children feel secure – a home, in fact. In most cases children know they are safe in the family and will be loved there. The family also explains the world to the child. For example, if a child is bullied at school, the parents will explain that this is wrong and doesn't happen very often. The family can continue to act as a refuge in this way even when children grow up. Married children sometimes 'go back to Mum' for a rest or for help when they have problems.

QUESTIONS

9 Which photograph gives an example of role modelling? [1]
10 Which other agency shown in Fig. 1 could also have taught the behaviour shown in Fig. 3? [2]
11 Give two examples from your own family of how it prepared you for living in the wider society. [4]
12 What were two methods used by your family to socialise you? Give an example of how each was used.[6]
13 What method(s) would you use to study how a young child learns how to eat with a spoon? What would be the advantages and disadvantages of your chosen method(s)? (See Section 1.) [7]

EXTENSION ACTIVITIES

1 **Find out** more information and write a paragraph about each of the following terms: sex-role socialisation, role modelling, norms, values, family subculture. Give an example for each.
2 **Explain** briefly how the family socialise children so that they can fit into society.
3 **Discuss** why, if all these agencies of socialisation are so influential, some people have 'bad habits' or don't conform.
4 **Make up a role-play** showing how your parents or teachers are often telling you what to do, and then what you really think as you appear to go along with it.

Fig. 4

Fig. 2

Fig. 3

THE FAMILY AND INDUSTRIALISATION

Industrialisation and family change

In Units 2.2 and 2.3 we have described the family as it is today. But sociologists disagree about whether the family has changed during the last 200 years.

The most important event during this period was the Industrial Revolution, which began in the eighteenth century. This was to change the working occupations of most of the population. Goods were produced in large quantities by machines. People went out to work in factories. Because the factories needed large numbers of people, new towns grew up. All of this meant new working conditions.

Some people say that these changes affected the family. Before the Industrial Revolution most people in Britain lived on the land. Families didn't move very much, and the extended family was more common. But the new industrial society needed a different type of family. It wanted people to move to where there was work. Skills were needed which the old family could not teach. The best workers were the people most in demand, regardless of their age. The nuclear family seemed to be the result of these needs.

Other changes tended to separate different generations in the family and encourage a nuclear type. Young couples moved around looking for work. When the towns became overcrowded new estates were built on the outskirts, where people could get houses to rent. In the twentieth century local authorities have built council houses so that young people can have a house of their own rather than having to live with their parents.

The growth of the welfare state has meant that people rely less on their extended family network than they once did. The welfare state provides schooling for children, medical care for all, and, most important, support for the family in times of unemployment. Young couples and their children can now survive without their kin and this is said to be the reason why family types have changed.

The unchanging family?

As we have just seen, there is evidence to support the idea that industrialisation changed family life. But there is other evidence which suggests the opposite – that the nuclear family was common *before* as well as after industrialisation. Consider the following example.

' Peter Laslett, a Cambridge historian, studied family size and composition from 1564 to 1821. He found that only 10 per cent of households contained relatives other than the nuclear family. This percentage is the same as for England in 1966. Evidence from the United States presents a similar picture. This low figure may be due in part to the fact that people in pre-industrial England and America married relatively late in life, and life expectancy was short. Laslett found no evidence to support the view that the classic extended family was widespread in pre-industrial England. '

Adapted from M. Haralambos, *Sociology Themes and Perspectives* (University Tutorial Press, 1980), p. 347.

QUESTIONS

1 According to Laslett, what percentage of families in the sixteenth century were of the nuclear type? [1]
2 Why does the writer mention the figure for 1966? [2]
3 What reason does Laslett give for the small percentage of extended families? [2]
4 What are two ways in which your family might help you to find a job or move to a place where there was work? [4]
5 Among which groups in modern Britain are you likely to find extended families? Explain why. (Look back at Unit 2.2). [8]

Has the family lost some of its functions?

Some sociologists claim that since industrialisation the family has lost some of its functions. They would claim that the pre-industrial family looked after its own needs without the help of outsiders. However, with industrialisation some of the functions once performed by the family have been taken over by other agencies. The family's health, for example, has been taken over by the Health Service. It is claimed that the family has lost its non-essential functions and only kept the three essential functions it performs best: the provision of a home, the production and rearing of children and the provision of a stable sexual relationship.

This idea is illustrated in Fig. 1.

FUNCTIONS OF EXTENDED FAMILY

FUNCTIONS OF NUCLEAR FAMILY

Recreational

Decision-making

Economic
(making a living)

Health

Educational

Religious

Provision of a home

Production and rearing of children

Stable sexual relationship

Fig. 1 Functions of the extended and nuclear family

QUESTIONS

6 An American sociologist, R. M. McIver, claims that the family has lost its non-essential functions, which have been taken over by other bodies. Complete the table below to show which agencies might have taken over these non-essential functions.

Function	Taken over by
Religious	Churches
Educational	
Health	
Recreational	
Economic	
Governmental	

7 Write down one example of when your family performs each of the following functions: a) health, b) educational, c) recreational. [5]

8 In Fig. 1 three functions are shown as carried out by the nuclear family. Which of these can sometimes be carried out by the state? [2]

EXTENSION ACTIVITIES

1 **Find out** more of the arguments for and against the idea that industrialisation caused a change from extended to nuclear families.

2 To what extent is the nuclear family *isolated*?

3 **Make a study** of the contacts between your immediate family (you and your parent(s)) and your other relatives. Keep a diary for four months in which you write down such things as when you see your relatives or get telephone calls from them. Record the reason for the contact. You could make a similar study using another method such as interviews or a questionnaire. Discuss what your findings tell you about your family.

4 **Investigate** the functions performed by your family. Make a list of the essential and non-essential functions shown in Fig. 1 and choose a way of recording when your family performs them.

THE EGALITARIAN FAMILY

QUESTIONS

Relationships in your family

1 Who is the most important person in your family?

Father ☐ Mother ☐ Both ☐ Grandfather ☐
You ☐ Other brother/sister ☐

2 Who makes the important decisions in your family, such as where you live or choosing schools?

Father ☐ Mother ☐ Both ☐

3 How much notice do your parents take of your opinion on family matters?

A great deal ☐ Some ☐ Not very much ☐
None at all ☐

4 Collect together all the answers from your class and display them as a pie chart (see Unit 1.6).

5 What patterns are shown by your results?

6 How do the results relate to the different types of family which we explored in Unit 2.2?

The debate about family relationships

You may have seen on television or read in books about the Victorian family where the father was very strict and dominated the family. He gave orders to his wife, and the children were often frightened of him. This is a very different picture from most families today, as the results of the above questions should have shown. But there is a disagreement among sociologists about how much change has taken place in family relationships.

Arguments for change

Peter Willmott and Michael Young carried out a survey on family relationships in the late 1960s. Some of their findings are shown in Figs. 1, 2 and 3.

On the basis of evidence such as this, Willmott and Young called the modern family *symmetrical*. By this they meant that husbands and wives in the family do different things but are more or less equal.

Fig. 1 On average 70 per cent of men help with cleaning, child care and cooking in the home.

Fig. 2 62 per cent of fathers play with their children.

Fig. 3 60 per cent of men had their wives with them last time they met a friend.

QUESTIONS

Your evidence

7 Look back at the answers of your class to the questions at the start of this unit. Do they support the idea that husbands and wives are equal in the family?

8 Do the answers provide evidence that children are listened to equally in the family?

Elizabeth Bott is another sociologist who thinks that family relationships have changed. She describes it as a change from *segregated* to *joint roles*. By segregated roles she means that the husband and wife used to have different things to do in the family. The husband's main job was to go to work and earn a living. The wife had to look after the children. Both used to have their own friends and interests.

This has now changed, Elizabeth Bott says. Husband and wife now have joint roles. Both do any of the household tasks and they have friends and interests in common.

11 Give two interpretations of Fig. 5:

    a) It shows that there has been a change in women's role in the family   [2]

    b) It shows that there has not been a change in women's role.   [2]

12 Do you think that husbands and wives should share family tasks equally? Give reasons for your answer.   [5]

13 What method(s) would you use to investigate whether the changes shown in the photographs were widespread?   [7]

Fig. 5

EXTENSION ACTIVITIES

1 **Think about** the statement that 'In spite of recent changes there are still important differences in the parts men and women play in the family.' What evidence exists to support this statement?

2 **Make a study** of decision-making in your family. Keep a diary of how decisions are made. These can range from what to have for tea to where to go on holiday. When you have a lot of examples, see who makes the decisions about which things—about food, leisure, the children, clothes, etc.

3 **Find out**, using books in the library, about the changing roles of men and women this century. Compare family life in 1900 with today by means of photographs and newspaper articles. Look at such things as jobs in the home, courtship, children's behaviour and household spending. Interview the oldest person you know about their parents.

Fig. 4

QUESTIONS

9 What changes in the family are represented by Figs. 4 and 5?   [2]

10 What evidence is there in Fig. 4 that this father regularly washes up?   [2]

ALTERNATIVES TO THE FAMILY

Do we need a family?

There has been a great deal of discussion about whether the family is something that human beings naturally form. The human baby needs an adult for several years if it is to survive by itself. This has led some people to claim that the family is necessary. However, just because a baby needs looking after, it doesn't mean that parents have to do the job. Any adult can look after a baby. There have been several attempts to replace the family as a group because it is felt that families make people too selfish, that people are interested in only their family and themselves.

Communes

You may link communes with the hippie groups of the 1960s or with people who wander around the country. But the idea has been tried out in Britain and the United States for more than a hundred years. There are many types of commune. One idea which they share is that they want to change the normal family structure and try to share more of their life. Sometimes family groups live together, helping each other with the children. In other communes, people all own the house jointly and share the domestic duties. This may seem a good idea, but few communes seem to have lasted for more than two generations.

A news report on communes

‘Lynn is part of a growing number of teens and young twenties who proclaim communal living as the solution to many of society's ills. They feel that within a carefully selected "family" they can do away with loneliness, insecurity and aimlessness and live more economically as well.

I visited several communes and talked with people living there and those who had left. Everyone commented on how contented they were living in a group, but several said they found it too much. Most thought it was a first step to marriage but they hoped to live in close-knit neighbourhoods after they had started a family. Many felt that the commune would eventually become very common.

"You have to realise that our isolated family structures set up in little houses are unnatural," said a short Scotsman at a Hampstead planning meeting. "Man is by nature a pack or tribal animal. He operates best when he feels other people around him who he can trust and be open with. In isolation he becomes suspicious, bitter and nasty."’

From S. Steiner, ‘Communes: Life in a Selective Family’, *Honey*, February 1971; reproduced in R. Ash, *Talking about the Family* (Wayland, 1973), p. 89.

QUESTIONS

1 What are two reasons given in the article for living in a commune? [2]
2 Why does the Scotsman feel that living in a normal family is unnatural? [2]
3 Can you think of two reasons why communes do not usually last for more than two generations? [4]
4 How would living in a commune be different from living in your own family? Give three differences. [6]
5 Using material from the passage, and ideas of your own, make a list of good and bad things about living in a commune. [6]

The kibbutz

Communes have mostly been small in size and have not usually lasted very long. In contrast the kibbutz system in Israel has existed since the 1930s and is very common. The Jews came from many cultures to settle in the newly created state of Israel. To try to unite them and make them think of Israel as their country, the early leaders encouraged a new type of grouping, the kibbutz.

This is a group of people who live in a village-like community and farm. They live as married couples, but they share most things. They have common places to eat and for entertainment. The children spend only a few hours with their parents. The rest of the time they spend together in the ‘children's house’. Some of the features of the kibbutz are shown in Fig. 1.

QUESTIONS

6 Describe two ways in which a kibbutz differs from a family. [2]
7 Do parents on a kibbutz spend more time or less with their children than your parents with you? Give reasons for your answer. [2]
8 Do you think it is a good idea that children do not have toys of their own and have similar sorts of clothing? Give reasons for your answer. [4]
9 If you were living in a kibbutz, what might you like and dislike about the system? [6]
10 Describe two similarities and two differences between life in a commune and life in a kibbutz. [6]

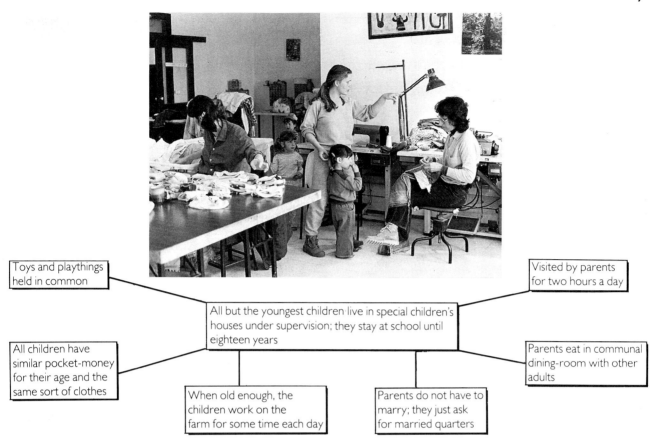

Toys and playthings held in common

Visited by parents for two hours a day

All but the youngest children live in special children's houses under supervision; they stay at school until eighteen years

All children have similar pocket-money for their age and the same sort of clothes

Parents eat in communal dining-room with other adults

When old enough, the children work on the farm for some time each day

Parents do not have to marry; they just ask for married quarters

Fig. 1 Family life in the kibbutz

The children's home

Another alternative to the family which is more common in Britain is the children's home. This is for children who are orphans or whose parents are unable to look after them. These homes are similar to a family, and the people in charge are called housemother or housefather.

They differ from a family in a number of ways. They are larger, usually having up to a dozen children in them. The children are not related and may spend only part of their lives in the home. The relationship of the children to each other and to the houseparents is not quite the same as with natural parents. There may also be other adults who help with the cleaning and cooking.

EXTENSION ACTIVITIES

1   **Compare** life in a commune or a kibbutz with life in a family.
2   **Make a list** of the aspects of family life that communes and the kibbutz are trying to improve.
3   **Make a study** of communes in Britain and other countries:

   a) **Find out** how they look after children, make decisions and live together. Set out the advantages and disadvantages of living together in this way.
   b) **Find out** about the famous American commune at Oneida.
   c) **See** if your local library has copies of the newsletter that communes in Britain circulate. This will give you more information, and you may be able to visit one.

4   **Read about** the kibbutz system. The Israeli Embassy in London will probably give you some information. Explain how the kibbutz movement began and how it has changed over time.
5   **Imagine** you are members of a commune. Role-play your weekly meeting. You live together, you grow your own food and have various craft workshops. Decide who is to do the various tasks in the commune: looking after children, working on the farm, making and selling craft products, repairing the house, cooking, cleaning.

2.7

MARRIAGE

QUESTIONS

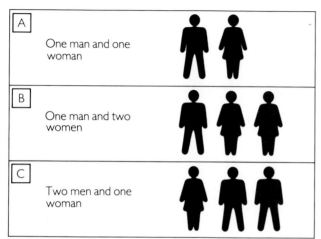

A	One man and one woman
B	One man and two women
C	Two men and one woman

Fig. 1

1 Which of the examples in Fig. 1 are marriages?

Defining marriage

It may surprise you to know that all three examples in Fig. 1 are types of marriage which are found in the world today. Our idea that a marriage should consist of one man and one woman is the commonest type found in practice. But many societies allow one man to have more than one wife, and some allow one woman to have several husbands. This makes it difficult to define marriage.

Marriage is best defined as a relationship between one or more men and one or more women which is recognised by custom or law.

Types of marriage

There are many types and arrangements of marriage, but these are the three commonest forms:

● *monogamy* – one husband and one wife;
● *polygyny* – one husband and more than one wife;
● *polyandry* – one wife and more than one husband.

Any marriage involving more than two adults is known as *polygamy*.

A number of explanations have been put forward for these different types. It has been suggested that polygyny (more than one wife) developed where there was a surplus of females. Similarly, where there was a surplus of men, or where they were likely to be killed, then women took more than one husband. However, these conditions are not found in all situations. For example, in parts of Africa there is a shortage of men, but they still have polyandry. All we can say is that religious ideas, traditions and economic factors all play a part.

Another variation in marriages is which partner is more or most powerful. If the dominant person in the marriage is male, we call it *patriarchy*; if the female is dominant, this is called *matriarchy*.

There are two other types of marriage which you may come across in Britain. A *common-law marriage* is where a man and woman live together permanently but have not gone through a ceremony. An *arranged marriage* is where parents choose the partner for their son or daughter.

Examples of arranged and 'free-choice' marriage

Mani Singh Sandhu married Hirshu Kaur Sandhu. She was chosen by his parents from Mungha, their village in the Punjab. The two had met a few times before the wedding was conducted according to Sikh rites. Divorce is very rare in Sikh families. See Fig. 2.

Fig. 2 A Sikh wedding ceremony

Alan Jackson (aged twenty-two) married Sara Purdy. They met at Sainsbury's, where Sara is a section manager and Alan a check-out assistant. They were married at All Saints Church, Harborne. One in three Western marriages ends in divorce. See Fig. 3.

Fig. 3 A Christian wedding ceremony

2   One of the above examples is of a *free-choice marriage.* Who makes the choice? [1]

3   One of the examples shows an *arranged marriage.* Who arranges it? [1]

4   What do you think the divorce rate for each kind of marriage tells us? [2]

5   Draw up two columns, 'For' and 'Against'. a) Put down the main arguments for and against free-choice marriages. b) Put down the main arguments for and against arranged marriages. [8]

(See also Unit 5.3 for more about arranged marriages.)

Changing marriage patterns

Fig. 4

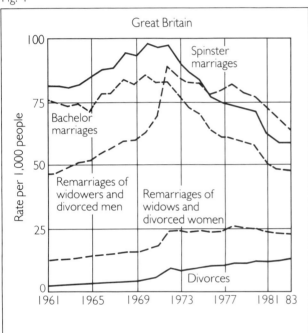

From *Social Trends*, HMSO 1986, p. 38.

Reasons for changing marriage patterns

A number of reasons have been put forward to explain why marriage has become less popular, as shown by Fig. 4. Changing attitudes mean that more people prefer to live together instead of getting married. Birth control is easier, and so couples can have a sexual relationship without having children. More job opportunities for women encourage them to remain independent.

Another change is that people are waiting longer before they get married. Again, there are several reasons. Young people are staying on at school longer, and more are going on to further and higher education. The number of white-collar jobs has increased; in these jobs it takes a longer time than in manual work to get on to higher wage levels. Since 1961 prices have risen sharply, so couples have to save longer before they can get married. This is particularly so for those who want to buy a home. More recently, unemployment has made marriage more difficult for some people.

6   A *spinster marriage* is one where the woman has not been married before. Between which years were the number of spinster marriages at their peak? [2]

7   How do sociologists know how many marriages take place? (See Unit 1.5 if you are not sure.) [2]

8   In your own words, describe the pattern of spinster marriages shown by Fig. 4. [6]

9   Draw a bar graph to show the rate of bachelor marriages in 1965, 1973 and 1981. [6]

10 Will you get married or not? Give reasons for your answer. [4]

1   **Write an account** of why marriage has become less popular over the last twenty years.

2   **Debate** the motion 'Marriage is unnecessary if you really love and trust each other.'

3   **Investigate** teenage marriage. Find out the figures from *Social Trends*. Look at the advantages and disadvantages. Interview three teenagers who are married and compare their answers with three older people who were married in their teens. What special problems are faced by teenage couples? Why is there such a high divorce rate among people who marry in their teens?

THE BREAKDOWN OF MARRIAGE

One in three marriages ends in divorce

Divorce and marital breakdown

Divorce rates continue to rise . . .

It is only when you see headlines such as the above that you realise how common divorce is. One in three marriages will end in divorce, and the rate is increasing. But if you check round in your class at present, there may not be a third who have divorced parents. The reason is that some divorces happen before children are born, or later in life when children have left home.

Other forms of marital breakdown

Divorce can be defined as the legal ending of marriage. But not all couples whose marriage has finished get a divorce. A legal separation is a temporary agreement to live apart. There are also 'empty-shell marriages' where the couple still live together, perhaps for the sake of the children or for financial reasons; but they do not love each other or have a sexual relationship. Sometimes a couple split up but do not get a divorce. They just live apart for the rest of their lives. These factors mean that the official divorce figures are not a full picture of marriage breakdown in Britain.

The pattern of divorce in the twentieth century

Fig. 1 The pattern of divorce, 1900–85

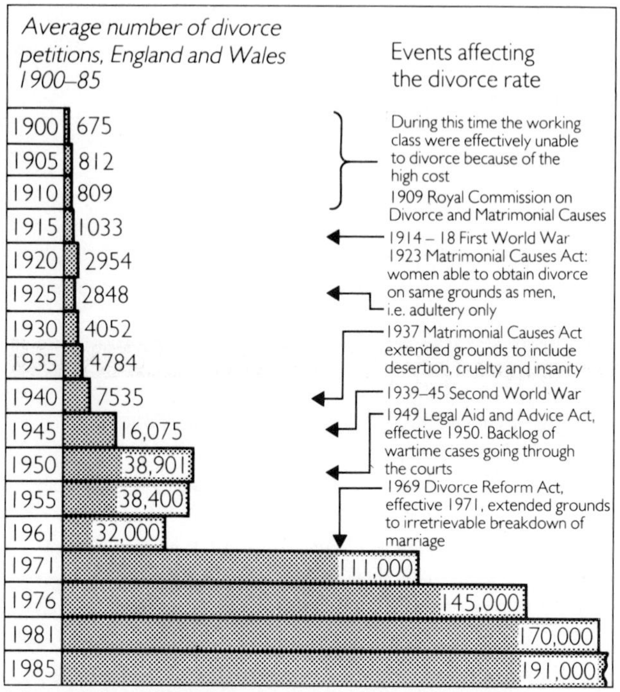

Average number of divorce petitions, England and Wales 1900–85	Events affecting the divorce rate
1900 675	During this time the working class were effectively unable to divorce because of the high cost
1905 812	
1910 809	1909 Royal Commission on Divorce and Matrimonial Causes
1915 1033	1914 – 18 First World War
1920 2954	1923 Matrimonial Causes Act: women able to obtain divorce on same grounds as men, i.e. adultery only
1925 2848	
1930 4052	1937 Matrimonial Causes Act extended grounds to include desertion, cruelty and insanity
1935 4784	
1940 7535	1939–45 Second World War
1945 16,075	1949 Legal Aid and Advice Act, effective 1950. Backlog of wartime cases going through the courts
1950 38,901	
1955 38,400	1969 Divorce Reform Act, effective 1971, extended grounds to irretrievable breakdown of marriage
1961 32,000	
1971 111,000	
1976 145,000	
1981 170,000	
1985 191,000	

Adapted from J.Nobbs, Social Science for GCSE (Macmillan, 1987), p.127.

QUESTIONS

1 Why was it difficult for the working class to obtain a divorce before 1910? [1]
2 Give two of the factors which affected divorce rates in the period 1910 to 1971. [2]
3 How do you know that the bars on the graph were not drawn to scale? Give one example. [4]
4 Give three reasons why divorce figures do not show the true extent of marriage breakdown. [6]
5 Describe the pattern of divorce since 1900. [7]

Reasons for the increase in divorce

?

Increased geographical mobility — Changing role of women — Industrialisation — Decline of religion — Urbanisation — Legal changes — Increased social mobility — Changing ideas about marriage

Fig. 2

6   Explain, using examples, each of the factors associated with divorce shown in Fig. 2.

The social consequences of divorce: a case study

Simon and Marjorie Jeffery were divorced two years ago. Simon met Kay at work and had been going out with her for nearly a year before Marjorie found out. They tried to keep the marriage going for the sake of their two children, but Simon wanted to keep on seeing Kay. After many arguments and much unhappiness they agreed to get a divorce.

Howard Jeffery (aged fourteen): 'I remember the night when Mum found out about Dad. There was a terrible row. Nothing seemed the same again. Even when they were not arguing I could see Mum felt unhappy. It was a relief when they got a divorce.'

Angela Jeffery (aged sixteen): 'I shall never forgive my father for what he did to us. I was just beginning my O–levels when it all blew up. There were terrible arguments. He agreed to give up the other woman but he couldn't. I wish we'd have moved somewhere else and tried to start again as a family. Parents should think more about their children when they do this sort of thing.'

7   What would you have done if you had been in Marjorie's position—asked for a divorce or tried to keep the marriage going? Give reasons for your answer.

8   Divorce is a very complicated process. Write a short paragraph explaining how each of the following factors could affect how the children in a divorced family felt about their parents afterwards: a) the age of the children, b) events leading up to the divorce, c) the financial situation of the parents, d) arrangements for the children after the divorce.

9   If you were a sociologist carrying out research on the breakdown of marriage, how would you decide whether or not a marriage had ended?

1   **Write** a description, giving reasons, of changes in the divorce rate during the twentieth century.

2   **Discuss** whether it is better to live with parents who do not love each other or to have divorced parents.

3   **Make a study** of divorce. Look at the changing patterns this century and at changes in the law. Find out how a divorce is obtained and the costs. Visit a court and write about the legal procedures. If you know someone well, and they don't mind, interview someone whose parents have divorced. Ask them the advantages and disadvantages. Collect newspaper cuttings and accounts of divorce cases. What are some of the problems arising from divorce?

4   **Find out** about second marriages. Find out from *Social Trends* how many people marry again. Why do more men than women remarry? If you know someone well, and they don't mind, interview someone who has married again. If there are children, how well do they get on together? Set out the problems faced by people who remarry. Find out about organisations which help people to find a partner, such as marriage and dating bureaux; how many are there in your area and how much do they charge?

PROBLEMS OF FAMILY LIFE

1 Look through the popular newspapers for one week and cut out all the stories about problems in families. Try to sort them into different problems and make them into a wall display.

Fig. 1

Husband took to drink

Baby Ann 18 months brutally beaten by parents

Battered wife found unconscious

Fig. 2

Critical views of the family

Units 2.1 to 2.6 show mostly a 'rosy' view of the family. They describe the different types of family and how the family prepares children for their place in society. This approach has been criticised because it looks only at the positive things the family does for society. It doesn't look at the problems involved.

Some people say that the modern nuclear family has an advantage because it doesn't have family ties and so can move to where there is work (see Unit 2.2). But this can produce difficulties. A husband and wife, when they are cut off from their other relatives, have only themselves to think about. This can lead them to quarrel more than they would if they belonged to a wider family network. Also, they don't have anyone to turn to if they have a problem.

The small family home is often pictured as very happy. But it may also be a place where there is wife-beating and child abuse. People keep themselves to themselves, and so neighbours do not like to interfere even when they know there is a problem. People often have little contact with their wider family, and the battered wife may have to stay with her violent husband because she has nowhere else to live. Fairy-tales and folk songs of wicked stepmothers and child murderers show that violence in the family is not new. But in the modern, isolated family it may be more hidden than it once was.

Another criticism of the family is that it restricts people's development. It has been said that the function of the family is to produce people who conform to society's rules. And so individuality may not be encouraged by parents.

A similar view is that the family teaches traditional gender roles. It teaches boys to be boys and girls to be girls. This often means preparing girls for an inferior position in society and leading boys to expect to get their own way.

QUESTIONS

Conflict between parents and children

2 Two views of the relationship between parents and children are shown in the photographs. Describe them. [2]

3 In Fig. 1 what do you imagine the father thinks of his daughter's appearance? [2]

4 In Fig. 1 what do you imagine the daughter thinks about her father's attitude to her appearance? [2]

5 Describe three areas where young people might come into conflict with their parents. Give reasons for your choice. [6]

6 Does living in a small nuclear family, compared with an extended family, make conflict between children and parents more or less likely? Give reasons for your answer. [8]

DAVID IS A SINGLE-PARENT FAMILY HE LIVES IN A FLAT WITH HIS DAUGHTER, DONNA AGED 2

AS SOON AS DAVID GETS UP HE FEEDS DONNA

DAVID TAKES DONNA TO A CHILD MINDER

DAVID WORKS IN THE POST OFFICE AS A SORTER

WHEN DAVID GETS HOME HE BATHS DONNA AND PUTS HER TO BED

IN THE EVENING, HOUSEHOLD CHORES INCLUDE IRONING

Fig. 3

QUESTIONS

Single-parent families

7 When you hear about single-parent families, do you normally assume that the parent is the mother or the father? Why? [1]

8 What special point is being made in the story of a single-parent family in Fig. 3? [2]

9 List two advantages for a child being brought up by only one parent. [2]

10 List two disadvantages for a child being brought up by one parent. [2]

11 Why do some women choose not to marry and to bring up their child themselves? [3]

12 Give four reasons why there are more single-parent families today than there were fifty years ago. [4]

13 Can a parent and child like David and Donna be called a family? Look back at the characteristics of a family given by Murdock in Unit 2.2. How many of these do they meet? [6]

Elderly people

The development of the nuclear family has led to another problem. When people get old and are part of an extended family, they are cared for by the family. In agricultural societies, such people are also respected because they have long experience of farming.

In modern societies, people have very different attitudes towards the elderly. Children often move away from their parents and may not want to look after them when they are old. It is often expected that parents will provide for their own old age or that the Welfare State will look after them. Because of the Welfare State and its social services, few old people die through neglect; but they may not be happy or feel respected, and will often be very lonely.

EXTENSION ACTIVITIES

1 **Describe** the problems that the nuclear family faces which are not found in the extended family.

2 **Look back** at Unit 2.6 and write about ways in which the kibbutz and communes might deal with the issues of old people and conflict between parents and children.

3 **Discuss** whether you would have your parents living with you when they are old and infirm.

4 **Role-play** a scene based on Fig. 1. Take the part of the father and daughter shown in the photograph and act out their discussion when the daughter tells her father she wants to go to an all-night party.

FUNCTIONS OF SCHOOLING

Why do you have to attend school?

As you sit in lesson after lesson, you must often have wondered what you were doing in school and why you *had* to attend. Most children look forward to the holidays but also they know that there are some advantages in going to school. Here are some of the answers given by fourth-year students to the question 'why attend school?':

Helen: 'To learn things.'
Promila: 'It will help me to get a better job.'
Andrea: 'School teaches me how to behave.'
Simon: 'I suppose it makes me a better person.'

Children were first made to attend school at the end of the nineteenth century. State schools were set up by the government because it was thought that Britain was falling behind other countries such as Germany and the United States which had introduced schooling for everyone. It is said that schools were necessary because the family could no longer prepare children for a modern, complex industrial society. Schools were also meant to train young people for their future jobs.

Training children for jobs and preparing them for their future roles are just two of the tasks schools are supposed to do. These are called the *functions* of schooling. (You may remember that we described the functions of the family in Unit 2.3.) Other functions carried out by the school on behalf of society are shown in Fig. 1.

Fig. 1 The functions of schooling

Political functions

Social control

Economic functions

Transmission of culture

Individual development

1 Find out about and describe each of the functions of schooling shown in Fig. 1.

2 Look at the replies given by our students at the top of this page to the question, 'Why do children have to attend school?' Fit each one to a function of the school by completing this chart.

	Functions
Helen Promila Andrea Simon	

3 Make a list of all the subjects you are studying this year which give you a skill or knowledge which could be used directly in a job, e.g. typing.

4 Make a list of all those subjects which you think prepare you indirectly for a job, e.g. maths and writing.

5 Make a list of those subjects which do not appear to be preparing you directly for a job at all.

6 Work out how much time you spend on each of these groups of subjects. Do your results support the idea that an important reason why children must attend school is that it prepares them for work?

Resistance to schooling

It is easy to believe that the school carries out all of the functions described in Fig. 1. But if it did this very well, then there would not be problems with teenagers or adults. Clearly the school doesn't always succeed with all students, and some take very little notice of the school.

Anti-school groups

A study of difficult children in a Midlands secondary school was made by Paul Willis. Here is part of an interview he had with a group of boys:

Joey: Of a Monday afternoon, we'd have nothing, right? Nothing hardly relating to school work. Tuesday afternoon we have swimming, and they stick you in a classroom for the rest of the afternoon. Wednesday afternoon you have games, and there's only Thursday and Friday afternoon that you work, if you call that work. The last lesson Friday afternoon we used to go and doss, half o' us wagged out o' lessons, and the other half go into the classroom, sit down and just go to sleep, and the rest of us could join a class where all our mates are.

Will: What we been doing, playing cards in this room, 'cos we can lock the door.

PW: Which room's this, now?

Will: Resources Centre, where we're making the frames [a new stage for the deputy head], s'posed to be.

PW: Oh, you're still making the frames?

Will: We should have had it finished. We just lie there on top of the frame, playing cards, or trying to get to sleep.

PW: What's the last time you've done some writing?

Will: When we done some writing?

Fuzz: Oh, ah, last time was in Careers, 'cos I writ 'yes' on a piece of paper. That broke me heart.

PW: Why did it break your heart?

Fuzz: I mean, to write, 'cos I was going to try and go through the term without writing anything. 'Cos since we've come back, I ain't done nothing. [It was halfway through term.]

From P. Willis, 'The Class Significance of School Counter Culture', in M. Hammersley (ed.), *The Process of Schooling* (Routledge & Kegan Paul, 1976), p. 188.

QUESTIONS

7 These 'lads' (as Willis called them) call boys who work hard in their school 'ear' oles'. What name is given to such people in your school? [1]

8 Give two examples from the interview of how the 'lads' avoid school work. [2]

9 Give three reasons why boys such as Joey do not work hard at school. [6]

10 Paul Willis chose to watch the boys in school and to interview them to carry out his research. What would be the advantages and disadvantages of these methods? [6]

11 Paul Willis called his book *Resistance through Rituals*. Discuss with your teacher what he meant by this. [5]

EXTENSION ACTIVITIES

1 **Write an explanation** of why in an industrial society all young people have to go to school.

2 **Compare** the socialisation functions of the school and the family.

3 **Discuss** the suggestion that young people should be allowed to leave school before the age of sixteen if they want to, provided they have a pass level in basic subjects such as maths and English. Do you think this would get rid of the trouble-makers in schools?

4 **Make a study** of either the pupils/students who 'play up' in your school/college or those who are considered 'good'. You could either interview members of your chosen group or carry out participant observation. Describe the individual members and what they do. If you had time you could interview both groups and compare their views on such topics as teachers, homework and the future. Compare your results with the findings of Ball (see Unit 3.5) or Paul Willis (see above).

EDUCATION IN ENGLAND AND WALES

The structure of education

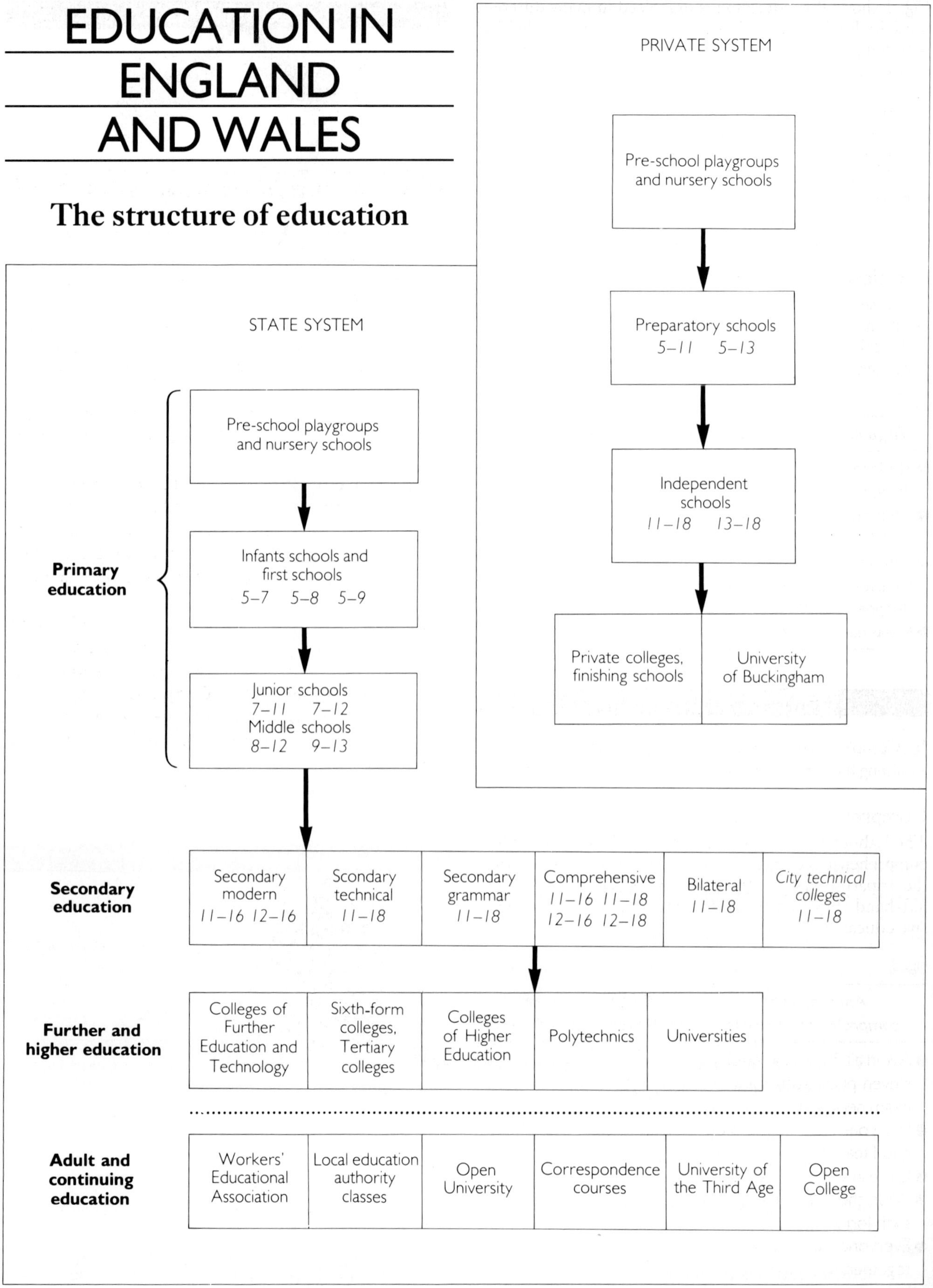

Pre-school playgroups and nursery schools

↓

Preparatory schools
5–11   5–13

↓

Independent schools
11–18   13–18

↓

| Private colleges, finishing schools | University of Buckingham |

STATE SYSTEM

Pre-school playgroups and nursery schools

↓

Primary education

Infants schools and first schools
5–7   5–8   5–9

↓

Junior schools
7–11   7–12
Middle schools
8–12   9–13

↓

Secondary education

| Secondary modern 11–16 12–16 | Secondary technical 11–18 | Secondary grammar 11–18 | Comprehensive 11–16 11–18 12–16 12–18 | Bilateral 11–18 | City technical colleges 11–18 |

↓

Further and higher education

| Colleges of Further Education and Technology | Sixth-form colleges, Tertiary colleges | Colleges of Higher Education | Polytechnics | Universities |

Adult and continuing education

| Workers' Educational Association | Local education authority classes | Open University | Correspondence courses | University of the Third Age | Open College |

Fig. 1 The education system in England and Wales

Fig. 1 shows that education is organised in many different ways in England and Wales. First there is the division between private and state education. Then within the state system there are arrangements for the change between schools at the ages of 7, 8, 9, 11, 12, 13 and 16. The only common factor is that all children must attend school between the ages of 5 and 16. This situation has come about partly as a result of different opinions about schooling. In the rest of this unit we look at some of these debates.

Debates in education

The eleven-plus: for and against selection

Fig. 2 sets out the arguments in favour of the selection of children at the age of eleven into grammar schools, technical schools and secondary-modern schools (the *tripartite* system).

Fig. 2

Arguments for selection	Arguments against selection
● Students learn best with those of similar ability	
● Able students are not held back by the less able	
● Non-academic students can have a special programme designed for them	
● It was easy to set up in 1944	

QUESTIONS

1 Complete the right-hand column in the table (Fig. 2) by listing the arguments against selection.

Comprehensive schools

The Labour government decided in the 1960s to introduce comprehensive education, and most areas changed from the tripartite system. In the following table (Fig. 3) the left-hand column sets out the advantages of comprehensive education.

Fig. 3

Advantages of comprehensive schools	Disadvantages of comprehensive schools
● Avoid all the problems of eleven-plus selection, e.g. exam nerves	
● Everyone has the benefit of good teachers	
● Large in size, many facilities	
● Wide choice of subjects in sixth form.	
● Everyone is educated together, no division between students	

QUESTIONS

2 From your own experience and reading, set out the disadvantages of comprehensive education by completing the right-hand column of the table. (Fig. 3)

EXTENSION ACTIVITIES

1 **Write an account** of the arrangement of schooling up to the age of sixteen in your area.

2 **Describe** both the advantages and the disadvantages of middle schools.

3 **Explain** the meaning of the following statement, and say whether or not you agree with it: 'Grammar schools are unfair to average pupils; comprehensive schools are unfair to able pupils.'

4 **Debate** the following motion: 'Only people with money have the choice of private schools, and so they should be abolished.'

5 **Make a study** of comprehensive schooling in your area. Find out when it was introduced and why. Interview someone who went to a grammar school, or who goes to a grammar school, about their experience there. Do the same for someone in a comprehensive school. Comment on the differences and similarities.

6 **Investigate** the Youth Training Scheme (YTS). Why was it introduced by the government? Describe the change from one year to two years. Interview some people who have been on YTS. What are the advantages and disadvantages? Look at the alternative schemes for unemployed young people, such as the Community Programme.

EDUCATION AND INEQUALITY

Fig. 1

In Unit 3.2 we looked at the structure of education in England and Wales, and at some of the changes which had taken place in it. The most important change at secondary level has been the introduction of *comprehensive schools* (Fig. 1).

Equality of opportunity

There are a number of advantages to comprehensive schools, as we saw in Unit 3.2. An important reason why they were introduced by the Labour government was to improve *equality of opportunity*. This is the idea that everyone in society should have the same chance to achieve their level, regardless of their background.

In Britain the first concern was that young people from the working class did not have equality of opportunity.

They did not have the same chance as middle-class youngsters to get O-levels, go to grammar schools, stay on in the sixth-form or go to university. Evidence for this is shown in Fig. 2 below.

More recently, sociologists have been looking at other groups who seem to be disadvantaged, such as girls and ethnic minorities. Evidence for this is given below.

In the next four units we will be looking at some of the explanations for these differences. In other words, why do middle-class children do better than working-class children, white children better than black children and boys better than girls?

But a word of warning: we shall be describing the overall pattern. If you compare the achievement of all working-class children with all middle-class children, they will do less well, but there will be many working-class children who do better than some middle-class children.

Fig. 2. Social class and educational achievement

Father's social class	% attending selective secondary schools	% obtaining O-level	% obtaining A-level	% attending university
I and II	71.9	58.1	26.9	20.1
III, IV and V	39.6	24.2	6.9	4.6
VI, VII and VIII	23.7	11.8	2.8	1.8

From A.H. Halsey *et al.*, *Origins and Destinations* (Oxford University Press, 1980), p. 184.

1   What percentage of children from social classes I and II go to university? [1]
2   What percentage of children of classes VI, VII and VIII go to university? [1]
3   At which stage is the difference in achievement between the children of social classes I and II and those of social classes VI, VII and VIII greatest: a) eleven-plus, b) O-level, c) A-level or d) university level? [2]
4   If classes I and II form 13 per cent of the population, what percentage of university students should come from these classes if there was equality of opportunity? Explain your answer. [4]
5   Describe and compare the pattern of educational achievement shown by the table for children of classes I and II and classes VI, VII and VIII. [12]

Issues of inequality

Girls and boys

Fig. 3

School-leavers intending to enter full-time further or higher education as a percentage of all school-leavers, by type of course (1983–4)	Boys %	Girls %
Degree	8.5	6.3
Teacher training	0.1	0.7
HND/HNC	0.5	0.4
BTEC	1.6	1.6
GCE A-level	3.8	4.6
GCE O-level	1.9	2.1
Catering	0.7	1.5
Nursing	—	1.7
Secretarial	—	3.7

Compiled from *Social Trends* (HMSO, 1987, p. 61, table 3.12.)

QUESTIONS

6   According to Fig. 2, did more boys or girls go on to study A-levels full-time in 1984? [1]
7   Which group had a larger percentage going to university – boys or girls? [1]
8   Compare your answers to 1 and 2. How do you explain the differences? [4]
9   Which occupational courses were taken almost exclusively by girls? [2]
10 Why are these occupations considered 'female' ones? [2]

Teacher's prejudice?

The Swann Report on *Education for All* (1985) blamed much of the school failure of young Afro-Caribbeans on 'prejudice and discrimination' both inside and outside school. An example of how a teacher may take a prejudiced view of pupils and their parents is given in the following extract.

'Mrs X sees her pupils as the products of largely unstable and uncultured backgrounds, with parents who are irresponsible, incompetent, illiterate and uninterested. Their mothers are seen as immature and unable to cope, having too many young children either by accident or design, while they are still too young. The teacher criticises them for creating "latchkey children" and for frittering away their money on toys and unsuitable clothing.'

Adapted from R. Sharp and A. Green, *Education and Social Control* (Routledge & Kegan Paul, 1975); quoted in Paul Widlake, *Reducing Educational Disadvantage* (Open University Press, 1986), p. 15.

QUESTIONS

11 Who does the teacher, Mrs X, think is to blame for her pupils' poor performance in school? [1]
12 Would you describe the teacher's attitude as understanding or unsympathetic? [1]
13 Do the teacher's views show that she has taken much interest in individual pupils? [1]
14 Explain each of these words, used to describe the teacher's view of her pupils' backgrounds and parents: unstable; uncultured; irresponsible; incompetent; illiterate; uninterested. [6]
15 What else does Mrs X blame the mothers for? [6]
16 Would a teacher such as Mrs X be likely to succeed with pupils who had learning difficulties? Give reasons for your answer. [5]

EXTENSION ACTIVITIES

1   **Describe** some of the problems of educational inequality found in Britain. Use evidence from this unit and from the newspapers and television.
2   **Find out** about and suggest ways of making education a more equal experience for all young people. Possibilities include: home–school liaison, community schools, smaller schools, better funding.

THE FAMILY AND EDUCATIONAL ACHIEVEMENT

The family and achievement

Blaming the family is a very old explanation for the poor school performance of children. You may hear your teachers say, 'She doesn't get any help from the home', or 'They don't care if he comes to school or not'. Home background was one of the first factors sociologists looked at when they were trying to explain why some children did less well than others – see Fig. 1.

Fig. 1 The family and educational achievement

Factor 1: material conditions of the home

Some researchers have suggested that the physical condition of the home may affect achievement. J.W.B. Douglas in his study found that children from poorer homes did less well in school than children from well-off homes. If the home is overcrowded and there is nowhere to do homework, children are likely to find it harder to work. Lack of books and equipment may also be a handicap.

Another common idea is that money, or the lack of it, can affect achievement. It is thought that poor families cannot afford the costs of uniform at grammar schools or cannot afford to let their children stay on in the sixth form. They have to leave and get a job. There may be some truth in this idea, particularly for very poor people. But some families who aren't very well off do let their children stay on at school. So attitudes may be as important as income levels.

Factor 2: child-rearing practices

Being intelligent or unintelligent is not the only factor influencing how well you do at school. You have to do your homework, present your work neatly and learn things which are sometimes boring. To do such things you need

Families pass on culture

Families have views about schools

Families encourage or discourage children

Families provide the conditions for learning

qualities of determination, self-control and being organised; they do not depend on being 'intelligent' in the sense of 'quick-witted'.

Qualities such as neatness and determination are thought to be taught during childhood. It has been suggested that some parents give in too much to their children and indulge them. The result is that they are less prepared to wait for their rewards. So instead of doing homework properly, they are allowed out to play with their friends or to watch TV. Homework is less likely to be checked by such parents, and their children are more easily bored by the lessons and do not pay attention.

The above child-rearing pattern is often – but not always – associated with working-class homes. In contrast, parents who encourage orderliness and hard work in their children are usually seen as having middle-class values. This 'middle-class' approach is more successful at producing good students.

Factor 3: values and attitudes

Something else passed on to children during their up-bringing are values and attitudes. It has been suggested that the values of the working class are less supportive of education than those of the middle class. Examples are set out in Fig. 2.

Fig. 2 Values and education

Working-class values	Implications for education
● Tend to think only of the present ● A sense of fatalism—they do not think they control their lives	Children encouraged to enjoy themselves when they are young; children feel there is little they can do to improve their position
Middle-class values	
● Tend to think of the future ● Optimistic—a belief in their ability to influence their future	Children encouraged to plan ahead and wait for their rewards; children believe they can be successful

Factor 4: language

An important idea about why some children do less well at school was developed out of the work of Professor Basil Bernstein. He had suggested that there were two broad types of language code: a *restricted code*, which people use when they know each other well and have a lot in common; and an *elaborated code*, which is used when people have less in common and there is a need to explain things.

The restricted code uses short, simple sentences, a limited range of descriptive words and such phrases as 'you know' and 'isn't it'. The elaborated code uses more complex sentences and a wider choice of words.

Bernstein said that working-class children were more likely to use a restricted code and middle-class children an elaborated code. This could be a handicap for working-class children in the classroom, because most school work is based on the elaborated code. The working-class child can use the elaborated code which the school requires, but has less practice in it than the middle-class child.

QUESTIONS

Fig. 3 Social class differences in achievement

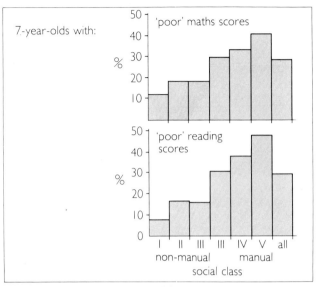

From *New Society*, 15 March 1984

1 Looking at the two graphs in Fig. 3 as a whole, are there more 'poor' students in maths than in reading? [1]
2 How much greater is the percentage of poor readers in class II than in class I? [1]
3 Why are there more children from classes III (manual), IV and V with poor reading scores than from classes I, II and III (non-manual)? [5]
4 What are the problems for teachers or researchers in deciding what is a 'poor' reading or maths score? [3]

EXTENSION ACTIVITIES

1 **Write** about how influences outside the school affect a child's educational achievement in school. Your answer should include the following: family, income, home environment, parental attitudes, language, child rearing.
2 **Role-play**, in groups, how different families react to children's homework. Prepare short scenes to show, first, the keen mother and father who carefully watch everything the pupil does, then the parents who take no interest in their children's homework. The role-play could begin with the child coming in from school and getting out the homework on the table.
3 **Make a study** of the discipline techniques used by families. Prepare a questionnaire to ask your friends how their parents punish and reward them. Compare the results of a small sample of boys and girls.
4 **Find out** from books about child-rearing practices and educational achievement. This is a complicated area, because studies have very different findings. Find as many studies as you can in your library and then sort them out in a clear and logical way. A good book to begin with is that by Olive Banks called *The Sociology of Education* (Batsford, 1969).

THE SCHOOL AND SOCIAL CLASS

> If the children pass it's because I'm a good teacher.
> If they fail it's because they aren't very clever and don't work!

Fig. 1

Fig. 1 shows the attitude of some teachers. They take credit for young people's success but blame them for their failure. In the 1960s sociologists began to look closely at schools and teachers to see what part they played in students' achievement. They found that some features of schools could be influencing differences in achivement.

Teachers' perceptions of children in terms of social class

QUESTIONS

In your own words, describe how teachers' expectations might influence the achievement of children they consider working-class, as shown in Fig. 1.

Teacher unfairness

Rist's study was a longitudinal observation of an inner-city, "urban ghetto school" in the USA. Twice each week he spent an hour and a half in the kindergarten (reception) class and in the second grade (aged eight). His thesis is that teachers have an image of an "ideal client"–a concept of the "sort of child" who does well–and relate to children in their class on the basis of this ideal client. Rist observed that within a week of starting school the teacher with whom he was working had grouped the children so that as one moved from the nine children seated around the table nearest the teacher to the ten furthest away, there was an increasing difference between them. The latter group were all

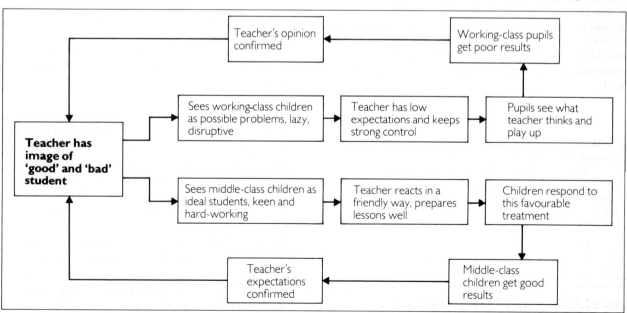

Fig. 2 How teachers perceive students in terms of social class

poorly dressed and generally unkempt, they did not take the initiative in classroom activities, were less adept at the use of "school language" and were more likely to come from homes with low income, large families and whose parents had had little education.

From P. Robinson, *Perspectives on the Sociology of Education* (Routledge & Kegan Paul, 1981), p. 110.

QUESTIONS

6 Which class appears to have misbehaved most in this school? [1]
7 Identify and explain two reasons why detentions were high in Band 2. [4]
8 Identify and explain two reasons why detentions were low in Band 1. [4]
9 How might you explain the low number of detentions in class 3MA? [3]
10 Give four reasons why detentions may not be a fair way of comparing the misbehaviour of classes. [8]

QUESTIONS

1 What sort of children were seated nearest to the teacher? [1]
2 Where do teachers in your school seat children who they think might be troublesome? [1]
3 Describe the teacher's 'ideal pupil'. [4]
4 What method of research did Rist use and why might he have chosen it for this study? [6]
5 What are three disadvantages of this method which he might have come across, and how might they have been overcome? [8]

Streaming

Another feature of schools which may be to the disadvantage of working-class pupils is *streaming* (or banding). This is where pupils are sorted into classes on the basis of their achievement. Studies have shown that pupils from poorer homes are over-represented in lower streams, and pupils from well-off homes are over-represented in upper streams.

This seems to affect children in a number of ways. Those in lower forms feel they have 'failed' so they don't work hard. Those in the top streams tend to get the best teachers, the newest books and the best rooms such as science laboratories. Teachers prefer to teach the higher streams, and they get a more academic syllabus. All this produces a reaction from pupils; the lower streams are more likely to behave badly, and the higher streams to co-operate with the school. Evidence for this is shown in Fig. 3.

Fig. 3 Banding and behaviour

Number of third-year detentions recorded for one school year		
Band 1	Band 2	Band 3
3CU 22	3WX 185	3MA 13
3FT 6	3BH 125	(remedial)
3ST 9	3TA 110	3UD 118
3GD 9	3LF 141	

From S.J. Ball, *Beachside Comprehensive* (Cambridge University Press, 1981), p. 25.

School resources

Sociologists have also looked at differences in the resources of schools, such as buildings, equipment and teachers. Schools in better-off areas are more likely to be newer and better equipped and to attract good teachers. In contrast, schools in inner-city areas which serve mainly working-class children tend to be old and not very attractive.

It has also been said that schools within the same local education authority may be treated differently. If a school is thought to be good, then it attracts good teachers; pupils work hard, and so it gets good results. The local authority is then more likely to give it extra resources such as a language laboratory. Poor schools, where staff do not like to stay, get poor results. So extra money is not spent on them. Where this happens they are likely to be schools used more by the working class.

Changes in school provision because of falling numbers of children are discussed in Unit 8.6 on local authorities.

EXTENSION ACTIVITIES

1 **Write** about the effect of streaming on children's educational achievement.
2 **Find out** the meaning of the following terms used in the sociological study of education; self-fulfilling prophecy, labelling, anti-school culture, compensatory education, educational disadvantage.
3 **Investigate** streaming or banding in your school. Keep these questions in mind: When does streaming begin. On what is it based? How many pupils change stream each year? What subjects and examinations does each stream take? Interview the headteacher or a senior teacher about why they have streaming. What are the attitudes of teachers to different streams? What are the reactions of pupils in different streams?
4 **Make a study** of homework. Ask friends in different years to keep a homework diary for a month, noting the type of homework and how long it takes them. Analyse the results by class and subject. Interview teachers and your headteacher about why they set homework. Carry out a survey of pupils on their attitude to it.

GENDER AND EDUCATIONAL ACHIEVEMENT

QUESTIONS

2 Using Fig. 1, list two subjects taken more by girls than by boys. [2]
3 List two subjects taken more by boys than by girls. [2]
4 What sort of career might the subjects taken mainly by girls lead to? [2]
5 What sort of career might the subjects taken mainly by boys lead to? [2]
6 How useful are GCSE entries for investigating the different subjects taken by boys and girls? [2]

QUESTIONS

1 If you are in a co-educational school or college, write down ten ways in which boys and girls are treated differently.

Heredity or environment?

In Unit 3.3 we looked at some of the differences between boys and girls. You may also be surprised to know that girls do better on average than boys at O-level and when getting two A-levels. But more boys get three A-levels and go on to university and higher degrees.

There has been a long debate about whether the differences in achievement between boys and girls are *natural* (caused by biological differences) or *environmental* (a result of the different way boys and girls are treated). This is a difficult question to decide. But in this unit we are going to look at some of the ways in which the school treats boys and girls differently and how it may affect their school achievement.

Fig. 1 The sex gap

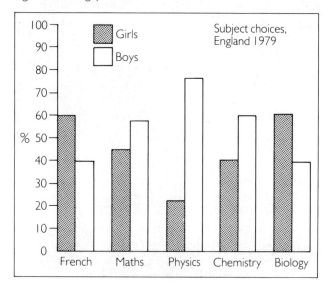

Teachers' perceptions

Look at your answer to question 1 at the start of this unit. You should have written down a number of ways in which boys and girls are treated differently. Michelle Stanworth, a sociologist, did a similar thing to this. She spent some time in a school observing how teachers treated boys and girls. She described how boys got more attention from the teacher because they were thought to be more difficult to teach. During the lessons, teachers talked more to the boys and favoured them in the topics they taught – choosing heraldry or wars, for example.

This extra attention might explain why boys feel more confident in school. Teachers might also influence the choice of subjects or careers, suggesting that some are more suitable for boys, others for girls. What would your teacher say if a girl said she wanted to be a North Sea diver?

QUESTIONS

7 If you wanted to investigate how teachers treat boys and girls differently, what methods would you use and why?

The hidden curriculum

The *hidden curriculum* means those things you learn in school which you are not aware of. For example, you probably are not aware that when you are taught to obey the rules of the school, this is preparation for obeying the laws of the world outside.

The school treats girls and boys in many different ways, and it has been said that this has some influence on their ambitions and achievement. For example, although both boys and girls may be made prefects, they may be asked to do different duties. The girls perhaps serve the tea to visitors, while the boys may take charge of the difficult classes.

These hidden messages are also passed on by the use of space in schools. Boys, with their games of football and cricket, push girls to the edges of the playground. All this may give girls the secret message that they are less important.

Hidden messages are also passed on by textbooks. We talk about *stereotypes* – when an occupation is shown to be always filled by one sex or another. For example, nurses are nearly always shown as female, chefs as male – see Figs. 2, 3 and 4.

QUESTIONS

8   Look at Figs. 2, 3 and 4. Which of the photographs does not show a gender stereotype?   [1]

9   Choose one of the photographs and explain why it could be described as sexist.   [3]

10   Are there any boys or girls in your class who intend not to follow stereotyped occupations? Give two examples.   [2]

11   How might photographs such as these influence behaviour?   [2]

12   Why might photographs such as these be described as part of the *hidden curriculum*?   [4]

13   What methods might you use to check whether school textbooks contained stereotyped images? Give reasons for your suggestions.   [8]

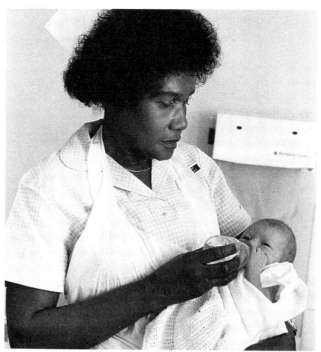

Fig. 2

Role models

Another way pupils may be influenced in schools is by the adults they see around them. If they see men holding the most important positions such as headteacher, head of science or head caretaker then this gives the impression that men are naturally leaders and more important than women. Even when men and women have the same position, such as deputy heads, you may find that the female head carries out 'women's tasks' such as being responsible for pupil welfare. Pupils see these differences as 'normal' and model themselves on them.

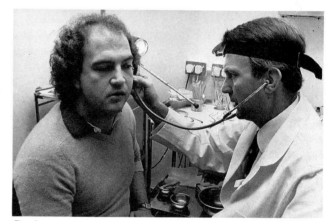

Fig. 3

EXTENSION ACTIVITIES

1   **Write an explanation** of what is meant by the *hidden curriculum*. How might it influence the achievement of either boys or girls?

2   **Discuss** what methods a) boys and b) girls use in your class to get round your teachers.

3   **Make a study** of role models in your school or college. Draw up a table of the important positions and whether they are held by men or women. (Don't forget non-teaching staff!) Describe and discuss the pattern of authority shown by your results. Examine the relationship between gender and subjects taught.

Fig. 4

EDUCATION AND RACE

Problems in talking about race

Fig. 1 Our multi-racial society

Fig. 2 Educational achievement of children of Afro-Carribean, Asian and other origin

	Afro-Caribbean %	Asian %	Other school-leavers %
CSE/O-level in English language	9	21	29
CSE/O-level in maths	5	20	19
One or more A-level passes	2	13	12
University places	1	3	3

From the *Rampton Report* (HMSO, 1981).

The photograph in Fig. 1 show the first problem in talking about race and educational achievement. There are so many different groups that it is impossible to say anything that applies to all of them. Some people from India have paler skins than many so-called 'white' people.

In this book we are going to use the term ethnic minorities to describe the different racial groups who have come to live in Britain in recent years. It will not be possible for us to deal with all the different minority groups, so we are going to look mainly at the achievement of children of Afro-Caribbean and Asian origin, because these have had most research done about them.

QUESTIONS

1 Which group of children get the poorest results in every subject and level? [1]

2 At which level do Asian children do better than other school-leavers? [1]

3 Why is it misleading to talk about 'Asian children' as if they were one group? [3]

4 Why has the author chosen to look at results in English and maths rather than other subjects? Do you think this is a suitable choice? Give reasons for your answer. [7]

5 List and comment on three other pieces of information you would need to know in order to use this table to compare the achievement of these groups of children. [8]

6 You have read in Units 3.3 and 3.5 about the existence of teacher prejudice and unfairness. What does this tell you about the *limitations* of the figures in Fig. 2?

Explanations of under-achievement

'Intelligence' and racist myths

Because poor, foreign-born and ethnic-minority children often do less well than average at school, the myth grew up that they were less intelligent. IQ tests were said to 'prove' this fact. However, it is now widely believed that IQ tests – and results at school – fail to take into account social background. How can we compare the intelligence of different groups unless they have grown up in identical situations?

Social factors

As you can see, this is a very difficult subject. So what we are going to do is to outline some of the factors, other than 'intelligence', which have been put forward to explain the differences in achievement shown in Fig. 2. As you will see in Fig. 3, these are mostly *social* factors, unconnected with what we call 'intelligence'.

Fig. 3 Factors influencing the achievement of minority children

EXTENSION ACTIVITIES

1 **Write** about why ethnic-minority children often do less well in school than other children.

2 **Describe** some of the problems sociologists face in trying to explain the differences in achievement between different groups.

3 **Hold a discussion** on why some of the words used to describe ethnic-minority groups are offensive.

4 **Make a study** of teachers' attitudes to different pupils: boys/girls, white/black, able/less able. Begin by looking at the studies carried out by sociologists: D. Hargreaves on good/bad pupils, Rex and Wilkinson on ethnic groups. Talk to your friends and write down examples from your own school or college. Try to describe the way teachers convey to pupils what they feel about them.

SOCIAL DIFFERENCES BETWEEN PEOPLE

If you were asked to write down a list of differences between people you might mention hair colour, gender, height, clothing, family background, talents, and so on. The list could be endless. These are all differences between people. Social scientists are also interested in differences between people, but mainly in those differences which affect people's position in society. Having brown hair is unlikely to make much difference to a person's position in society, but having half a million pounds or being a street sweeper is likely to have an effect upon how somebody lives and is seen by others.

Fig. 1

Patterns of difference in other societies

It seems that there has never been a society in which people have been considered equal. There are always differences between groups which affect the way they are treated by other people. In some early societies, such as among the Australian Aborigines, work and food were shared out equally. But for the Aborigines people's social position depended on their age. Boys and young men were low down on the social scale, but as men grew through the stages of hunter, warrior and 'elder' they were more and more respected as decision-makers. (Like many early societies, the Aborigines treated males very differently from females – see Unit 4.6 on gender and inequality.)

Other societies have developed other ways of treating people differently. In a *caste system*, people are born into their place in society and cannot change it during their lifetime. This is the traditional social system of India. A person's caste decides their occupation and also who they are considered free to marry or mix with socially. The Hindu system has five main castes: priests and nobles; rulers and administrators; merchants and farmers; manual workers; and 'untouchables'.

Slavery is a system based on dividing society into two groups: free people and slaves. Slaves have no rights and are owned by their masters/mistresses, who have complete control over them. Slavery was common in the ancient world, existed in the United States till a little over 100 years ago, and still survives on a small scale in some parts of the Third World.

The *estate* (or *feudal*) *system* existed in Europe in the Middle Ages. Each social group was known as an estate. At the top was the King or Queen, who was considered the rightful owner of all the land. He or she gave some land away to the nobles and clergy in return for services–either fighting-men or food. The nobles did the same for lesser gentry who served them. Below the gentry in the social structure were craftsmen and freemen, and at the bottom were the serfs, who were little more than slaves.

The modern pattern

Some aspects of the earlier systems exist in modern industrial societies. We still have remains of the estates system in Britain – the landowning aristocracy. And sometimes – for example, in the legal profession – we tend to give extra respect to the views of older, more experienced people, as the Aborigines did.

However, a modern society does not just have one simple structure or 'family tree' in which everybody knows their place. Most people agree that we have a *class system*, but it is less easy to define than the earlier systems, and different writers have highlighted different aspects of it. But most people agree that the differences between people in modern society are basically economic ones–differences in wealth and income. Economic differences are reflected in other differences – in housing, education, occupation, power, status, health and other aspects of people's lives.

How can differences be measured?
Some of the differences between people in modern society are fairly straightforward to identify and measure. Others are harder to measure because they depend on people's feelings (sometimes called *perception*) about their position.

QUESTIONS

Social differences
A list of differences between people is given below. Describe how you would observe and measure each of these differences in a population. You could choose to take the national population for 1, 2 and 3, and your local area for 4 to 7.

1   Economic differences–differences in wealth and income.
2   Occupation differences–between different types of paid work.
3   Differences of gender, race and age.
4   Power differences–differences between people in terms of how much control they have over their own and other people's lives.
5   Differences of status–how people are looked on by others.
6   Differences of class-consciousness–some people feel strongly about belonging to a particular social class, while others do not.
7   Differences in culture, values and upbringing.

Power and authority are discussed in Unit 7.1. The other areas of difference are looked at in the following units.

EXTENSION ACTIVITIES

1   **Find out** about, and write a description of, either slavery, caste or the estate system.
2   **Describe** how social class in a modern society differs from a caste or estate system.
3   **Invite** a Hindu student to speak to the class on caste in Britain today.
4   **Discuss** the role of the monarchy and the aristocracy in the social system of modern Britain.

MEASURING ECONOMIC DIFFERENCES

Differences in wealth

Fig. I Marketable wealth in the UK

Percentage of wealth owned by	1971	1983
Most wealthy 1% of population	31	20
Most wealthy 5% of population	39	27
Most wealthy 25% of population	86	78
Most wealthy 50% of population	97	96

From *Social Trends* (HMSO, 1986). p.92, table 5.22.

QUESTIONS

1 By what percentage did the wealth owned by the top 1 per cent of the population change between 1971 and 1983? [1]

2 By what percentage did the wealth owned by the top 50 per cent of the population change between 1971 and 1983? [1]

3 What percentage of the nation's wealth was owned by the bottom 50 per cent of the population in 1983? [1]

4 Using examples from your own family, explain the differences between wealth and income. [5]

5 Describe the pattern of ownership of wealth in 1983 as shown by Fig. 1. [6]

6 Describe and comment on how the pattern of ownership of wealth has changed between 1971 and 1983 as shown by Fig. 1. [6]

Wealth and income

What is the difference between *wealth* and *income*? Wealth means goods which are *owned*, such as land, buildings, machinery and household goods. Income, however, means in-coming wealth, such as wages and profits.

Differences of wealth are often more extreme than those of income. It is the possession of land and property that separates the very rich from most of the population, who do not usually own anything more than their basic necessities of housing and a car, with perhaps a few shares in privatised companies. However much people may move from job to job and raise their income, there is relatively little change in the wealth owned by the most wealthy half of the population, as Fig. 1 has shown.

Differences in income and earnings

Apart from the very wealthy, whose income derives from land and other forms of ownership, income depends mainly on *occupation* – on the paid work we do. There are wide differences in what people may earn, even in a society like Britain which has fewer extremes of rich and poor than many other countries. Even so, some people earn less than £2 per hour for casual work such as cleaning, while chairmen and directors of large and successful companies are paid up to £1 million a year.

These large differences are justified in terms of the *division of labour* in society. High incomes are said to be the reward for hard work and developing special skills (see Unit 4.3 on occupations and social class). However, there are many other factors which affect incomes, apart from people's skills. One example is the use of power, which is discussed in Unit 7.2.

Some people argue that the lowest income groups should receive more. There are organised groups of people concerned about low incomes, including the Child Poverty Action Group and trade unions. Also, there is concern about low incomes and poor working conditions on humanitarian grounds. This was the motivation behind the trade unions in Britain at the end of the nineteenth century as they battled for better pay and conditions for dockers, textile workers and other poorly paid people.

Fig. 2 Differences in earnings

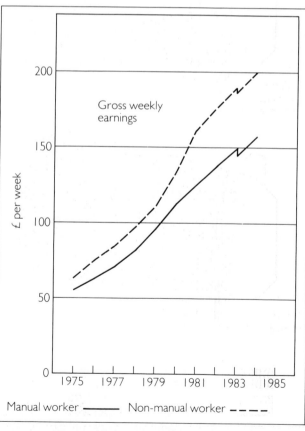

From *Social Trends* (HMSO, 1986), p. 87, table 5.15.

7 Estimate from Fig. 2 the average earnings in 1975 of
a) manual workers and b) non-manual workers. [2]
8 Estimate from Fig. 2 the average earnings in 1985 of
a) manual workers and b) non-manual workers. [2]
9 Using the information from questions 1 and 2, work out
the increase in earnings of both manual and non-manual
workers over the period 1975–1985. [6]
10 Using examples of your own, explain the difference
between earnings and income. [4]
11 Which of these two groups, manual or non-manual, is
most likely to have income other than earnings? Explain
your answer and give examples. [6]

12 Which of the four groups in Fig. 3 had the greatest
percentage of people owning their homes outright? [1]
13 Which of the four groups had the greatest percentage of
people renting homes from the council? [1]
14 Describe the pattern of home ownership of any one of
the groups. [6]
15 The percentage of people owning their own home
outright is similar for each social class. What differences
are not shown by these figures? [4]
16 Complete the following table from the pie charts. [8]

	Owned outright %	Owned with mortgage %	Rented from council or private %
Non-manual	36		
Manual	30		

Differences in housing

Fig. 3

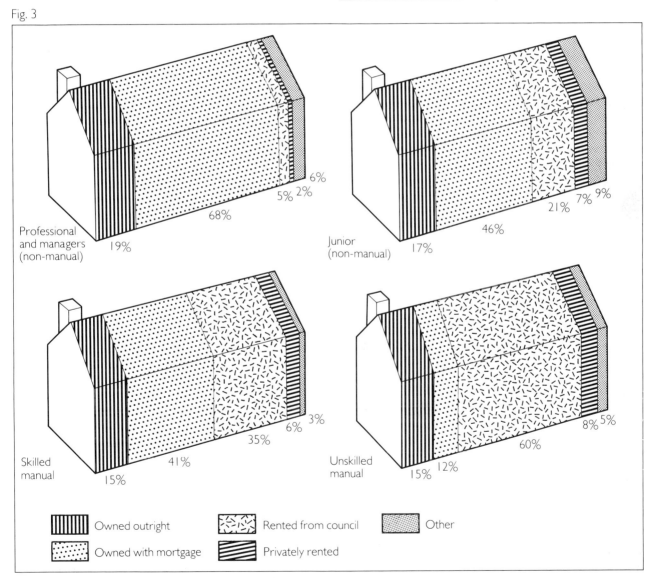

Professional and managers (non-manual): 19%, 68%, 6%, 5%, 2%

Junior (non-manual): 17%, 46%, 21%, 7%, 9%

Skilled manual: 15%, 41%, 35%, 6%, 3%

Unskilled manual: 15%, 12%, 60%, 8%, 5%

|||||| Owned outright
∴∴∴ Owned with mortgage
≀≀≀ Rented from council
▨ Privately rented
∵∵ Other

Based on *Social Trends* (HMSO, 1985), p. 126, table 8.7.

OCCUPATIONS AND SOCIAL CLASS

QUESTIONS

1 List the occupations in Fig. 1 in order of the importance of their position in society. Look at the photographs and choose the job you think is most highly rated. Give this number 1. Then choose the one you think is next, and so on.

2 Set out a table like this, with the occupations down one side and the number ranking down the other. Collect the results from the rest of the class.

Occupation	Ranking						
	1	2	3	4	5	6	7

3 For which occupations is there most agreement about ranking and which the least?

4 How do you explain the agreement and disagreement?

What is social class?

Class is a very difficult thing to define. Besides depending on a person's occupation, it also has something to do with their wealth, their education, their housing and their general life-style.

There are many possible approaches to defining social class. And there is also disagreement about the importance of defining class. For example, some sociologists believe that it is not very helpful to divide people up into rigid categories, as if they were different kinds of fish or minerals. All people are different, and we are all a mixture of habits and ways of doing things that might be called working-class or middle-class.

Fig. 1

Barwoman

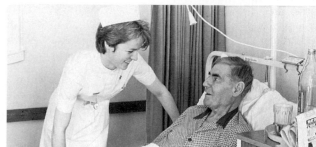

Nurse

Solicitor

Newspaper seller

Teacher

Bricklayer

Pop singer

Karl Marx's ideas

Many writers, following the ideas of Karl Marx, who wrote more than one hundred years ago, have tried to analyse Western societies mainly in terms of the conflict between two great social classes: the *capitalists* or *bourgeoisie*, who owned the factories, businesses and land; and the *workers* or *proletariat*, who owned nothing but their power to work and sell that work for wages in order to live. Marx thought that these two groups would always be in conflict in such societies. The workers would not like working for someone who made a profit out of them. The capitalists were anxious to make their employees work as hard as possible in order to make profits.

When Marx wrote this, he thought that a revolution was certain to happen. The owners would, he believed, become more and more powerful, while the workers would gradually realise they were being exploited and would join together to overthrow the system.

This has not happened. But Marx's ideas are still useful because they point to the basic conflict between workers and employers.

Functions of the class system

We have already looked at functionalist views of the family and education. These are the views of sociologists who think that each feature of a society can be looked at in terms of its possible function for that society. So, for social class, they ask what function does dividing people into groups serve? They say that this arrangement is for the benefit of society as a whole.

In a society, some tasks are very demanding. Others require special skills. To get people to take on these demanding jobs or to use their special skills, society gives them extra rewards. These rewards may be money, or extra status. So, to functionalists, dividing a society into classes, some of whom get more than others, is a way of encouraging people to undertake particular necessary tasks. A social class is therefore a group of people who have similar skills or do similar jobs and get similar economic rewards.

Practical approaches to social class

Although there is no common agreement on how we are to define social class, sociologists often need to be able to divide people into classes for their research. This is considered necessary so that one piece of research can be compared with another.

There are a number of these scales of social class. The best known is the *Registrar General's Scale*. This is used for the Census and for other official surveys. It consists of about 30,000 occupations. These have been grouped on the basis of their general social standing into six social classes:

- Class I: Higher professions, e.g. doctor, lawyer.
- Class II: Other professions and technical/managerial/intermediate, e.g teacher, nurse.
- Class III (non-manual): Skilled non-manual, e.g. salesperson, supervisor.
- Class III (manual): Skilled manual, e.g bricklayer, electrician.
- Class IV: Partly skilled, e.g. postal worker, telephonist.
- Class V: Unskilled, e.g. driver's mate.

QUESTIONS

9 Match the occupations shown in the photographs in Fig. I to the Registrar General's Scale of social class.

EXTENSION ACTIVITIES

1 **Describe** two ways in which social class may be defined.
2 **Make a display** to show different social classes. Cut out pictures from newspapers and magazines to correspond to each of the Registrar General's classes.
3 **Carry out a study** of pupils' ideas of social class. Find some photographs of people in different occupations. Show them to samples of pupils either of different ages or in different groups. Draw up a sheet to record their answers. Set out your results and comment on them.
4 This is a difficult project. **Make a study** of Karl Marx and his ideas on social class. Find out how modern thinkers have modified his ideas. Draw a map to show which countries in the world claim to be Marxist. Find out why some people are strongly opposed to Marxist ideas, and why others strongly support them.

QUESTIONS

5 Look back at the photographs in Fig. I. Explain the high position of the solicitor in terms of the division of labour. [4]
6 How would the division of labour explain the low ranking of the barman? [4]
7 What position did you give the pop singer in Fig. I: high, middle or low? Give three reasons for your answer. [6]
8 Explain why functionalists might have difficulty explaining the following:

a) The high class of people with titles regardless of their jobs. [3]
b) The ranking of social workers or nurses. [3]

SOCIAL CLASSES IN BRITAIN

The working class

The Registrar General sees classes III (skilled manual), IV (semi-skilled manual) and V (unskilled manual) as the working class (Fig. 1).

For Marx, the working class were those who did not own the means of production. More recently, David Lockwood has suggested that the working class contains three groups: *proletarian* – the traditional working class in industrial cities; *deferential* – people with low incomes who accept the leadership of their 'betters'; and *privatised* – a newly affluent group who are concerned with their family, money and possessions.

The middle class

There is some debate about whether we should talk about the middle class or the middle class*es*. The Registrar General sees classes I (professional), II (managerial and technical) and III (clerical and minor supervisory) as the middle class (Fig. 2).

J.H. Goldthorpe identified four groups within it: the old-established middle class, such as owners and independent professionals; the newly established middle class, such as managers; the old marginal middle class, such as the owners of small businesses; and a new marginal middle class, such as routine white-collar workers.

QUESTION

Working class and middle class compared

1 Drawing on information from Units 4.1, 4.2 and 4.3 and your own experience, write out and complete the following table.

Characteristic	Working class	Middle class
Values	Belief in the class solidarity of working people	Society consists of many groups which you can move into with your own effort
	Sometimes the welfare of the group is more important than individual freedom	Individual freedom of choice is all-important
	Live for the present, enjoy life while you can	Plan for the future, give up pleasures today so as to be better off in the future
	You can only get on with the help of your family and fellow workers	You get ahead by your own individual efforts
Voting	The majority vote for the Labour Party (but a large minority do not)	Majority vote for the Conservative Party (but many do not)
Trade-union activity	Many join trade unions	Less inclined to join trade unions, prefer professional associations
Work	Often paid by the hour, work involves physical activity, statutory holidays, few perks, no company pension, extra earnings from overtime and piecework, liable to unemployment	Salary, work with 'head', holidays longer than average, company perks, pensions, annual increments, security
Housing		
Education (see Unit 3.5)		
Language		
Child rearing (see Unit 3.5)		
Clothing		
Food		
Leisure		
Family life (see Section 2)		

Fig. I A working class family

Fig. 2 A middle class family

Fig. 3 The upper class at Ascot

The upper class

To many of you, the upper class may seem like a shadowy group left over from the past. But it still exists (Fig. 3). Because it is rich and powerful it can buy privacy and resist sociologists asking it questions!

At the very top is the Queen, the Royal Family and the traditional aristocracy. They live in country houses on large estates. Although connected with land they also have investments in property and industry. This traditional aristocracy has been joined by other rich people who have made their money from industry, commerce or banking and finance; for example, the Sainsbury and the Guinness families (Fig. 4).

Fig. 4 The top ten richest people in Britain

1	The Queen	£3,340 m
2	Sir John Moores (Littlewoods Pools and mail order)	£1,700 m
3	Garry Weston (Food)	£1,500 m
4	Duke of Westminster (Land)	£1,400 m
5	Sir James Goldsmith (Food)	£1,000 m
6	Sainsbury family (Food)	£1,000 m
7	Vestey family (Meat)	£1,000 m
8	Robert Maxwell (Printing/Publishing)	£700 m
9	Cayzer family (Ships)	£600 m
10	Clark family (Shoes)	£500 m

From a list compiled by *Money* magazine, February 1988.

QUESTIONS

2 Who is the richest person in Britain? [1]
3 Who on the list in Fig. 4 are part of the traditional aristocracy? [2]
4 Who on the list are part of the new rich upper class? [3]
5 According to a survey carried out by *Money* magazine in February 1988, Paul McCartney's wealth is estimated to be £79 million. What are the arguments for and against Paul McCartney being a member of the upper class? [6]
6 If you won a million pounds on the football pools, what would you have to do to become accepted as part of the upper class? [8]

EXTENSION ACTIVITIES

1 **Distinguish** between the middle and the working class and discuss the differences between the two.
2 **Discuss or debate** the following:

   a) Does social class matter in Britain today?
   b) What are the problems involved in marrying someone from a different social class to yours?

3 **Make a study** of the upper class. Find some books about the aristocracy and the very rich and identify the different groups. Look for reports about their activities in the newspapers. How do these groups spend their time?
4 **Develop** a method of classifying the working class. Take up to five characteristics from the comparison table earlier in this unit and develop a questionnaire to test for them. Take a sample of your friends who come from working-class backgrounds and see how they answer the questions.

CHANGES IN THE CLASS STRUCTURE

QUESTIONS

Have things changed for the better?

1 Compared with my grandparents, I think my generation is better off ☐ the same ☐ worse off ☐.

2 Compared with my grandparents, I think young people have more ☐ the same ☐ less ☐ money to spend on the things that interest them.

3 Compared with my grandparents' day, I think it is easier ☐ the same ☐ harder ☐ to be successful and become well off.

4 Collect the answers from other students in your class to questions 1, 2 and 3, and present the results as bar graphs.

5 Comment on the results.

Changes in the class structure

British society has changed greatly during the last 100 years. The small mills of the Industrial Revolution gave way to larger factories. Modern industries such as car manufacturing replaced older ones such as textiles.

In the 1960s, the wealth of most people in Britain increased. More people benefited from further education. New opportunities for people in occupations such as photography, pop music and advertising also helped break down some of the class barriers. In recent years we have seen supermarkets take over from corner shops, and new technology and the decline of traditional industries put masses of men and women out of work. Many jobs in industry are now being replaced by jobs in smaller businesses.

All these changes have affected the number and type of jobs available. And as we saw in Unit 4.3, occupations are an important aspect of the class structure. In Unit 6.4 we consider in more detail the occupational changes of recent years.

In general, class divisions in Britain today are more complex and harder to identify than in the past. Reasons for this include:

● Most of the population are better off than ever before.
● Since the 1960s young people have tended to break away from their parents' life-styles and to follow patterns of behaviour which are 'classless' (see Unit 4.10). Even after such people enter middle age and have families, they often live less according to the 'rules' of class behaviour than their parents did.

● The old class system was dominated by the traditional family pattern of the male bread-winner and female housewife. As one-parent families, unmarried couples and working women have become more frequent, these patterns have changed.
● The multiracial community which has developed during the past twenty years has broken up some of the old patterns of British life.

Changes in the working class

Workers in heavy industry, though fewer in number than they used to be, have achieved through trade union action better wages and conditions. And a greater proportion of the population is now employed in *services* (e.g. tourism and catering) and white-collar (non-manual) work than before.

In this way the traditional working class of manual workers has decreased in size, and among skilled workers wages have improved. People who twenty years ago would have been called 'working class' are nowadays more likely to drink French wine, own shares and vote Conservative – all signs of what used to be defined as being middle class.

But while some of the working class are much better off, there are others who are becoming poorer. These are the unskilled workers, the unemployed and their families, and old-age pensioners, whose living standards have fallen in recent years. In this way the working class is said to have stretched – with a greater range of prosperity than before. This is said to divide the class.

The picture has been complicated by the recent growth of the main ethnic minorities – Afro-Caribbeans and Asians – in the population. Many of these, such as Asian professionals and business people, have joined the middle-class occupations. The result has been a blurring of the distinctions between the classes.

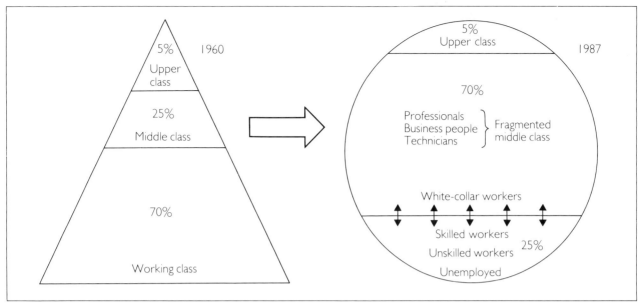

Fig. 1 The changing class structure

Changes in the middle class

Marx predicted that there would only be two classes. Instead we seem to have many sub-groups within each class. The middle class, too, has changed. It has been said that there are so many groups within the middle class that they can no longer be called a class. Small shopkeepers, professionals and office staff have such different working conditions, qualifications, levels of income that they have been called a *fragmented* middle class.

One of these groups, the office workers (clerks), has been the subject of debate. Photocopiers, word processors, large offices and so on have changed their working conditions so much that the job is now similar to manual work. The work may also be less skilled and lower paid than some types of manual work. Not everyone agrees that office work is similar to manual work, however, and many office workers do not see themselves as working class.

QUESTIONS

6   How have *two* of the following affected the British class structure during the past twenty years: a) prosperity, b) occupational change, c) young people's life-styles, d) working women, e) a multiracial community?

7   'We are all middle class now.' What does this mean? Is there any evidence to support this claim?

EXTENSION ACTIVITIES

1   **Make a study** of middle-class occupations. Using the Registrar General's scale, draw up a list of different middle-class occupations. Each person should find out the average salary, entry qualifications, working conditions and promotion prospects of one occupation. Draw up a table. Comment on whether your information supports the idea that the middle class is fragmented.

2   **Carry out** a similar study to that in extension activity 1, but this time on the working class. Take a set of working-class occupations and find out their wages, working conditions and qualifications. Also, obtain information on levels of social security and unemployment benefit. Discuss whether your findings support the theory that the working class has 'stretched'.

3   **Make a study** of the social class position of one family. (You could use your own family and imagine you were a social scientist studying it from the outside.) Describe and comment on such things as parents' occupation, housing, family structure, attitudes and values, voting behaviour, leisure patterns. Discuss what these characteristics tell you about the social class of the family you have studied. Your conclusion might be that class position is a difficult thing to establish.

GENDER AND INEQUALITY

Sex and gender

Sex refers to biological aspects of being male or female – features you are born with and cannot normally change. *Gender* refers to social and cultural aspects of being male or female. These are parts of our behaviour that we have been taught or have learned from other people.

QUESTIONS

1 List how boys and girls are treated differently in the family. Use the following headings: names, clothes, toys and games, books, food, expected behaviour, freedom.
2 Divide the following into either sexual or gender characteristics: a) hair on chest, b) interested in children, c) breasts, d) aggressive, e) emotional, f) beard.

Socialisation into gender roles

People's sexual characteristics are mostly fixed at birth. But our gender characteristics result from socialisation and therefore can change and vary from society to society. In our society the process of treating boys and girls differently begins as soon as they are born. We have names, clothes and toys which indicate gender. Boys are brought up to be boys, and girls are brought up to be girls.

Some people have claimed that girls are better at some things than boys and vice versa. For example, girls apppear to be better at language skills and boys at tasks involving shapes and spatial skills. However, both of these could be caused by the different ways they are bought up. Boys are given more construction toys and encouraged to make and do things. This may explain why they are better at construction-type tasks. Girls, on the other hand may be spoken to more by their mothers and this may increase their verbal skills. It is impossible to test out these sort of ideas.

Because children are influenced by many things, parents, friends, the media and so on, we cannot talk about any behaviour as being 'natural' to boys or girls. All the behaviour which we, in our society, think of as 'male' or 'female' is found in some other society attributed to the other sex. This has been illustrated by an anthropologist, Margaret Mead, who studied a number of societies living on islands in the Pacific Ocean. The people living on these islands were from a similar stock, but had been separated long enough to develop their own cultures. In the following extract Margaret Mead describes three of these tribes and how the behaviour thought to be 'natural' to men and women varied.

> The Arapesh tribe made very little distinction between the ways of behaving of the different sexes.
>
> Assertiveness or aggressiveness, which in our society are usually attributed to men, are not characteristic of the behaviour of either sex among the Arapesh, among whom there is a uniform lack of ambition.
>
> As far as heavy carrying work is done in this primitive society, it is performed by the women, who are supposed to be equipped "naturally" with specially strong foreheads for the purpose . . .
>
> Among the Mundugamor, a tribe of recently "pacified" head hunters living some distance away, aggressiveness was a characteristic of both men and women in equal measure. Love-making was a battle between the partners. Children were reared with extreme disregard, many first born being drowned, with adults showing little affection for children.
>
> In a third tribe, the Tchambuli, some of the attributes often ascribed to men and women in our society seemed actually to be reversed. Men adorned themselves, and gossiped, and were selected by the women, who made sexual advances, did all the trade upon which the society depended, although the men made many of the traded items. Women were dominant and aggressive, and female homosexuality was common.

Adapted from M. A. Coulston and C. Riddell, *Approaching Sociology* (Routledge & Kegan Paul, 1970), pp. 28–9.

QUESTIONS

3 What was one difference in behaviour between men and women in the Arapesh tribe? [1]
4 What does the example of the Arapesh tribe illustrate about the characteristics of men and women? [2]
5 What characteristic which we associate with men was found in women in the Mundugamor tribe? [1]
6 What characteristics which we regard as female were practised by the Tchambuli men? [3]
7 What characteristics, which we associate with men were common among the Tchambuli women? [3]
8 Can you think of any characteristics in our society, other than sexual ones, which you think distinguish men from women?

Fig. 1

Changing attitudes to sex and gender

People have become aware that the way we treat young children in terms of their gender may not always be for the best. The women's movement has shown that women often suffer throughout their lives because they were forced into female patterns of accepting second-best or limited choices when young.

Schools are now making efforts to give boys and girls an equal chance in such traditionally 'girls only' or 'boys only' subjects as cookery and woodwork (Fig. 1).

In appearance and dress, too, some of the differences between male and female have disappeared. Both sexes wear trousers (jeans), have long hair and short hair, wear ear rings and make up. These changes have been very rapid. If you ask your parents they will tell you that if a boy had worn ear rings and make up when they were young he would have been laughed at and called a girl. It will be interesting to see how far this 'unisex' trend goes and whether it represents real changes in attitudes or just superficial ones. You may care to discuss this in class.

EXTENSION ACTIVITIES

1 **Write** about whether men and women will ever be equal in our society. Give reasons for your views.

2 **Role-play** a disco in reverse! Girls should act out how they think boys behave towards them when they meet at a disco. Boys should act out how they think girls behave when they meet them in a disco.

3 **Make a study** of gender socialisation. If you have a young child in your family, make a study of how he or she is socialised into gender roles. Make your study over three months. Observe and record with a diary or a camera aspects of this process such as clothes, toys and games, treatment by adults.

4 **Investigate** the differences in social characteristics between men and women in our society. Use information from *Social Trends* and newspapers. Look at areas such as employment (See Unit 4.7), education (see Unit 3.6), health, crime, leisure and politics. Display your information to make the maximum impact on the people who will see it.

WOMEN, INEQUALITY AND WORK

Gender and work inequality

In Units 3.6 and 4.6 we saw examples of gender inequality. Women have lower levels of post-school educational achievement than men. They also have lower levels of earnings. In most areas of working life women do less well than men. Women form 1 per cent of bank managers, 5 per cent of MPs, 2 per cent of university professors and 20 per cent of senior teachers. (See also Unit 7.8 on representatives and élites.)

Reasons for inequality

We saw in Unit 4.5 that many differences between the sexes – the *gender* differences – are not 'natural' but are taught by society. Some people have suggested that because women have to bear children, and are often physically weaker than men, they are bound to do less well at work.

Others have explained gender inequalities in terms of a Marxist view of society. Having women thought of as inferior, they say, benefits capitalism because it divides the working class and makes men feel superior; it also allows women to be used as cheap labour.

Whatever the cause, if women are unequal at work they are likely to be unequal in everything else.

Women and paid work

Women have always worked, especially working-class women. Before the Industrial Revolution women traditionally did much of the farming work. In the nineteenth century they worked in factories, mines and the large country houses.

In the late nineteenth century middle-class women began to work in occupations such as school-teaching and medicine, which they had not entered before.

Today, even with high unemployment, a majority of women have some paid work, though much of this is part-time. Also, of course, virtually all women (and many men) do a large amount of unpaid work in the home and local community.

Women's work is usually paid less than men's work.

Different occupations

One difference is that men and women work in different occupations. Most nurses and home helps are female, while all coal-miners are male. Some 75 per cent of secretaries, hairdressers and machine-sewers are female; 75 per cent of building, gas and electricity workers are male. Occupations employing women are usually lower-paid than mainly male occupations.

QUESTIONS

Fig. 1 Employees in employment by industry, 1984

	Males	Females	(thousands)
Construction	849	120	
Energy and water supply	531	82	
Manufacture of metal and mineral products, chemicals, engineering and vehicle construction	2,073	539	
Distribution, hotels, catering	2,042	2,428	
Transport and communication	1,035	269	
Banking, finance, insurance	1,009	963	

From *Social Trends* (HMSO, 1987), p. 73, table 4.8.

1 In which group of occupations in Fig. 1 are there almost equal numbers of male and female workers? [1]
2 In which of the groups of occupations are there more female workers than male? [1]
3 Give three reasons why few females are employed in the construction industry. [3]
4 Display as a bar graph the distribution of male and female employees in the following industries: distribution, hotels and catering; banking and finance; manufacturing. [6]
5 Explain how having equal numbers of male and female employees in an industry may still not mean that they are equal. (Banking might be a good example to take.) [9]

Different jobs within occupations

When men and women work in the same occupation they are often found at different levels. In primary teaching, for example, there are more females than males. But when you look at headteachers, then there are more male headteachers than female, and females tend to occupy more of the lower level posts in schools. This is shown in Fig. 2.

Fig. 2 Full-time teachers in primary schools

	Males	Females
All teachers	46,784	156,103
Headteachers	13,552	10,295

From Department of Education and Science, *Teachers* (HMSO, 1977), vol. 4, table 20, pp. 32–3.

In many other occupations, the situation is similar. For example, in the law and in journalism, women tend to remain in the lower grades of the job, while the senior positions are mostly filled by men.

Gender differences in earnings

Fig. 3

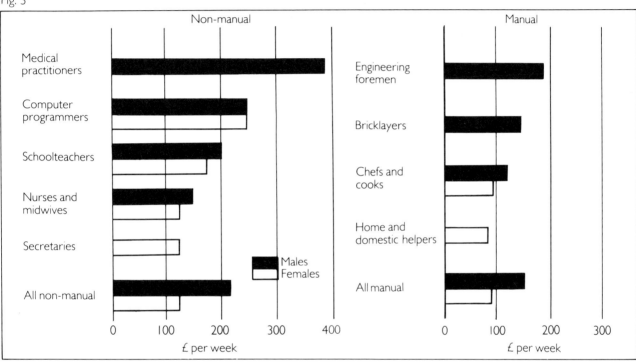

From *Social Trends* (HMSO, 1986), p. 80, table 5.5.

QUESTIONS

6 Give one occupation shown in Fig. 3 in which: a) most of the workers are male; b) most of the workers are female. [2]

7 Who earns most in the following occupations, men or women? a) schoolteaching, b) nursing, c) chefs and cooks. [3]

8 From Fig. 3, estimate the differences in earnings between male and female workers in a) manual and b) non-manual occupations. [2]

9 For which group is the difference in earnings greater, manual or non-manual? [1]

10 Write one sentence summarising the differences in earnings shown by Fig. 3 between men and women in both manual and non-manual occupations. [2]

EXTENSION ACTIVITIES

1 **Write** about a) why women have different jobs from men, and b) any changes that have taken place in the pattern of female employment during the twentieth century.

2 **Collect** photographs and articles showing men and women doing untypical jobs for their sex. Comment on which you have found more of, men doing 'women's jobs' or women doing 'men's jobs'.

3 **Design** a poster encouraging either boys or girls to take up an occupation not normally associated with their sex.

4 **Make a survey**, using a questionnaire, of the jobs the students in your class hope to get. Ask them for the reasons for their choice. Analyse the results by sex. Comment on whether their choices represent a continuation of the patterns we have discussed in this unit.

RACE AND INEQUALITY

In Unit 3.7 we looked at some of the evidence which shows that there are racial inequalities in Britain today. This inequality can be shown in three major areas: housing, employment and education – see Fig. 1.

Fig. 1 Racial inequalities in housing, employment and education

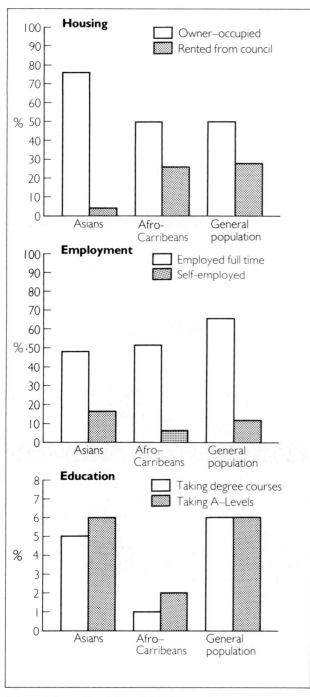

Adapted from *Social Trends* (HMSO, 1985).

1 Looking at the information in Fig. 1, which group seems to be the most disadvantaged in Britain? Support your answer with statistics from the graphs. What additional information could you try to find to support or challenge your conclusions?

Racial prejudice

Racial prejudice can be defined as an unfavourable attitude held towards another group on the basis of race. It is a very difficult thing for sociologists to measure because the definition itself is not very clear.

A survey of racial prejudice

One attempt to measure the extent of racial prejudice in Britain was made by Mark Abrams. His research is summarised in the following extract.

A sample of 2,500 white residents from five different areas were asked a series of questions, from which four social issues were chosen as crucial measures of prejudice:

1 Whether they would avoid having black or Asian neighbours even if they were professional people.
2 Whether they regarded black or Asian people as their inferiors solely on the basis of skin colour.
3 Whether the authorities should refuse housing to black or Asian tenants even if they had been on the waiting-list the required time.
4 Whether a private landlord should refuse accommodation to black or Asian tenants if he or she knew they would care for the property.

On the basis of the answers given, Abrams claimed that 10 per cent of whites were prejudiced (three or four hostile answers), 17 per cent were 'prejudice inclined' (two hostile answers) 38 per cent were 'tolerant inclined' (one hostile answer) and 35 per cent were tolerant (no hostile answers). Abrams concluded that prejudice was relatively rare.

Adapted from A. Pilkington, *Race Relations in Britain* (University Tutorial Press, 1984), pp. 32–3.

2 If people gave one hostile answer, how would Abrams have classified them: as tolerant, tolerant inclined, prejudice inclined or prejudiced? [1]
3 Why did Abrams conclude that prejudice was rare? [2]
4 Abrams's results could be interpreted to show that 65 per cent of the population was prejudiced. Explain how this could be done. [4]
5 Abrams carried out his survey in 1966. Do you think the results would be the same if he carried it out today? Give reasons for your answer. [6]
6 Do you think this is a suitable method of measuring prejudice? Give reasons for your answer. [7]

Racial discrimination

One criticism that could be made of research such as Abrams's survey above is that the answers people give to questions are often the answers they think investigators want to hear. People give the best possible account of their attitudes, but in practice the way they behave towards black and Asian people may be different.

Racial *discrimination*, unlike prejudice, involves taking action to disadvantage a person or group because of their race. All the evidence suggests that discrimination is still widespread in many areas of life in Britain.

The Policy and Economic Planning Unit, based in London, has produced a series of reports which show that discrimination is taking place in housing, employment, education and other areas of our social life. Fig. 2 shows one experiment used to measure discrimination. Actors telephoned for jobs which had been advertised. Discrimination was measured by seeing how many were offered the job or an interview.

7 What clue did each actor in Fig. 2 give to his racial identity? [1]
8 How did the researcher judge whether the actor was being discriminated against? [1]
9 Why do you think a white person was included in the experiment? [2]
10 Why do you think a Greek person was included in the experiment? [2]
11 According to these results, which group faces the greatest discrimination? Quote the evidence to support your answer. [4]
12 Did you find that the disadvantaged group was the same as the group in Fig. 1? Support your answer with evidence. [5]
13 What are two disadvantages of this experiment as a method of measuring discrimination? [5]

1 **Explain** in your own words the meaning of prejudice. Describe one of your own prejudices. (We all have some; it doesn't have to be racial.)
2 **Discuss**, in small groups, ideas for solving the problems of race relations in Britain today.
3 **Debate** the motion that 'The law is not the way to deal with prejudice and discrimination.'

Fig. 2 An experiment to test for discrimination

Result: percentage of cases where the actor did not get offered the job or an interview (based on four experiments):

Afro-Caribbeans	Indians	Greeks
27%	28%	11%

4.9

RACE, INEQUALITY AND EMPLOYMENT

Two contrasting views

There have been two contrasting myths about the ethnic minorities in Britain. On the one hand, newspaper headlines like 'Asian workers work too hard – so say workers in factory in West Bromwich' suggest that members of the ethnic minorities work harder than white workers and so threaten their jobs. On the other hand, the same minorities are seen as people with large families who get more than their fair share of social security.

The second myth is certainly wrong. In 1974, before unemployment rose to later record levels, 93 per cent of Afro-Caribbean males were in employment, compared to only 91 per cent of white males. The contrast between females was even greater; 74 per cent of Afro-Caribbean women went out to work, compared to only 43 per cent of white women. The figure for Asian women was lower, at 33 per cent.

Job levels and ethnic minorities

Fig. I

Job level	White %	Afro-Caribbean %	Pakistani/ Bangladeshi %	Indian %
Professional/ management	23	2	4	8
White-collar	17	6	4	12
Skilled manual	42	59	33	44
Semi-skilled manual	12	23	38	27
Unskilled manual	6	9	20	9
Unclassified	1	1	1	1

From D. Smith, *Racial Disadvantage in Britain* (Penguin, 1977), p.73.

Fig. 2

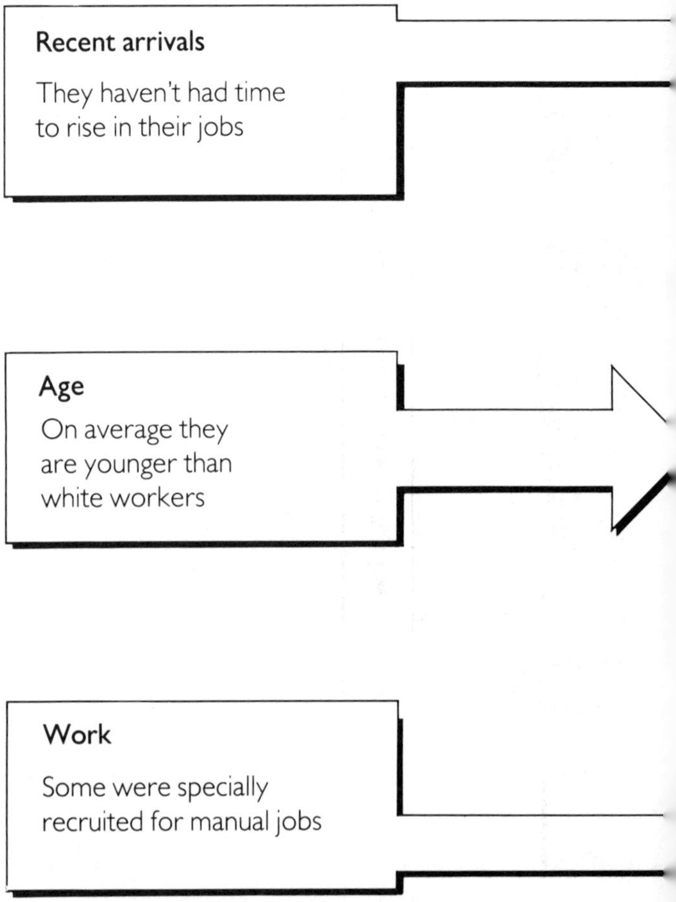

Recent arrivals

They haven't had time to rise in their jobs

Age

On average they are younger than white workers

Work

Some were specially recruited for manual jobs

QUESTIONS

1 Which ethnic group has the greatest percentage of semi-skilled and unskilled workers? [1]
2 At which level of occupation is there the greatest difference between Afro-Caribbean and white workers? [1]
3 Redraw Fig. I to divide the occupations into manual (skilled, semi-skilled and unskilled manual) and non-manual (professional/management, white collar). The first has been done for you:

Job level	White %	Afro-Caribbean %	Pakistani/ Bangladeshi %	Indian %
Non-manual	40			
Manual	60			

4 Using information from Fig. I, compare the job levels of:
   a) Afro-Caribbean with white workers. [6]
   b) Pakistani/Bangladeshi with white workers [6]
   c) Indian with white workers. [6]
   d) Indian with Afro-Caribbean workers. [6]
5 Take any two racial groupings and suggest reasons for the difference. [8]

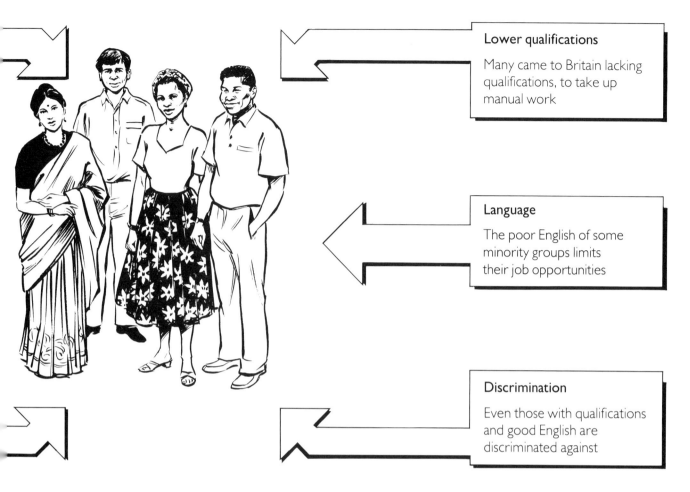

Lower qualifications

Many came to Britain lacking qualifications, to take up manual work

Language

The poor English of some minority groups limits their job opportunities

Discrimination

Even those with qualifications and good English are discriminated against

Reasons for job levels of ethnic minorities

❝Job levels of racial minorities tend to be skewed towards lower levels so that all tend to be under represented in non-manual jobs, especially the higher ones, and over-represented in manual jobs, especially the lower ones.❞

A. Pilkington, *Race Relations in Britain* (University Tutorial Press, 1984), p. 84.

Income levels

As we have seen in Fig. 1, Asian, Afro-Caribbean and white workers do not have similar patterns of employment. They are also unequal in another way. Even within the same occupations, ethnic-minority workers get paid less. This is as true of doctors as it is of labourers. The reason is that within any type of job there is often extra pay for holding positions of responsibility. Ethnic-minority people hold fewer of these posts, so their wages on average are lower than those of white workers.

In unskilled jobs, Asians and Afro-Caribbeans take home more pay than white workers, because they do more shift-work and more of the better-paid unpleasant work.

Unemployment

All sections of the population have been affected by unemployment, but the ethnic minorities have suffered more. Between 1972 and 1981 total unemployment increased by 138 per cent, but for ethnic minorities it increased by 325 per cent – nearly three times faster. In 1984 only 10 per cent of white males were unemployed compared with 34 per cent of Asian and 23 per cent of Afro-Caribbean males.

There are many reasons for this. As more recent arrivals in many jobs, they are often the first to be laid off under the 'last in, first out' principle. They are also over-represented in the occupations and industries that have been most affected by the economic decline – semi-skilled and unskilled manufacturing jobs. But there is also no doubt that in some cases members of ethnic minorities suffer from discrimination when it comes to redundancy.

EXTENSION ACTIVITIES

1 **Compare** the job levels of ethnic minorities with those of white workers. Why are black and Asian people concentrated in the poorest jobs?

2 **Discuss** how a company which has to make some workers redundant should decide who to sack. What criteria (such as age or length of service) should be used?

3 **Design** a poster or logo which a company could use to show that it is an equal opportunity employer.

AGE INEQUALITIES

QUESTIONS

When can you do what?

1 How old do you have to be to:

	Ages
buy cigarettes?	11 13 14 15 16 17 18
own property or land?	11 13 14 15 16 17 18
get married without parents' consent?	11 13 14 15 16 17 18
buy alcoholic drinks in a pub?	11 13 14 15 16 17 18
place a bet?	11 13 14 15 16 17 18
have a job?	11 13 14 15 16 17 18
drive a car?	11 13 14 15 16 17 18

Changing definitions of childhood

Your answers to the question above should have reinforced what you already know, that any person under the age of eighteen is not considered an adult and therefore does not have full rights and privileges. We tend to think that children or young people are too young to have a job or have a drink in a pub, but ideas on when someone is a child or an adult have changed a great deal over the last 100 years.

In the nineteenth century people as young as five worked all day in the fields or in factories. David Livingstone, the famous explorer, worked sixty hours a week in a factory when he was only twelve.

In the past people were either considered babies or were treated as adults. There was little difference in clothing, habits or activities between them and older people. If you look at paintings in the great houses you will see that the children are dressed in the same way as their parents and did the same things.

Childhood and adolescence are a modern idea. Social historians have said that after the early period of the Industrial Revolution there was less need for children to work. So it was gradually made illegal. At the same time compulsory schooling occupied children. You tend to feel grown up when you leave school, and the school-leaving age has been rising. It was nine in 1870, eleven in 1900, fourteen in 1945 and is sixteen today. There is even talk of raising the school-leaving age to seventeen.

The extension of childhood in this way means that we now have a group of people who are physically and mentally mature, without family responsibilities but who are still dependent on their parents and who are not treated as adults. This is the origin of the *youth culture*: the development of fashions, activities, ideas and values held by young people who are not considered to be full adults.

Youth groups

Fig. 1

Fig. 2

Fig. 3

2 Look at Figs, 1, 2 and 3. Name the type of youth group shown in each of the photographs. [1]
3 What kinds of fashion, music, ideas and activities do you associate with each of the groups shown in the photographs? [4]
4 If you wanted to find out more about the ideas and attitudes of groups such as these, what methods of social research would you use and why? [10]

Youth cultures

Not everyone joins a youth group such as those shown in Figs. 1, 2 and 3. Many young people conform to their parents' ideas. Sociologists have tried to explain why some people become punks or rockers. One suggestion is that these and other teenage groups help children to become independent of their parents. They also provide an opportunity for 'dating and mating' – the chance to find a partner without having to take the first person you meet.

Another explanation is that these youth cultures are a reaction against different aspects of society. The hippies of the 1960s, for example, were partly a reaction against the materialism of a society (especially in the USA) that seemed to have become too commercialised. The punks were said to be a reaction against the grim reality of unemployment for young people who hadn't done well at school in the 1970s. The foul language and anti-social behaviour of the punks may be criticised by older people, but to some extent they were reacting against a social system that they thought had failed them. Similar feelings can be found among Rastafarians, who dislike the materialistic values of modern society.

Girls and youth culture

5 How does the setting of the girls' youth culture shown in Fig. 4 differ from that of the youths shown in Figs. 1, 2 and 3? [2]
6 Give two reasons why girls are often more controlled by their parents than boys and so form fewer youth styles. [4]
7 Do you know of any mainly female youth groups? Describe them. [4]
8 What part do girls play in the male youth groups you know? [4]
9 Girls may be physically weaker than boys but they have their own ways of holding their own. List three ways in which they do this. [6]

EXTENSION ACTIVITIES

1 **Make a study** of the treatment of young people by newspapers and magazines. Collect newspaper stories and photographs. Divide them into groups according to the subject of the story: for example, young people as anti-social rebels, young people as helpers, young married people.
2 **Act out** the reaction of the police to different types of young people. One person should be a police officer who meets different people late at night: a girl, a young man in a suit, a hell's angel, a punk, etc.
3 **Investigate** one youth group, male or female. Find out how sociologists have explained your chosen group. Watch a group in your area. Describe their clothes, music, activities and values. See if they will agree to be interviewed. Discuss some of the problems you met in carrying out this sort of study.

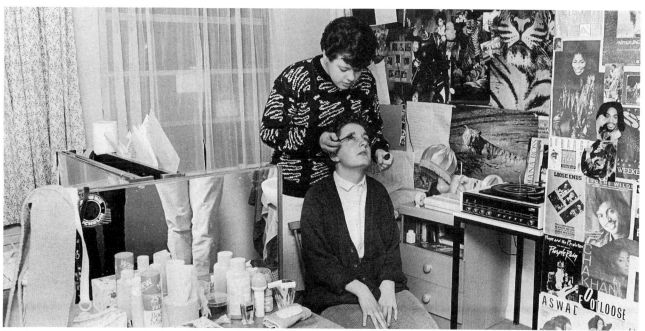

Fig. 4

POVERTY

What is poverty?

A common-sense definition of poverty would be the amount of money needed to secure the minimum needed for a healthy life. This is a definition of *absolute poverty*. However, the problem is how to decide what is the minimum. An alternative definition is *relative poverty*. This is where people cannot afford the minimum diet and living conditions expected in the society in which they live. Using this definition, the actual amount of money thought necessary would vary from society to society.

Sociologists have tried to measure how many of the population live in poverty. They have also tried to explain and describe why it happens. In this unit we look at two of these ideas: the cycle of poverty and the cycle of disadvantage.

The cycle of poverty

A famous survey on poverty was carried out in York at the beginning of the century by Seebohm Rowntree, a social reformer. He found that even the very poorest families did not live the whole of their lives in great poverty. At some periods they were better of than at others. They were at their most prosperous just after they got married when both of the adults could work. However, this time was short-lived because children soon came along. At this point the mother could not work and the family income was halved. The family would remain in poverty until the mother stopped child bearing and the children left home. There might be a brief period of more prosperity in late middle age or before retirement. The *cycle of poverty* is shown in Fig. 1.

1 According to Fig. 1, at which points in the family's life is it most comfortably off? [2]
2 Describe two types of family who might be caught in a cycle of poverty. [2]
3 At which points in the life cycle does the family fall below the poverty line? [2]
4 Take any one point at which the family falls below the poverty line and explain why it happens. [4]
5 Why is the family quite well off in middle age? [4]
6 Imagine you were a member of a family living in poverty. Write an account of one day in your life which draws attention to some of the key features of your situation. [6]

Fig. 1 The cycle of poverty

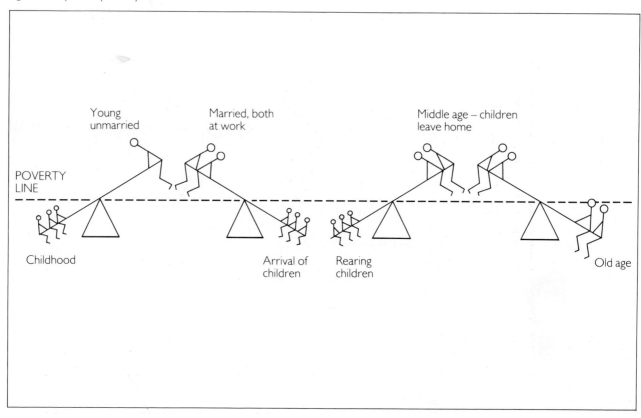

The cycle of disadvantage

Rowntree's cycle of poverty describes the fortunes of a family during its lifetime. The *cycle of disadvantage* is a term to describe the way in which poverty lasts from one generation to another. Poor parents have children who, in turn, are poor, and they have children who are poor. The reasons for this chain of poverty is that the adults never get into a position where they can give their children a better start to their lives.

EXTENSION ACTIVITIES

1 **Describe in your own words**, using examples, either the cycle of poverty or the cycle of disadvantage.
2 **Discuss** why some families find themselves living in poverty.
3 **Work in small groups.** Imagine you were living in a flat alone. Work out the minimum you think you would need each week a) to be above absolute poverty and b) to be above relative poverty. Think of your rent, food, clothing allowance, etc.
4 **Make a study** of poverty in the Third World. Look at the extent of poverty in the world and how it is measured. Find out about international relief agencies and describe their ideas on how to deal with this problem. (See also Unit 9.6 on international influences.)

Fig. 2 The cycle of disadvantage

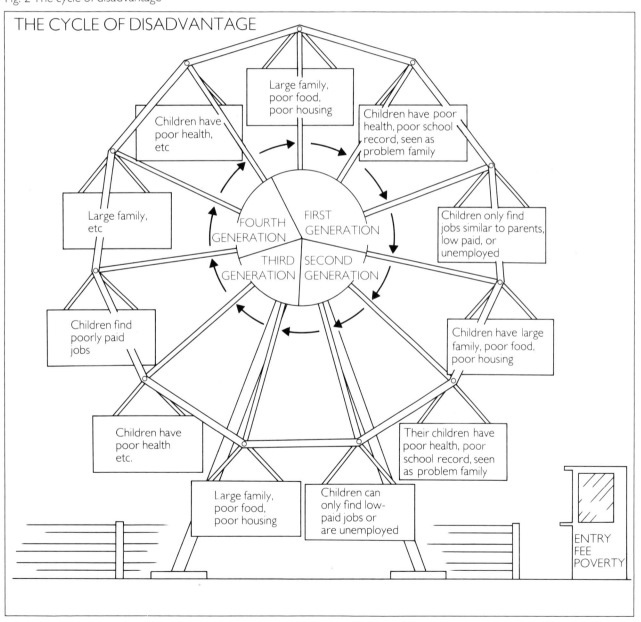

67

SCARCITY AND RESOURCES

Scarcity

Moira: Coming to the disco tonight, then?

Shelley: Can't. I've got too much homework. I've not done my Social Science course work yet.

Moira: What about you, then, Karen?

Karen: Sorry, Moira, I've promised to baby-sit. I'm getting paid for it and I need the money for my holidays.

Moira: Isn't anyone coming down the disco? I feel like going out tonight.

Julia: I can't come. I've no money left.

Moira: That's only because you spent it on that eye make-up.

Julia: That's my choice, isn't it?

Nazima: It's no good looking at me. I'm not allowed to go to discos.

Albert: (*To his friends.*) I wouldn't mind going to the disco.

Moira: My dad's been telling me I ought to stay in and save up a bit more. I think perhaps I'll stay home tonight and listen to some records.

In the discussion above, Shelley is concerned about the scarcity of time, Karen and Julia with their shortage of money and Nazima with the limits on her choices, and we are left in doubt about whether Moira is really interested in the need to save for the future. They are all concerned with the problem of scarcity.

Section 4 was concerned with problems of inequality and poverty. In this section we shall look further at the problems of the lack of resources available to satisfy all wants and needs, and at the choices which have to be made on the use of those resources.

Scarcity is the main problem with which we shall be concerned here and in Section 6. Scarcity exists in all countries, although we may think of it most often in relation to the poorest countries of the world, where large numbers of people lack adequate food or clean water, or eat the following year's roots or seeds because of extreme hunger.

Scarcity, and therefore the need for choice, exists even in the most affluent societies, however. This is because there appears to be no limit to human wants, and so choices have to be made. We shall be concerned with choices about what to produce, about how to produce the goods and services and about who will receive the product.

Choices are concerned with what to consume today and who should consume the goods and services which have been produced. Choices are also concerned with the uses which are made of the resources that are available.

Resources

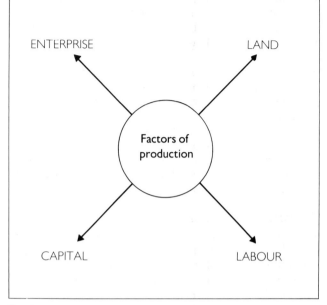

Fig. 1

The resources which are used to produce goods and services are sometimes called *factors of production* – see Fig. 1. They include:

- *land* and natural resources which are essential to any production;
- *labour* – all the efforts of people to produce goods and services;
- *capital* – this means buildings, equipment, tools and goods which are not yet finished; and
- *enterprise*, which means the organisation of the business and risk-taking.

This section is concerned with all of these factors of production and with the choice about how to use them. The problem is that there will never be enough resources to satisfy all the wants and needs of the world.

Some resources have changed over time. The activities of producing and consuming goods and services have had effects on the environment, and therefore effects on such activities as fishing, forestry and agriculture. (See Units 5.7 and 5.8 on the environment.)

The amount of capital has increased as a result of investment in new buildings and equipment. Also, the quality of capital has changed as a result of technical developments. (See Unit 6.2 on economic growth.)

The labour force has increased as a result of a fall in the death rate and an increase in the number of women seeking work. (See also Unit 4.7 on women, inequality and work.)

The labour force

The labour force consists of people in work (including self-employment) and the unemployed who are seeking work. The size of the labour force varies between countries and over time depending on the following:

- The number of people and their ages; this is affected both by natural population growth (births exceeding deaths) and by migration (people moving into or out of a country or area).
- The school-leaving age, the numbers attending colleges and the age of retirement.
- The extent to which members of the household work without taking paid employment (e.g. family farms and unpaid work in the home).

Women in the labour force

There are many factors affecting the proportion of women in the labour force. Some of these are considered in Units 4.6 and 4.7 on gender, inequality and work. Social attitudes are important in influencing the number of women in work. Other factors include the assistance available with the care of children and the types of job available. Women are less likely to work if family income is high but more likely to work if their earning power is high compared with that of their husbands. Legal rights may also influence the number of women employed; for example, since 1975 women have had the right to return to their jobs after maternity leave in some cases.

Age distribution

Fig. 2 shows the age distribution of the population of the United Kingdom in June 1985.

Fig. 2

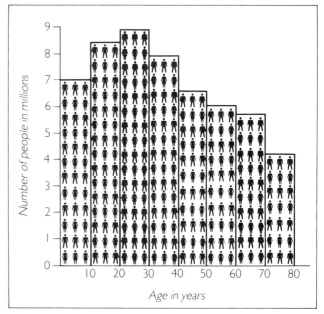

Adapted from *Monthly Digest of Statistics* (HMSO, February 1987), p.16, table 2.2

QUESTIONS

Shortage of labour

1 Form groups to act as advisory bodies to the government of a group of islands in the South Atlantic where there are labour shortages. Produce a set of proposals:

   a) to increase the number of married women in work;

   b) other measures to increase the size of the labour force.

2 Write a report on your discussions, giving your group's recommendations and the arguments for them.

3 State whether you personally disagree with any of your group's recommendations and explain why.

QUESTIONS

4 Which age group has the largest share of the population?

5 There are more people in the 30–39 age group than in the 0–9 age group. How would you account for this?

6 Discuss whether the total labour force is likely to increase or decrease by 1995.

7 The number of young people entering the labour force is declining. What are the likely implications of this for the skills of the labour force and the need for training?

EXTENSION ACTIVITIES

1 **Conduct a survey**, under the guidance of your teacher, to find out why many people work part-time. Ask whether they would prefer to work full-time or not to be in paid employment at all. (See also Unit 1.4 on surveys and sampling.)

2 a) **Identify any changes** which are taking place in the local or national labour force; for example, the numbers employed and their age, sex, race, origins and occupation. (Possible sources include: your local reference library for statistics published by your local authority; and the reports of the Census, or *Social Trends* for national figures.)

   b) **Discuss** the reasons for any changes in the labour force revealed by your investigation.

OPPORTUNITY COST

What is opportunity cost?

We all have to make choices, because we do not have enough resources for all of the things we would like to do or to buy. We have to choose from a number of alternatives, and it is therefore possible to measure the cost of what we do by the alternatives which are sacrificed. The sacrificed alternative is known as the *opportunity cost* of any action.

Examples of opportunity cost include the following:

Decisions about what to buy

If I go into McDonald's I have to choose whether to buy a hamburger or a cheeseburger, or whether to sacrifice other purchases I might have made in favour of a quarter-pounder, or whether to have a milk shake.

Decisions about how to spend our time

Other decisions which we face are far more complicated and require more thought. We may need to choose whether to study art or music at school; there may not be enough time or space on the timetable for both. The opportunity cost of studying art is giving up the music which might have given us greater pleasure, and vice versa. Choices have to be made about whether to stay at school or to look for work at the age of sixteen. The opportunity cost of working on a Saturday may be the sports which could have been enjoyed, or the homework which could have been completed, or the sleep which could have been gained (Fig. 1).

Business decisions

Businesses, too, must make decisions which involve opportunity cost. For example, there are decisions about what they will produce and about how they will produce the goods and services they have chosen. A decision which faces many businesses at present is whether or not to install computers, and if so which jobs will be replaced or changed by the use of computers.

Decisions by communities as a whole

Sometimes communities have to make decisions which involve opportunity cost. For example, a decision by a local council about whether to spend more money on a school requires consideration of the opportunity cost – perhaps the youth centre or day centre for the elderly which could be provided instead. The government decides whether to spend more or less, and what to buy.

The government must make decisions about what will be provided by the state for everyone, regardless of income (such as health care and education), and which goods and

Fig. I

services should be bought and sold. Decisions must be made about which services should be privatised, who should be taxed and how the country's income should be shared out.

Problems of inequality were considered in Section 4. The sections which follow will consider problems in the use of resources, and government policies to deal with these problems.

QUESTIONS

1 By choosing to build a new hospital, a community is unable to afford to build a new school. Briefly explain the economic principle which this example illustrates. (Question from Southern Examining Group specimen paper, worth 2 per cent on a paper of two hours' duration.)

2 Mary O'Hara and her daughter, Helen, run a shop which Mary inherited from her parents. Mary has no rent to pay. She pays her daughter a very low wage, although a friend has told Helen she could earn twice as much in the new supermarket which has opened locally. The money received by the business each year is greater than the money spent on Helen's wage, new stock, heating, rates and other expenses. Recently, however, there have been fewer customers, and the profit is low. Mother and daughter are thinking about selling the shop. Mary would retire, and Helen would go to work in the supermarket.

a) What is the opportunity cost to Mary and Helen of continuing to run their own business? (Think about the alternative work Helen could do and the alternative ways of using the capital of the business.)

b) Would there be any advantages to Mary and Helen in continuing to run their own business?

3 What are the opportunity costs of the development described in the article in Fig. 2?

4 Would there be any opportunity cost in deciding not to allow the building of the houses in Fig. 2?

EXTENSION ACTIVITIES

1 **Find one newspaper article** from your local or national newspapers which provides a good illustration of decisions to make changes involving opportunity cost.

The following questions relate to the newspaper article which you have chosen.

a) What would be the opportunity costs of making the changes described in the newspaper article you have found?

b) Would there be any opportunity cost in deciding not to make the changes described in your article?

c) Does the newspaper article appear to support or oppose the changes? Give reasons for your answer.

Fig. 2

School fields sell-off under attack

A TEACHERS' union has slammed the sale and development of school playing fields in Redbridge.

It was revealed at the recent Professional Association of Teachers' annual conference that 17 sites in the borough risked being sold for housing estates to be built on.

The conference unanimously resolved to call on the government and local authorities to block any further cuts in school sporting facilities.

The Central Council for Physical Recreation, which carried out the study which produced the figures, fears that physical education lessons in Redbridge will suffer as a result of the sale of the land.

A spokesman for the CCPR said: "Financial restraints imposed by central government have forced a nationwide sale of fields where outdoor sports have been played by schools.

"Traditional grass games have instead moved indoors onto hard surfaces while private development companies have taken over the fields."

But Redbridge Council has hit back at the report saying that, rather than cutting back on recreational facilities, it has increased them considerably in the last five years.

A council spokesman said: "In Redbridge we take recreation very seriously and in recent years have established a sports promotion unit.

He pointed out that the council had recently bought Oakfield playing fields, a 60-acre plot of land in Forest Road, Barkingside, from the Inner London Education Authority.

Two examples of sites for sale in Redbridge given by the CCPR, were Fullwell Avenue and Loxford Lane.

But the council spokesman said the land at Fairlop would accommodate schools using the Fullwell Avenue land and that the Loxford Lane land had been sold because it was under-used by schools.

From *Yellow Advertiser*, 8 August 1986.

d) Which groups of people and organisations are likely to seek to influence the changes? Explain why they would be involved.

See also Units 7.5 and 7.6 on pressure groups.

USE OF RESOURCES

The use of any resources requires decisions, and all decisions involve opportunity cost.

Meena's case: a family argument about resources

The situation

Dear J.,

Thank you for the birthday card. Now I am 16, there are lots of problems at home. I think I told you that I want to go to college next year to take a business studies course. I certainly don't want to get married yet. And I don't want to go into my parents' business. I just want to do the things other girls do for a few years and not be rushed into anything.

Well, the main problems have arisen since my grandmother came to stay from Delhi. My parents seem to notice more when I don't behave just as they wish and they seem to be reluctant to let me talk about an office job, or even to let me go shopping for clothes with my school friends.

The real trouble is that Grandmother wants me to marry her friend's nephew, Mukesh, and wants my father to arrange a meeting. I don't know what to do. Everyone seems so keen on the idea and they will be very angry if I don't agree. Please can you meet me soon to talk about it?

Best wishes,
Meena

Fig. 1

The grandmother

You have heard that Meena's grandmother is more traditional in her outlook than Meena's parents. She has told her sister-in-law that if Meena is not soon married to a nice boy she will get into bad ways, and no good family will want her as a daughter-in-law. Grandmother would like to arrange an introduction in the hope that Meena and Mukesh will like each other and perhaps get married. She points out that she had no choice at all about whom she should marry and she has been quite content.

The father

Your parents have seen Meena's father, Ravi, and found that he has not been well recently and he would like Meena to help in the family business. Last time he tried to employ someone he found the employee was cheating him. However, he wants to do whatever is best for his daughter.

The brother

Meena's brother, Praful, has pointed out that he had to leave school and get a job because the family could not afford to support him. He thinks that Meena should do more to contribute to the household. However, he does have some sympathy for Meena, and she thinks he might be persuaded to help her.

QUESTIONS

1   Work as four groups. Each task should be undertaken by one group, which appoints a reporter to present a summary to the class. (Choose as a spokesperson someone whom you think does not usually say much in class. Make notes to help your spokesperson report back, and be prepared to help him or her if necessary.)

Group A. Imagine that you are the grandmother and a group of her friends. What do you consider to be the opportunity costs of delaying Meena's marriage? What would be the benefits to her and the family of her getting married soon? Do you all agree?

Group B. You are Meena's father, Ravi, and a group of his friends. What would you see as the opportunity costs of Meena going to college? Make a note of all the arguments you would consider which involve opportunity cost.

Group C. You are Meena's brother, Praful, and his friends. What do you think Meena should do? Take account of the costs and benefits to Praful and the family as well as to Meena herself.

Group D. You are some of Meena's school-friends. Present your arguments about what you think Meena should do, taking into account the costs and benefits of going to college.

2   Following your discussions, take the role of J. who received the letter. Reply to Meena, advising her.

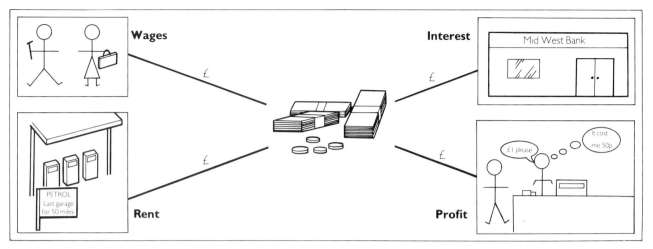

Fig. 2

Payment for the use of resources

The use of the factors of production – land, labour, capital and enterprise – involves a cost (see Fig. 2). In the case of labour, this cost is referred to as *wages* (although the wage of a non-manual worker who is paid monthly is called a *salary*). The return for the use of capital is *interest*. For land (including buildings), and sometimes for other resources where there are shortages, the payment is *rent*. The reward for enterprise (the taking of risks and bringing together of the other factors) is defined as *profit*.

Wages and profits

Praful is earning a reasonable wage (above the national average for manual work) working in a semi-skilled job in a large car-assembly plant. His friend, Michael, has started a small record-producing company. He records the music of groups which are not well known and sells the records, mainly through mail order and clubs. He wants Praful to join him. He claims to have found a group which will set new trends in music. Praful would receive a low wage at first but he would also receive a 20 per cent share in the profits.

QUESTION

3   Discuss the action which Praful should take.

To let or not to let?

Michael's father, John, has inherited a small flat worth £40,000. He does not wish to live in the flat but he has to decide whether to:

● rent it out;
● allow Michael to use it for his record business;
● sell it and put the money in a deposit account;
● sell it and invest the money in Michael's business in return for a 50 per cent share in the profits.

QUESTION

4   Assess the possible advantages and disadvantages to John of each of these alternatives.

Household income

Fig. 3 shows the sources of household income in the United Kingdom in the years 1974, 1979 and 1984.

Fig. 3

Source of income	Income % before tax		
	1974	1979	1984
Wages and salaries	67	66	61
Income from self-employment	9	8	9
Social security benefits	9	12	13
Other	15	14	17

From *Social Trends* (HMSO,1986). p. 77, table 5.1.

QUESTIONS

5   Draw suitable charts to illustrate the figures given in Fig. 3.   [5]
6   Wages and salaries as shown in Fig. 3 include 'income in kind' such as free meals and housing. Such benefits are sometimes called *fringe benefits*. Make a list of any other payments in kind which form part of some workers' incomes.   [5]
7   During the period 1974 to 1981 social security benefits (including pensions) increased from 9 per cent to 13 per cent of total income. Can you give any reasons for this?   [10]

  You can obtain further details of these benefits showing the increase in retirement pensions (the largest item), supplementary allowances (second-largest item), child benefit (third largest) and other allowances from a copy of *Social Trends*.

PROFITS AND SUPPLY

Profits

In previous units we have considered the use which is made of resources and the distribution of income. Profits are a form of income and are the rewards for taking risks and for organising production. Without the possibility of a profit the owners of business organisations would be unwilling to risk their own resources in the business. They could simply put their money in the bank and gain interest.

Profits are calculated by taking the difference between the revenue received by the seller of a good and the costs, such as labour and materials, which must be paid by the seller.

Profits are important in all economies in the non-communist world. Some goods and services are provided by governments and charities which do not always aim to make a profit. But in this section we are particularly concerned with production by businesses which aim to make as much profit as possible.

Businesses change the type or amount of goods they produce in order to increase their profits. This may be illustrated by the behaviour of a market stallholder called Pat, who sells greengrocery. Pat notices that a stall nearby is selling something different such as fresh herbs and that lots of people are buying these herbs at a price well above the cost from the wholesale market. The following day Pat also purchases some herbs from the wholesaler and starts to sell them. Pat even sells the herbs a little cheaper than the other stall holder in order to attract customers.

This example illustrates one of the advantages of competition. It shows that producers who are acting to maximise or increase profits may at the same time increase the variety of goods available to the consumer. They may also reduce prices.

Sometimes, however, the actions of producers in pursuit of profits are not entirely good for consumers. This is shown in the following examples.

● Large companies may take over other producers to reduce competition and so raise prices.
● Businesses may fail to take account of the effects of their activities on the environment or on their customers' health.
● Producers are unlikely to provide goods and services for those who cannot afford to pay for them.

All of these problems will be considered in later units.

Profits thus provide the main motivation for businesses to take risks – and there is always some risk and uncertainty. For example, there may be uncertainty about changes in demand or in the costs of production, or the risk of problems caused by the weather or strikes.

Risk and profits

1 Look at the lists of businesses on the stock-market pages of a national newspaper. Work in groups of three to decide on four businesses which you think would be very risky and show large fluctuations in profits, and four which would be likely to show only small fluctuations in profits.
2 Make a note of your reasons.
3 One person from each group should report back to the rest of the class.
4 Compare your analysis with that of the rest of the class.

EXTENSION ACTIVITIES

Local businesses
There may be local businesses which have closed (Fig. 1) because of falling profits or losses.

Fig. 1

1 **Collect** any available information on why some businesses have closed; e.g. why did small grocers close or why have the record shops closed?
2 **Discuss** whether there have been any changes in the last year in the shops close to your school or college. If so, what changes have taken place?
3 **Identify** which types of retailing appear to have become more profitable and have therefore attracted more businesses and which have declined. Can you give reasons for these changes? (You may find articles in local or national newspapers about retailers expanding or changing.)
4 **Discuss:**

   a) reasons why a local council might need detailed information on the businesses in an area;
   b) what methods could be used to obtain detailed and accurate information on the changes taking place in the businesses in any area;
   c) how you would store this information so that it could be easily updated;
   d) how photographs could be used to show changes in businesses in the area. What would be the uses and limitations of photographs as part of a report on your local area?

Supply

Supply and price

The quantities of goods which are sold and the prices at which they are sold depend on two groups of people: the customers and the producers. The producers determine the supply of goods and services.

We can draw a *supply curve* to show the preferences of producers, Normally, as price rises, the production of a good becomes more profitable, and more producers aim to sell it. This is illustrated in the following figures and Fig. 2 relating to a new type of computer software. These show that an increase in price from £10 to £11 leads producers of this software to raise the quantity supplied from 20 to 22, and so on.

Fig. 2

Price	£5	£10	£11	£12	£13	£14
Quantity supplied	10	20	22	24	26	28

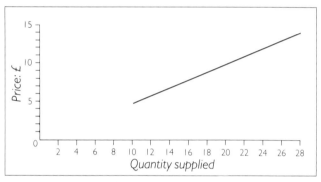

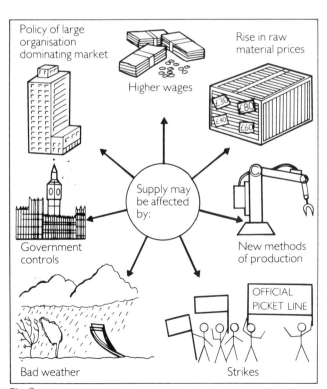

Fig. 3

Producers may be prepared to sell more at any price if the conditions affecting supply change (Fig. 3). Common changes include changes in the costs of production, such as higher wages or an increase in raw material prices, or a change in the methods of production.

Supply may be affected by interruptions to manufacturing, such as strikes or bad weather, or by seasonal factors. Supply may also be affected by government controls, or by the policy of a large organisation that dominates a market.

Supply of computers

David: I can't find any games for my Ultra-Video computer.

Leon: That's probably because it's so new. There might be some games if you wait awhile.

Jasmine: The school bought a computer three years ago for £500 and it now costs £250. I think it was a waste of money.

Louise: My mum works in a computer shop and she says that prices are going down all the time, and the computers are getting better.

Peter: My gran says that all the prices go up all of the time, and the quality of everything gets worse. She won't believe that some things come down in price.

Daniel: I've heard that the Ultra-Video computer factory has had a big strike, and there won't be many of their computers in the next month or two. The prices of computers might even go up because of higher wages. In any case, the microchips come from the United States, and the dollar has become more expensive.

Leon: I don't believe it. Computers have to come down in price because there will be newer and better ways of making them. If they make more, expensive equipment can be used to produce the computers faster and for less money.

Daniel: Well, I want a computer now and I don't believe that prices will fall. My brother might be able to get a discount on one for me.

Leon: You wouldn't catch me spending my money on a computer anyway.

QUESTIONS

5 Make a list of the reasons given above why the supply of computers might fall, and why it might increase. Explain which you find more convincing.

6 Peter's gran does not believe that prices fall. Make a list of four prices which have fallen and four prices which have risen in the last year. Explain why at least five of these prices have changed. (You may be able to get some ideas from your family and friends or from newspapers to help you answer this.)

DEMAND, WANTS AND NEEDS

The difference between needs, wants and demand

The wealth which is created depends not only on the producers of goods and services but also on the consumers and what they prefer to buy. We have to distinguish between the things which people may feel they want or need, and the things which they are able and willing to buy. People may *need* or *want* goods but not be able to pay for them; or they may prefer to spend their limited income on other goods and services.

People in some of the developing countries need more food, better seeds and more irrigation equipment. Producers and sellers of goods, however, are not usually influenced by wants or needs. Producers in the private sector, such as companies, sell goods and services in order to make a *profit*. They are therefore concerned with consumer *demands* rather than needs.

The term *demand* is used to describe the consumer wants which are backed up by purchasing power – that is, the quantities of goods and services which consumers are able and willing to buy. We can measure the goods which people buy only by considering them over a set period of time. We therefore use the term *demand* to describe *the quantities of goods which consumers are able and willing to buy in a given period of time.*

Housing repairs: an example of needs

Fig. 1

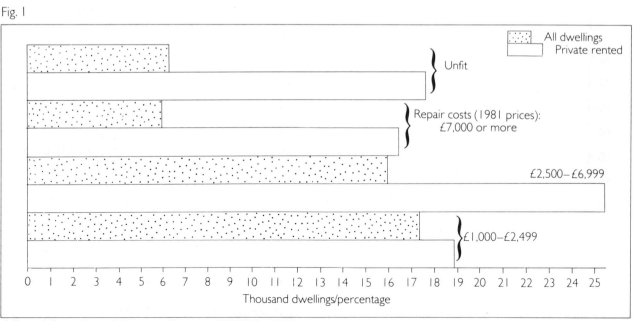

Adapted from *Annual Abstract of Statistics* (HMSO, 1986), p. 19, table 13 and p. 22, table 21.

Needs

1 Working in groups of four or five, make a list of three products for which the need is greater than the demand. Why is this so in the case of the examples you have chosen? (Do not use the examples given above.) Would it be possible to measure the needs you have chosen?

2 One person from each group should report back to the rest of the class. Does the whole class agree that a genuine need has been identified?

   (You are likely to find that needs are not easy to identify. In fact, they are very difficult to measure precisely unless agreement can be reached on the level of service or satisfaction which should be provided.)

Housing repairs

3 What does Fig. 1 tell you about the percentage of households which are in dwellings needing repairs?

4 Work in groups to make lists of reasons why landlords and tenants do not pay private builders to carry out the repairs and improvements.

5 Examine the reasons why rented houses and flats are more likely to be in a state of disrepair than other dwellings. (Before you answer, think about this question. You may be able to obtain ideas from your family and friends before you discuss this in class.)

6 Apart from disrepair, what would you consider in assessing the housing needs of an area?

7 Can you assess housing needs in your area? Your lending library may have local-authority statistics which estimate housing needs, or you could invite someone from the housing department or a pressure group (such as Shelter) to talk about housing needs. Then write a summary of what you think are the main housing needs in your area and what choices face the local authority.

Demand and price

Whether you demand a product is likely to depend on your income and preferences and on the price of the product. For most products a smaller quantity will be demanded as the price is increased. For example, the lower the price of chocolate bars, the larger the quantity of chocolate demanded and vice versa.

In considering the demand for a product, we are assuming that the quality does not change. For most goods, a *fall in price* will lead to an *increase in the quantity demanded*, assuming that all other things (such as the quality of the product and the incomes of consumers) remain unchanged.

The photograph of customers at the Harrod's sale (Fig. 2) illustrates a reduction in price which attracts an increase in the number of customers.

We can represent the relationship between price and quantity of demand by means of a graph – see Fig. 3. The line showing the amount which would be bought at each price is known as the *demand curve*. In the example given below, parents were asked whether they would buy a copy of the school magazine if it were produced at different prices. The figures below and Fig. 3 show how many parents were prepared to buy at each price.

Price	140p	120p	100p	80p	60p	40p	30p
Quantity demanded	65	90	120	160	220	310	400

On the graph, the line *DD* is the *demand curve*.

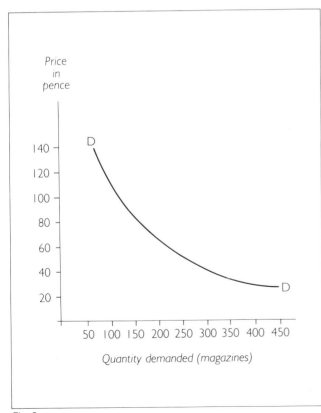

Fig. 3

Fig. 2

QUESTIONS

8 Choose a product which can be displayed in the classroom (perhaps a book, a pen or a bar of chocolate, or a school magazine).

9 Choose six price levels which are likely to result in some customers for the product. Find out by questioning the people in your class the maximum of the six prices which each person would be prepared to pay.

10 Draw a demand curve for this product – that is, a graph to show price on the vertical axis and the maximum number of purchasers on the horizontal axis.

EXTENSION ACTIVITIES

1 **Discuss** the likely effect of a 20 per cent increase in the price of school or college lunches on the number consumed each day in your school or college.

2 **State** how you might obtain estimates of the prices which people are prepared to pay for meals in your school. (See also Unit 1.4 on surveys and sampling.)

3 **Conduct a small survey** in your school or college to find out whether a 20 per cent fall in price would be likely to lead to a fall of more or less than 20 per cent in the number of meals consumed.

4 **Discuss** whether a price increase would affect your school or college more or less than other local schools/colleges which serve similar meals. (Factors to consider include the availability of alternative meals, the price of the meal at present, the incomes of the consumers and the number of students eligible for free meals.)

5 **Organise** a class debate on one of the following motions: *either* 'All school meals should be provided free' *or* 'School/college meals should be abolished'. Make a note of the main arguments which were advanced for and against the motion.

6 **Assess** which set of arguments listed in 5 is stronger: those for or those against the motion? Give your reasons.

CHANGES IN DEMAND

Changes take place in the goods and services which people plan to buy. You are probably aware of changes in your own income and preferences so that things you wanted very much a year ago may seem less important now, and you demand other things in their place.

Factors affecting demand

If you think about the factors which affect the demand for any product (for example, a particular record by a favourite group, or the goods or services produced by the organisation for which a friend or relative works), some of the following factors are likely to be included on your list.

Incomes

For most products, the higher the level of income the greater is the quantity demanded. For example, as incomes increase, people are likely to buy more records, clothes and good-quality furniture.

In some cases an increase in income may lead to a fall in the demand for the goods: such goods are known as *inferior goods*. The goods which are regarded as inferior for this purpose depend on the income and preferences of the people concerned. For example, people who are close to starvation may spend *more* on basic foods (such as flour, bread, rice and potatoes) as income rises. Most people in Western countries spend less on basic foods as income increases.

Substitutes

Some products may be regarded as substitutes for each other. There are many examples, and you can probably think of several. Some of the obvious substitutes include tea as a substitute for coffee, butter for margarine, oranges for apples.

The demand for any product is affected by the price of the substitute product. For example, if the price of tea rises, the demand for coffee may be expected to increase.

Complementary goods

Some goods are affected by the prices of other things which are used with them (that is, they are complementary rather than substitutes). Examples include video players and video cassettes, motor cycles and crash-helmets, a particular make of computer and the software for that computer. A fall in the price of video players increases the demand for video cassettes; a fall in the price of motor cycles increases the demand for helmets, and so on.

Seasons and climate

The weather affects the demand for some goods. A period of sunshine is likely to increase the demand for ice-cream. An increase in rain may cause a sudden rise in the demand for umbrellas or plastic mackintoshes.

You may find examples in the newspapers of people changing their holiday plans because of the weather, or of traffic jams on the routes from the cities to the coast when the weather is fine.

Fashion and tastes

Many products are affected by changing tastes or fashion. Clothes and records are obvious examples. The type of food eaten in Britain has also changed in recent years to reflect ethnic diversity and influences, and as a result of foreign travel by British people and greater awareness of the effects of diet on health.

Population and social trends

Changes in the size and age distribution of the population affect the demand for some goods and services. As the average age of the population in Britain rises, there is increased demand for nursing-home accommodation and sheltered housing; there is also a falling number of children in the schools.

The increase in the proportion of women who work outside the home (economic activity) also affects the goods and services which will be demanded.

Marketing

Organisations may aim to increase the demand for their product by a variety of marketing techniques including advertising, sports sponsorship, competitions and free gifts.

QUESTIONS

Demand changes

1 Make a list of the five items you would be most likely to buy if your income (pocket-money or income from a part-time job) were to increase by 50 per cent. Is there anything you would buy less of? Give your reasons.

2 Compare your list with those of two people sitting near you. Are there any similarities or any major differences of view on what you would buy more or less of?

3 Make a list of three examples (other than those given above) of each of the following: substitute goods; goods for which the demand is affected by trends in fashion; goods which are affected by the weather; goods and services affected by the fact that more women have paid jobs.

4 Find four examples of marketing techniques used to try to persuade your household to buy goods in the last week. Explain how each of these techniques tries to influence people.

5 Four school-leavers have decided to start their own business producing hot curried snacks called 'Spicey'. What would affect the demand for Spicey? How would they find out what the demand is likely to be?

Football in demand

6   What do the figures given in Fig. I tell you about attendances at football matches?

7. Describe the factors that could explain the changes in the number of people attending football matches.

8   What methods would you use to test your ideas in 7 above?

Fig. I

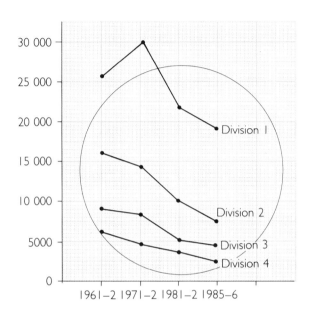

Adapted from *Social Trends*, 1987, p. 169, table 10.12.

Baby boom

Fig. 2 describes the Polish baby boom.

9   What problems are caused by an increase in the number of babies?

10 Why have problems particularly occurred in Poland (see Fig. 2)?

11 What goods and services are people likely to demand more of as the birth rate increases?

12 Explain the likely effects in ten years' and in sixteen years' time of an increase in the birth rate this year.

    See also Unit 2.2 on the family.

EXTENSION ACTIVITIES

1   **Write a report** to assess the demand for one of the following.

    a) Choose a local business organisation. You may do this individually or in groups as directed by your teacher. Find out what affects the demand for one product of this organisation. You may obtain ideas by thinking about the factors listed above and discussing whether any of these apply, or by reading local newspapers, or by asking anyone you know who works in the business. Write your assessment of the factors affecting demand in about 600 words.

    b) Or you may consider the factors affecting the demand for a service provided for a fee by the local authority, such as swimming-pool attendances or the use of a sports centre.

    c) Or choose one fashion product, such as a particular style in sweaters or socks or trousers. What affects the demand for this style?

2   **Hold a debate**, or discuss in writing, the following statement: 'Advertising is good for industry, good for consumers and benefits society.'

Queues grow for nappies as Polish baby boom bites

From Jackson Diehl, in Warsaw

ALMOST every afternoon at Smyk, a large children's store in Warsaw, a line of pregnant women forms in front of a counter on the second floor where supplies for babies are sold.

Each woman shows a clerk a card certifying pregnancy, and in return is handed a red plastic basket containing pyjamas, tee-shirts, sweaters, bibs, blankets and small cotton towels. The basket is not a gift. Buying everything in it could cost a prospective mother the equivalent of three or four months of a typical salary.

The line at Smyk is just one of the peculiar customs pregnant women in Poland have come to accept as normal in recent years. Unlike most of the rest of Europe, this country of 37 million is experiencing a baby boom, and state-provided services, from maternity wards to bib manufacturing, have not kept up. The result is not only inconvenience. In the last year, poor hygiene and supplies have caused the deaths of groups of newborn babies in hospital maternity wards at least twice, with a total of 14 dead.

Many women complain about less serious infections picked up by their infants at the hospital and about crowded maternity wards where doctors' visits, sanitary materials and even clean sheets can only be obtained with bribes. "It's a disaster," said Mr Jerry Holzer, director of the Institute of Statistics and Demography and Warsaw's State School of Planning. "We demographers reported at least 10 or 15 years ago that another wave of children was approaching and that investments in services were needed. But nothing was done."

The boom of births began in 1982 and peaked in 1983, when a record 720,000 babies were born. Since then, the numbers have declined.

Demographers, however, said Poland continues to have one of the highest rates of population growth in Europe.

Fig. 2

From the *Guardian*, 31 July 1986.

THE ENVIRONMENT (I)

Social costs

When nuclear power-stations develop faults and send radioactivity into the water or the atmosphere, when chemical waste is dumped in rivers, when someone plays a stereo so loud that other people are driven indoors or when someone in a café smokes while you are eating, *social costs* are involved.

Social costs are costs of an activity which are borne by society as a whole.

Consumers may inflict damage on other people by activities such as smoking or riding a motor bike noisily or recklessly. Producers may inflict damage on the environment or on people not directly involved in producing their product. This damage is a social cost. It must be paid for by those who are not receiving any direct benefit from the consumption or production.

The social costs involved in production include the pollution of the air by industry (which may even affect people in other countries), explosions which can destroy homes and possibly lives or cause injuries, congestion on the roads by large numbers of delivery vehicles and the destruction of forests which provide a habitat for wildlife and benefit the world's atmosphere by producing oxygen and absorbing carbon dioxide.

Social benefits

We have discussed the social costs which may arise from any activity. There may also be *social benefits*. Social benefits are the gains which society as a whole obtains from an activity. For example, if industrial buildings and homes are kept in a good state of repair and painted regularly, and if gardens are planted, then the whole neighbourhood may gain. Some of the benefit is difficult to measure, such as the enjoyment people may gain from looking at the gardens.

QUESTIONS

Social costs and benefits

1 Choose a local issue which illustrates social costs and benefits. It may be the siting of a nuclear waste dump, or a new airport, or a motorway. Find out by reading newspapers, and possibly by contacting the people involved, the views of those who support the development and of those opposed to it.

2 Divide into groups. Each group should take the role of one of the parties involved, such as a group opposed to the development on environmental grounds, a residents' action group, a group or company supporting the development, the local authority and a government department. Select at least one spokesperson from each group and hold an informal meeting to discuss the issues.

3 Write one of the following:

a) a report on the meeting for some of the councillors who were unable to attend; or

b) a newspaper article for the local paper describing the meeting and summarising the issues – include both the costs and the benefits to the local community.

EXTENSION ACTIVITIES

1 **Examine the social costs** involved in three of the following activities:

● Smoking.
● Driving a car.
● Drinking alcohol.
● The use of lead weights in fishing.
● Attendance at football matches.
● Glue-sniffing.

Obviously not all of these activities can be banned all of the time. For each activity you have chosen:

a) **Note** the steps taken by the state to make the social costs as low as possible.

b) **Discuss** whether the controls are adequate or excessive.

c) **Debate**: choose one of the activities and hold a debate on the motion that it should be banned.

2 There are plans to open a chemical factory 300 metres from your school. The company involved has already experienced a serious explosion at one of its factories producing the same product. A group of parents and teachers have visited a factory making this product and complained about the smell of the chemical within about 300 metres of the site. Vehicles carrying inflammable and toxic chemicals would pass close to your school.

a) **Discuss** whether there are any reasons why the local authority might give planning permission to this company to build its factory. Is it possible that the benefits to the community might be greater than the costs?

b) **Write a letter** to the local newspaper expressing your objections to the site of the chemical factory, or your support for the proposed factory.

Damage to the environment – an illustration

Fig. 1 shows some of the damage to the environment caused by industry, farming and the disposal of waste and rubbish.

QUESTIONS

4 Who would have to pay the costs of preventing each of the types of pollution shown in Fig. 1 from damaging the environment?
5 What would be the benefits of protecting the species shown in Fig. 1, and who would gain these benefits?

Fig. 1

ACID RAIN: Some parts of Britain have been covered by a layer of acid snow as black as soot, killing off plants and wildlife also damaging trees and soil

BEACHES: Because of 'diluted human sewage' pumped into the sea around 40% of Britain's beaches are unfit for bathing

BIRDS: At least 36 species have shown serious decline (like the golden eagle) in the last 35 years through loss of habitat

TREES: 40% of our broad-leaved woodland trees (oak, elm, sycamore and beech) have disappeared since the war.

BATS: Several of 15 species are now at great risk of extinction. The Mouse-Eared is down to the last male

DIPPERS: One of our rarer birds, are in danger of extinction because of reduced food supplies in many of our rivers

OTTERS: Are rare or have totally disappeared in most parts of the country because of pollution in our rivers and streams

POPPIES AND CORNFLOWERS: Are being wiped out due to farmers using chemical herbicides and fertilizers.

FROGS: There were 500 per acre in Huntingdonshire in 1940, now there are less than 1 per acre

SWANS: 30 years ago the river Thames between Sunbury and Pangbourne was home to 1,300 swans. Now there are fewer than 200

BUTTERFLIES: Out of a total of 55 British species 1 has become extinct, 10 are in serious danger and 13 have declined.

AMPHIBIANS AND REPTILES: 4 out of 12 are in danger of extinction.

DRAGONFLIES: 1 in 10 are extinct. 15 out of 44 species are now extinct or endangered

FISH: Tail-less trout have been found in Scotland. Many Lochs and Lakes cannot support natural fish population

From the *Sunday Mirror*, 19 April 1987.

THE ENVIRONMENT (2)

Unit 5.7 considered the social costs of wealth-creation. This unit is concerned with some particular examples of damage to natural resources.

The soil

Throughout the world people are aiming to produce more food and obtain more energy and raw materials for growing populations, industry and building. As they do so they use up resources which have taken hundreds or thousands of years to form. This is particularly evident in the case of the soil.

There are many reasons for the erosion of topsoil. Severe problems of erosion are most likely to occur where the soil becomes very dry during droughts and may then be blown away or washed away by torrential rain, as in a tropical climate. The topsoil is washed down the hillsides into the streams and out to sea. As the soil becomes thinner, it becomes harder to grow crops.

The problems of soil erosion increase as trees and hedges are removed. Forests, hedges and woodlands are continually being cleared to provide more land for farming and housing, and to provide wood for paper-making, construction and firewood. In Britain many hedges have been removed to allow for the use of modern farm machinery. As land is cultivated more intensively, by growing more crops, problems of soil erosion increase.

QUESTIONS

Soil erosion

1 Which groups of people lose most as a result of soil erosion?
2 What action could be taken by farmers and by governments to reduce soil erosion?

Acid rain

Acid rain is a form of pollution affecting most of the world. It is the result of burning coal and petrol, and the effects include damage to water, wildlife, trees and buildings.

Causes of acid rain

Acid rain is caused by sulphur dioxide and oxides of nitrogen. Seventy per cent of the acidity in British rain is due to sulphur which comes mainly from the burning of fuel in power-stations. The remaining 30 per cent comes from oxides of nitrogen, and more than two-thirds of this is from car exhausts.

Fig. 1 illustrates the formation of acid rain. Some of the chemicals are deposited close to the source. Others form acids which are deposited in rainfall; a large proportion of the acid produced in Britain falls in other countries, particularly Scandinavia, the Netherlands, Belgium and West Germany.

Effects of acid rain

Excess acidity in the rain has a number of effects, including:

● The pollution of lakes and rivers so that the stock of fish in them diminishes. This also affects the birds and wild animals which eat fish and insects, and it has badly damaged fishing and the tourist industry in Norway and Sweden.
● Forests are dying in Canada and Europe, although experts disagree on the evidence of the link between this and acid rain as compared with other types of pollution. In West Germany it is estimated that 50 per cent of the trees are seriously damaged, and this has seriously reduced the habitats of animals and birds.
● Food production is affected when the soil becomes acidic; for example, cereal yields go down.
● There is evidence that acid rain, by entering our drinking water, could be responsible for the increase of some diseases such as chest and kidney problems.
● Buildings are damaged by acid rain, causing concern about the stonework of the great cathedrals of Europe.

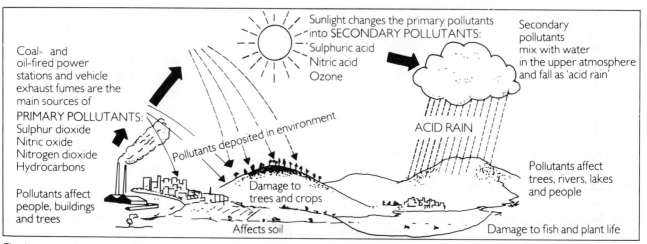

Fig. 1

Measures to combat acid rain

Political action: We all suffer the costs of other people's pollution. As individuals we can attempt to reduce the pollution we cause, but this involves costs to us, and the benefits affect other people. Pressure groups such as Friends of the Earth campaign on the issue of increasing government action to reduce pollution and encourage individual and community action. (See also Units 7.5 and 7.6 on pressure groups.)

No single country can solve the problem of acid rain alone, and Britain exports far more acidity than it imports. Acid rain from Britain particularly affects Norway and Sweden and northern West Germany. By 1985 twenty-two countries (excluding Britain) were committed to reducing sulphur dioxide emissions to 30 per cent of 1980 levels within fifteen years. This step would require the fitting of flue gas desulphurisation units to twelve of Britain's power-stations and could raise electricity prices by 1 per cent for ten years. The European Community has gone further and proposed a 60 per cent reduction in sulphur dioxide emissions.

New Technology: This could be developed to reduce pollution from car exhausts, and manufacturers could be required to fit the technology which is available. However, each car user may be reluctant to pay higher prices for this if other road users continue to cause pollution.

Energy conservation: The energy consumed in road transport and domestic heating may be reduced by using cars less and by increasing the insulation of buildings.

QUESTIONS

Action on acid rain

6   Explain why acid rain has increased in the last forty years.
7   What evidence is there of a need for government action to deal with acid rain? Why has there not been more action by the government?
8   Why is international co-operation necessary?
9   Discuss what action individuals can take to reduce the pollution which causes acid rain. What costs would be involved in taking such action?
10   Find out why the use of lead-free petrol is advocated by some groups, and discuss the reasons why people may be reluctant to buy lead-free petrol.

The deteriorating Great Lakes

A legacy of the last Ice Age 12,000 years ago, the five interconnected Great Lakes – Superior, Michigan, Huron, Erie and Ontario – hold one-fifth of the entire world's fresh water. More ships pass through them than through the Panama Canal, and 37 million Canadians and Americans depend on their water for drinking, irrigation, recreation and industry. Still, as the near death of Lake Erie in the late 1960s so dramatically demonstrated, the Great Lakes are extremely vulnerable to the pressures of civilisation. And now they face the greatest threat in their history: pollution from toxic chemicals.

Scientists have identified nearly 1,000 man-made chemicals in the Great Lakes, flowing out of factories, leaking chemical dumps, sewage plants, farmers' fields and even from the air itself – which transports not only acid rain but toxic chemicals from faraway smokestacks. They are invisible, but they build up gradually in the tissues of living things. In Lake Ontario, the most polluted of the five lakes, authorities have banned the sale of some commerical fish species because of toxic pollution. And many experts say that the water of the Great Lakes may soon not even be safe to drink – without advanced purification technology.

From an article by Pat Ohlendorf in the Canadian magazine *Maclean's,* 26 August 1985.

QUESTIONS

11   What would be the likely views of each of the following on the pollution of the Great Lakes?

   a)   The directors of a United States chemical company on the shores of Lake Erie.
   b)   A farmer using artificial fertilisers on the shore of Lake Erie.
   c)   A schoolteacher running an environmental education centre on the Canadian shore of one of the Great Lakes.

12   What steps would you take to control the social costs of North American industry and agriculture?

EXTENSION ACTIVITIES

1   Governments have attempted to clean up some of the dumps of toxic waste and to ban certain types of waste disposal affecting the Great Lakes. Critics say that they have not gone far enough and that more action is necessary if the pollution is not to cause cancers and birth defects in the future.
   Examine the reasons why government action is necessary to control environmental pollution, and why it cannot be left to industry.
2   International co-operation may be necessary to control pollution, as in the case of the Great Lakes.
   Find other examples from recent newspapers or television reports where international co-operation is needed to control damage to the environment.
   Discuss why action is needed and what form it should take.

THE STANDARD OF LIVING

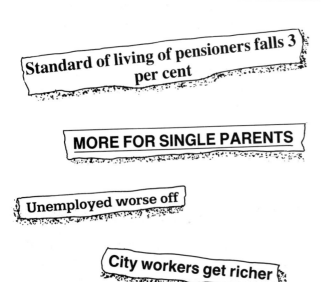

Standard of living of pensioners falls 3 per cent

MORE FOR SINGLE PARENTS

Unemployed worse off

City workers get richer

Comparisons are often made concerning the standard of living of people today compared with earlier years, or how well off some groups are compared with others. The phrase *standard of living* is used to describe how well off people are in terms of goods and services. Poverty was the subject of Unit 4.9, and poverty may exist at a time when most people are able to buy more goods and services.

Measuring the standard of living

There are many problems in measuring the standard of living. Consider, for example, whether people are better off or worse off than they were in the 1970s. Incomes have risen since the 1970s, but so have prices. We are therefore concerned with the increase in *real* incomes – this means the increase in money incomes after allowance has been made for increased prices.

It is difficult to compare the standard of living now with the past because of changes in the goods and services which are available, such as electrical and electronic goods, computers and videos, and services provided by the state such as health care and education.

The average standard of living may increase, but not all groups will be affected equally. Some groups can experience an improvement in their standard of living, while other groups such as the unemployed find that their standard of living has fallen. (See also Unit 4.11 on poverty and Unit 4.5 on changes in the class structure.)

Measurement of the standard of living does not usually take account of goods and services which are not paid for, such as unpaid work in the home. It also does not include the work which is undertaken for cash and not recorded by the government (the so-called *hidden economy*).

Changes in the standard of living

Fig. 1 The length of time necessary to pay for selected commodities and services (Great Britain)

	(Married couple with husband only working)					
	1971		1981		1985	
	hours	mins.	hours	mins.	hours	mins.
1 large loaf (white sliced)		9		8		7
1 pint fresh milk		5		4		4
1 lb of rump steak		54		57		47
Weekly electricity bill	1	04	1	14	1	06
Cinema admission		29		34		31
LP record (full price)	3	16	1	49	1	37

Adapted from *Social Trends* (HMSO, 1987), p. 106, table 6.9.

QUESTIONS

1 *Social Trends* is published annually and is available in most reference libraries. Find the latest edition available in your school or college library, or in your local reference library. Add the most recent figures available to Fig. 1. [5]
2 A pint of milk is shown as requiring only 4 or 5 minutes of effort. Cinema admissions require about 30 minutes. Does this mean that milk is a smaller and less important part of the total family budget than cinema admissions? [2]
3 What, if anything, do the statistics in Fig. 1 tell you about the standard of living now as compared with 1971? [4]
4 The table shows the earning power of married men in employment whose wives do not work. There are some groups of people whose standard of living may have changed in a different way from the group described in the table, such as the unemployed, pensioners, households where the main wage-earner is female and households where the husband and wife both work. Would you expect these groups to have increased or fallen in number since 1971? (Use statistics from *Social Trends* to support your answer if possible.) [5]
5 The standard of living of retired people is likely to be different from that of working men and women. Discuss why this is so. [4]

Housing standards

New goods and services are introduced into people's homes, and expectations change. For example, households in Britain today may expect to have their own bath, hot water and an inside toilet. Other examples include refrigerators and television sets.

Fig. 2 The rise in homelessness

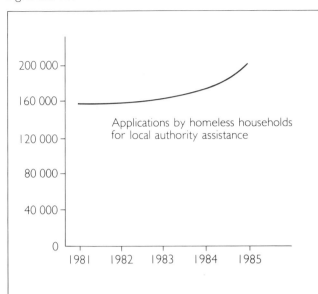

Applications by homeless households for local authority assistance

From Shelter, *Housing Factsheet 1*, May 1986.

Fig. 3

6 Discuss whether Fig. 2 provides any evidence of a change in the standard of living.   [5]
7 An improvement in housing might indicate that the standard of living has risen. What other statistics might be used to indicate a change in the standard of living?   [4]
8 What, if anything, does Fig. 3 indicate about the standard of living of the family in this picture?   [3]
9 What additional information, apart from Fig. 3, would you need to be able to draw conclusions about this family's living standards?   [5]

See also Unit 4.11 on poverty.

EXTENSION ACTIVITIES

1 **Interview** a sample of retired people. (Discuss with your teacher the number of people to be interviewed; you could begin with just one or two interviews and consider developing this into a longer project if you wish. (See Unit 1.4 on surveys and sampling.)

   a) How do they think the standard of living has improved in the last forty years?
   b) Are there any ways in which the interviewees in your sample feel that people now are worse off?
   c) Are there any factors which make comparisons with the past difficult – for example, differences in local services such as shops, or differences in the types of goods available? (Give details.)

2 **Find out** about the standard of living in another country in order to compare it with that of Britain. You may do this by drawing on your knowledge of both countries and using information from geography reference books. You may also interview people who have lived in the other country.

   a) Is there any evidence that people have a higher standard of living in the country you have chosen than in Britain? (Think about the type of evidence you would need to look for, such as income levels, food, housing and medical care.)
   b) Is there any evidence that people are worse off in that country than they are in Britain?
   c) Are there any factors which make comparisons difficult – for example, differences in temperature which affect heating requirements, or differences in the amount of unpaid help usually received from families and the local community, or different inequalities of income?

ECONOMIC GROWTH: BENEFITS, COSTS AND CAUSES

In Unit 6.1 we considered how the production of more goods and services can lead to a higher standard of living. Even a small annual increase in a country's income can accumulate steadily over the decades and lead to a considerable improvement in the standard of living.

Like the standard of living, growth is measured in *real* rather than money terms. This means that we consider the growth in the real goods and services available, not the increase in their prices. The term *economic growth* describes the increase in output per person over a period of time, usually one year.

Benefits of economic growth

Economic growth has many benefits for the country concerned. The extra goods which are produced may be enjoyed by the residents of the country, or they may be sold overseas, and other goods and services may be imported.

Governments may wish to provide additional benefits for the population such as better education, health care or care for the elderly. If the income of the country is increasing sufficiently, then the government may spend more on defence or on benefits for some people without making other people worse off.

Costs of growth

The costs of economic growth include damage to the environment. We may achieve faster growth by building more nuclear power-stations, destroying forests or using up natural resources rapidly. (See also Units 5.7 and 5.8 on the environment.)

Economic growth may also destroy the way of life of some communities, such as some of the Indian tribes of Brazil and North America. These tribes have suffered deaths from diseases for which they had little or no immunity (such as measles and chicken-pox). They have also lost their traditional hunting and fishing grounds, and their way of life has been destroyed as communities have broken up following the development of industry, mines or roads in their areas.

Growth in the south-east of England has led to the loss of much of the 'green belt' – the area of land free from urban and industrial development which was planned to encircle London.

An increase in economic growth may be achieved by allowing people to work in very poor conditions (Fig. 1) and even to suffer accidents or damage to their health.

Although greater wealth may be used to improve working conditions, higher output in the short term may be achieved by longer working hours, heavier workloads and poorer working conditions.

Fig. 1 Boys working on a building site in Bangladesh

Causes of growth

There are many different views about the main reasons for economic growth. The following reasons are usually discussed.

Technical change and investment

Scientists and engineers are constantly developing new machines which produce goods faster and more efficiently than before. These inventions can lead to economic growth, but only if the newer and better machines are produced and used.

Economic growth thus requires investment in new equipment, buildings and machinery. It is necessary to invest in new machines which produce goods faster and require less labour to operate or maintain them.

Two important requirements for economic growth are, therefore, technical change and investment.

Management and labour

Economic growth is affected by a number of different aspects of the labour force. These include:

- *management efficiency* – the organisation of labour by management so that people are used most effectively and do not, for example, have time wasted between different tasks;
- *the labour force* – the health of the labour force, the education and training of the workers and other factors which are harder to measure, such as the attitude to work;
- *co-operation between labour and management* – the extent to which labour and management see a common interest in trying to increase production, and in avoiding disputes.

Problems in achieving growth

Economic growth is not easy to achieve in any country. Many developing countries are finding it increasingly difficult to improve their growth rates, for the following reasons.

First, people may be unwilling to use resources to produce machines for the future when those resources could be used to buy imported consumer goods for the present. To obtain these imports, a country must export goods, including possibly food or crops grown in place of food. In any country, investment involves an *opportunity cost*, and that opportunity cost is mainly the sacrifice which must be made in goods and services for consumers. (See also Unit 5.2 on opportunity cost.)

Second, investment is encouraged by a growing market for consumer goods. Producers are more likely to want to buy new machinery if there are more people able to buy the goods in their country. There has to be a balance therefore between higher investment and consumer spending.

Third, some countries have borrowed from international organisations and banks but have then experienced difficulties in repaying the loan. This has happened in Latin America, where countries borrowed heavily and were then faced with higher interest rates and falling prices for their products. Banks are now less willing to make new loans to these countries.

Other factors can also influence investment, such as expectations of war or disorder in an area, or opposition to investment because of the effects on people's working lives or on the environment.

Island in the sun: a case study

Consider a small but beautiful island where the population of 60,000 people has traditionally made a living by farming and fishing and a small amount of tourism (Fig. 2). There is concern that the population is increasing because of the fall in the death rate. In order to provide jobs and incomes for the growing population, it has been suggested that tourism should be developed. A foreign hotel company is interested in building a large holiday complex. There would be chalets for 1,500 visitors, swimming-pools, saunas and other recreational facilities. A government adviser has been appointed to report on the advantages and disadvantages of the proposed development.

Fig. 2 Entertaining the tourists

QUESTIONS

Group A should take the role of the hotel company and prepare arguments to present to a government adviser on the advantages of the development.

Group B should take the role of the people who have retired to the island or bought expensive holiday homes there.

Group C should take the role of the people who are trying to earn a living and bring up their families on the island.

1 Each group should present their case at an inquiry held by the government adviser.

2 Take the role of the government adviser and summarise the arguments in a written report. Include your recommendation on whether or not the development should be allowed.

3 You may live in, or know of, an area where efforts are being made to attract tourists in order to provide jobs. Discuss the advantages and disadvantages of the expansion of tourism in this area.

EXTENSION ACTIVITIES

1 **Obtain information** about any developing country from newspapers. (Some newspapers, for example the *Guardian*, occasionally produce supplements on particular countries.) You may also collect information from television programmes (make notes and video recordings if possible). Do not forget to look at atlases and the geography section of your library, and to talk to anyone you may know from the country.

2 **Make a list** of the main economic problems of this developing country.

3 **Discuss** any developments taking place which could increase this country's growth in the future.

6.3

NEW TECHNOLOGY AND WORKING CONDITIONS

QUESTIONS

1 Using the views in the discussion, and any ideas of your own, make lists of the arguments for and against the introduction of new technology in British industry.
2 Comment on whether the fears of new technology given in the discussion are justified.

Unit 6.2 was concerned with the importance of new technology to economic growth. We shall now consider the effects of new technology on employment and working conditions.

A conversation in the factory canteen:

Sean: Have you heard about the new machines? They won't need anyone to operate them. Even the loading of materials into the machines will be automatic. And it will all be completely accurate – no waste or mistakes.

Terry: I've heard, all right! They say it's so that we can keep up with the foreign producers and that it will make our jobs more secure. If you ask me, it's just to make more profits.

Lucy: My dad says that this company is not making any profit, and if something isn't done quickly it will close down.

Mark: Well, he would wouldn't he? He's not going to lose his job.

Sayeeda: I've heard that the union is trying to get an agreement that only volunteers will lose their jobs and that there will be good redundancy money.

Anna: I was hoping that my son Ian might get a job here when he leaves school. Doesn't seem much chance now.

Carol: Who'd want a job here! The work is boring. If it's automated there might be something more interesting for young people to do.

Wayne: But even the skilled jobs are disappearing. It's cheaper now to replace a part than to mend it. They're cutting back on managers and office workers. And they won't retrain everyone to use the new machines.

Lucy: I know you'll say this is just my dad's view again, but if we don't introduce new machines other countries will, and there will be less jobs than if we compete. If the new machines mean higher incomes for some, there will be jobs producing goods and services for these people with higher incomes.

Examples of changes in working conditions

There are many examples of jobs which are changing because of the introduction of new machines. Computers have taken over the repetitive jobs and some of the skilled work in such activities as banking, retailing and printing. You may be able to provide other examples from your family's experience and what you have read in the newspapers.

Banking

Computers are now used for a wide variety of banking tasks. These include preparing customer accounts, record-keeping, sorting cheques, paying cash from automated teller machines (sometimes seen in the walls outside banks) and even making decisions about whether to grant a loan. Computers are also used, with telecommunications, to send financial and banking information around the world and to provide information in the home or the bank branch.

Retailing

New technology is changing many retailing jobs. The supermarket cashier, for example, now passes the goods over an automatic scanning device which reads the price, records the selling of the item and automatically sorts the information so that new stocks of goods can be ordered.

Printing

In some cases the new technology can take away part of the skill from a job. This is sometimes referred to as 'deskilling'. For example, printers used to serve as apprentices for five or six years to learn just one of the printing crafts. As a result of computerisation, workers can be trained quickly to do jobs which used to need a long apprenticeship. The skilled printing workers have traditionally all been members of a trade union; many of them have been unhappy about the way their work has changed, or even disappeared, in the newspaper printing industry.

In Unit 6.4 we shall consider some of the jobs which have declined in recent years, and others which have expanded.

Fig. 1

Fig. 2

The Ford Motor Company

Look at the photographs of car assembly on the production line at the Ford Motor Company – Figs. 1 and 2. Cars are usually produced on assembly lines . In Fig. 2 each worker remains in one part of the factory and performs a repetitive act (such as welding car doors) on parts of cars which move down a conveyor system from one worker to another.

Fig. 1 shows most of the welding being done by robots. There are fewer people working in this area of the plant. From the management point of view, robots have several advantages. They are always accurate; they do not get tired or have accidents or hangovers; they do not stop for tea-breaks; and they never 'work to rule' or go on strike for better pay or conditions. The introduction of robots at Ford is typical of the car industry both in Britain and overseas.

The number of workers at Ford Motor Company has fallen. This is partly because of decreasing sales of cars and the increase in foreign competition. It is also because some tasks can now be performed entirely by machine, as shown in the photographs. Some workers have volunteered to leave with financial compensation (they have accepted *voluntary redundancy*). Others have been moved to other jobs in the company (this is known as *redeployment*). Many workers are reluctant to volunteer for redundancy if they are unlikely to obtain new jobs elsewhere.

Work in three groups: a) shop stewards (trade-union representatives in the workplace), b) industrial relations managers and c) other managers (such as finance and marketing). Each group should decide on the most appropriate view to take of the introduction of the new technology.

Hold a meeting of union and management representatives to negotiate the introduction of the twenty new automated production areas and arrangements for 500 redundancies out of a work-force of 1,500 in the factory.

Report on the decision which you think would be made and the reasons for this decision.

4 Discuss the view that the introduction of robots is likely to lead to fewer jobs in the UK car industry in the future.

5 Do you think that the jobs now performed by fully automated machines, as shown in Fig. 1, would be attractive to most school-leavers if the robots were removed? Give reasons.

6 What method would you use to find out how workers feel about production-line work? Explain the advantages and disadvantages of using the method you recommend.

EXTENSION ACTIVITIES

1 **Collect information**, from newspapers, television, unions and employers about the introduction of new technology which has led to an industrial dispute. What are the issues and what are the views of each side? (You may need to use more than one newspaper to obtain details of both sides.) Comment on this and why it may be necessary.

2 **Interview** someone whose job has changed through the use of new technology. What have been the effects of the new technology on the numbers employed and on working conditions in your interviewee's workplace? Comment on the views about new technology held by the person concerned.

QUESTIONS

3 A car factory is considering the introduction of computer-controlled machinery which would eventually require only 20 per cent of the present work-force to produce the same number of cars.

OCCUPATIONAL CHANGES

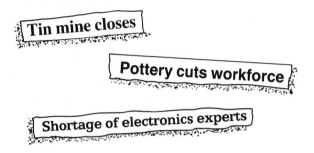

In Unit 6.3 we looked at changes in employment because of new technology. Changes also take place because the demand for some goods increases while the demand for other products falls.

Changes are taking place in the types of work which people do and the places where that work takes place. In this unit we shall consider changes in people's occupations and the employers for whom they work. Changes in the location of jobs will be considered in Unit 6.5, and unemployment in Unit 6.7.

The four sectors

Employment is often considered in terms of primary, secondary, tertiary and, sometimes, quaternary sectors. These are defined as follows:

- *primary sector* – employment in such areas as agriculture, fishing, mining and quarrying;
- *secondary sector* – mainly manufacturing and construction;
- *tertiary sector* – services such as banking, insurance, hairdressing, catering and retailing;
- *quaternary sector* – the new areas of employment such as computing, research and development. Some writers include these quaternary activities in the tertiary sector.

The British economy has experienced a gradual decline in the relative importance of the primary sector and an expansion, especially in recent years, of employment in services. These changes are typical of many industrialised countries, and the reasons for this include the following:

- *Greater efficiency*, as in agriculture and mining, so that less labour is required to produce an increased output.
- *Deindustrialisation* – employment in manufacturing increased for much of the nineteenth and twentieth centuries, but has declined in recent years. More than 9 million people were employed in production and construction in 1979, and this figure had declined to less than 7 million in 1986.

- *Expansion of services to industry* – services to industry which have expanded include banking, advertising, market research and catering. There are a number of explanations for this. First, as industry expands, it demands more commercial services. Second, in recent years large companies have made more use of specialist organisations for services such as catering, advertising and research, rather than employing their own staff. Third, Britain has expanded its service sector as industry and trade have grown around the world because other countries have purchased services (such as banking) from Britain.
- *Expansion of consumer services* – services to consumers have increased as the standard of living has improved and the working week has become shorter. These include leisure services such as theme parks and catering, and personal services such as hairdressing. Other consumer services which have expanded include education, health and banking.

Changes in occupational distribution

Fig. 1 Employment in various sectors in the UK, June 1979 – June 1986

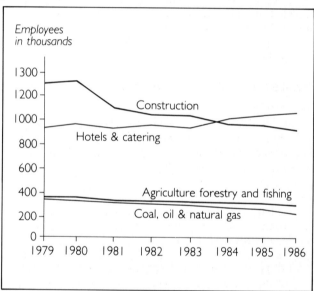

Adapted from *Monthly Digest of Statistics* (HMSO, August 1986), p. 18, table 3.2.

QUESTIONS

1 In which of the sectors shown in Fig. 1 has employment increased most? [1]
2 What does Fig. 1 tell you about changes which have taken place in the numbers employed in four sectors of the economy? [5]
3 Explain the trends in a) construction and b) hotels and catering. [6]
4 Give four reasons why people in declining occupations may have difficulty in transferring into alternative types of work. [8]

Private and public sectors

People may be employed in either the public sector or the private sector.

Private sector

The private sector includes employment in business organisations, charities, trade unions and other associations. There are two main categories of worker in the private sector: the self-employed and employees.

Public sector

Employment by the public or government sector includes *central government* (such as workers in the Department of Health and Social Security and the Inland Revenue), *local authorities* (such as teachers and social workers), *public corporations* (including coal-miners, railway workers and employees of new town development corporations), the *National Health Service*, (including hospital workers and family doctors) and the *armed forces*.

The extent to which services are provided by the public sector depends partly on political decisions and values and on changes over time. Some goods are unlikely to be provided at all by the private sector, and others may be provided by either sector. (See, for example, Unit 9.2 on the Welfare State and Unit 9.3 on the question of ownership.)

Private and public sector employees: a family case study

Michael is the son of a Yorkshire coal-miner. He went to agricultural college but found there was a lack of well-paid jobs for someone without the capital to start his own farm. He worked for a while in Essex as a builder running his own business. His business survived the fall in property prices in 1974, but in 1981 buildings were hard to sell, and he decided to give up his business and move to Kent to run the restaurant he had been building. The restaurant was very successful, and he has now retired. Michael's daughter is a doctor in a National Health Service hospital in Cardiff. Her special interest is in the expanding field of the care of the elderly (geriatrics). His son is an agricultural worker.

Fig. 2

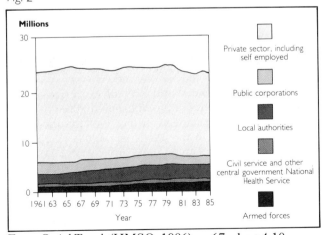

From *Social Trends* (HMSO, 1986), p. 67, chart 4.10.

QUESTIONS

5 Which two of the five types of employment in Fig. 2 have shown the largest increase? [1]
6 Which have shown the greatest decline since 1965? [1]
7 Using the statistics in Figs. 1 and 2, discuss the extent to which the experience of Michael's family (case study) may be considered typical of changes in working patterns in the last twenty years. [6]
8 What evidence is there of social, occupational and geographical mobility in Michael's family? [6]
9 Michael has changed his type of work and the part of the country in which he works. Why do some workers find such changes of work or movement to a new area difficult? [6]

EXTENSION ACTIVITIES

1 **Find examples** of the occupations or types of employment which are declining in your area. You may obtain this information from local newspapers, from reports and statistics in your local library or from local-authority sources.
2 **Find out** from the newspapers and from discussions with people involved why these occupations are changing.
3 **Work in groups**: one group of trade unionists and employers from the expanding industries, one group from the declining industries and one group of councillors and advisers from the local authority. The groups should discuss the cause of the decline and the effects on the local area; they should decide who has the responsibility for dealing with the problems.
4 **Form a panel** made up of representatives from each group to report back to the rest of the class and to answer questions.
5 **Write a report** of the final panel discussion as it would be written for a local newspaper.

REGIONAL CHANGES

In some parts of Britain jobs are expanding, while in other areas there is a general picture of decline. In this unit we shall consider the factors which lead to these changes.

Local industry

1 What is the main industry of the area in which you live? [2]
2 What other industries are there in the area? [3]
3 Read the following and account for the location of one of the main industries in your area, referring to some of the factors mentioned. [5]

Factors affecting the location of industry

Raw materials

Mining and quarrying, and industries which require bulky raw materials, have tended to locate close to natural resources such as coalfields and iron ore. In some cases these industries move as new sources of mineral wealth are discovered or as changes take place in the techniques of obtaining or processing materials. Mining, for example, has expanded in Leicestershire and Nottinghamshire due to new coal seams being found, whereas in South Wales it has declined.

Fuel and power

Industries which required large amounts of energy developed near to coalfields. In the last fifty years, however, coal has been replaced by electricity as the main source of power. Industries using electricity can locate anywhere, and industry has developed in the south of England and the West Midlands, away from the major coalfields.

Markets

Industries producing products which are bulky or awkward to transport have been sited close to the places where the goods will be sold. Industries developed around major centres of population which provided markets for the goods. Some services cannot of course be transported; retailing, hairdressing, catering and building services depend on the prosperity of the local area for their customers. If a coal-mine or a factory closes, the local services also decline.

Infrastructure

Road and rail links to other areas affect the access to markets and raw materials. Markets and shopping areas tend to develop at good route centres. The availability of suitable land, factory space and houses is also important.

'Footloose' industries

Some industries, such as electronics, can choose any of a variety of locations and have therefore been described as 'footloose'. They tend to develop close to other organisations in the same field, in areas where the labour force has the right skills and which are attractive but close to motorways and airports.

Government influence

Governments influence the location of industry, in some cases by directly employing people in areas of high unemployment. Financial assistance, information, advice and in some cases factories or factory sites are provided by a variety of agencies including the European Community, the Department of Trade and Industry, urban and new town development corporations, development agencies such as the Scottish Development Agency and local authorities.

Local developments
Read the following on changes in the location of industry and discuss the answers to the questions in relation to your own area.

4 Approximately when were most of the houses, offices or factories in your area built?
5 Why were they built at this time?
6 What are the main changes which have taken place in local industry in the last forty years?

Changes in the location of industry

In the 1930s there was unemployment in the traditional coal-mining, shipbuilding and textile industries, but newer industries were expanding. The expanding industries included car manufacture in the Midlands and the manufacture of consumer goods such as furniture in the areas where incomes were rising, particularly the Midlands and the South-East. By the late 1930s rapid expansion was taking place in the manufacture of weapons and ships for defence as it became increasingly obvious that war could not be avoided. This led to the revival of some industries such as shipbuilding in the North-East.

Following the Second World War the expansion of the manufacturing industries of the Midlands and South-East continued. Services expanded in the South, particularly in the London area. In the 1950s and 1960s employers in the more prosperous areas found difficulty in recruiting enough labour to fill the available job vacancies. The unemployment rate nationally was very low, but even so there was a regional problem, with lower unemployment and more jobs available in the South-East and fewer in the valleys of South Wales, in Glasgow and in northern parts of England including Merseyside.

In recent years the manufacturing sector has declined. The expanding sectors have included the hotel and catering industry (largely for business and overseas visitors) and financial services; both of these have expanded in the London area. The electronics industry has also expanded in the South, especially in the counties along the M4 motorway from London to the West.

The areas of decline include the inner cities. Some industries have moved out of the older inner-city areas to the outer suburbs and new towns, leaving declining services, poor housing and high unemployment. Some of these areas were formerly ports – the dockland areas are discussed in Unit 6.6.

The regional picture

Fig. 1 shows the areas of highest unemployment in the United Kingdom.

Fig. 1

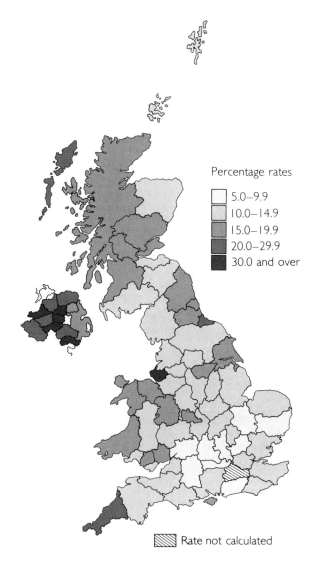

Percentage rates

☐ 5.0–9.9
☐ 10.0–14.9
▨ 15.0–19.9
▨ 20.0–29.9
■ 30.0 and over

▨ Rate not calculated

From *Regional Trends* 22 (HMSO, 1987), p. 108.

QUESTIONS

Regional unemployment

7   Account for the high unemployment in any two of the shaded areas in Fig. 1.   [3]
8   Account for the relatively low unemployment in any non-shaded area.   [3]
9   What evidence is provided by this map for and against a North/South divide in employment in Britain?   [4]

EXTENSION ACTIVITIES

1   If you live in or close to an area of high unemployment, there may be government schemes to assist your area.

   a) **Investigate** the assistance available in your region or town.
   b) **Design** a publicity brochure setting out the attractions of the area for industry.
   c) **Examine** and make notes on the features of the local area that would be unlikely to be included in such a brochure but serve to make the area less attractive to new industry.

2   **Compare** employment and developments in your own area with another area familiar to you, perhaps where you used to live or where you have visited a friend or relative, either in Britain or overseas. You may use photographs to illustrate some of the contrasts. (Note: the comparison should not list the features of each area separately, but it should compare the areas under several subheadings such as main industries, population growth, rate of unemployment, declining industries, expanding industries, changes in the infrastructure and reasons for change.)

3   **Examine** the case for, and the case against, each of the following (this could be prepared in three or six groups, with each group reporting back to the class):

   a) Workers from the North of England, Wales and Scotland should be prepared to travel to the South-East to work and return to their families at weekends.
   b) Workers from areas of high unemployment should be given priority for council accommodation in the South-East.
   c) Companies should be given large government grants to move to areas of high unemployment.

4   **Write** the arguments for and against the view that the workers in areas of high unemployment should move to the parts of the country where there are more jobs. (Take into account the various constraints which make relocation difficult for many people, such as the cost and availability of housing, family and social ties and children's education, as well as the advantages of moving.)

THE DOCKLANDS: A CASE STUDY

The areas around the main ports of Britain have traditionally been important industrial areas and major employers of labour. These dockland areas, particularly in cities such as London, Liverpool, Bristol, Cardiff and Glasgow, have declined in recent years. They are examples of areas where there are considerable problems because of the rapid decline in jobs. The London docks provide one example of decline and change in a docklands area.

Fig. 2 Derelict docks

Fig. 1 Greenland Dock, 1952

The docklands before their decline

Fig. 1, shows the London docks when there was still plenty of activity on the River Thames close to London. London has been a port for centuries and was an important international market centre for many goods including sugar, tea, spices and ivory, besides many other goods from the Far East. Before the Second World War many trades and services existed in the dockland areas to serve the local communities and sailors. There were repairers of ships and makers of ropes and barrels, pubs, shops, sellers of provisions, and of course the dockers and transport workers. There were also the industries which processed the imported goods such as sugar refining and spice packaging.

The activity in the docks provided incomes for the workers which they spent on goods and services in the local area. So this too helped to provide a demand for the services of the local builders, shopkeepers and publicans.

Reasons for the decline

Fig. 2 shows part of the London docklands in decline. By the 1970s most of the jobs had gone from the docks close to London. The reasons for the decline of the docks were as follows.

First *competition* from Europe has grown. With the loss of the Empire, particularly after the Second World War, Britain was no longer the main centre for European trade with the rest of the world. Other ports such as Rotterdam expanded in Europe, and ports on the east coast of England became more important.

Second, the use of *air transport* for goods and people increased enormously.

Third, the use of *containers* developed. Goods are packaged and sealed in containers, miles inland, away from the ports. This takes away all the work of unloading, stacking goods in warehouses and restacking them on ships which had formerly been done by dockers. The equipment at the traditional ports became obsolete. In a similar way, the growth of the transport of goods across the Channel on lorries which drive on to the ships (*roll-on, roll-off cargoes*) led to the development of new ports with new facilities.

Fourth, *road transport* has greatly improved. Proximity to railway routes and canals is no longer so important, and goods can be taken to Dover or Harwich for a shorter sea crossing than from London.

Fifth, the developments described above were also linked with the growth of *larger ships*, so the new ports developed downstream (for example, at Tilbury – Fig. 3)

Fig. 3 Malem docks at Tilbury

where the water was deeper. The docks closest to the centre of London, and for similar reasons Manchester, were among the first to close.

Sixth, in the 1960s the dockers secured better conditions of employment. Many of them had formerly been employed on a casual basis by the day, and they were now given better security. However, this raised *labour costs* and may have accelerated the decline of the jobs in the docks. ·

The pattern of decline

As the docks closed, the surrounding area also declined. Warehouses fell into disrepair; the factories processing and packaging imported materials such as spices closed; and people moved away to the newer towns and suburbs. Pubs and shops closed because of a lack of custom, and some areas became derelict. In other areas small parks and gardens were built.

Problems and solutions in the docklands

The problems

New industry was not attracted easily into the docklands area. There were many reasons for this:

● Road transport was poor, and the warehouses were not easily accessible or adaptable to modern industry. Many of the houses were old or had been replaced by unpopular tower blocks. As incomes declined in the area, so did other services.
● It is often cheaper to build on a new 'green-field' site than to demolish and redevelop.
● Planning responsibilities were divided between several local authorities. For some years there was a lack of an effective overall plan.
● Many of the workers who had lost their jobs in the docks did not have the skills required in expanding industries. People with skills which can be used elsewhere, such as electricians, are often among the first to move away.

The attraction of new industry

In 1981 the government formed the London Docklands Development Corporation (LDDC). Similar urban development corporations were formed in other areas such as the docklands of Merseyside and Clydebank. The LDDC aims to attract industry by selling land to developers and improving transport and derelict land. Financial incentives and easier planning permission have also been introduced.

New industry has been attracted into the London docklands, as shown in Fig. 4, such as newspaper printing and the financial institutions which have gradually spread eastwards from the City of London. Tourism and leisure developments have taken place in the Merseyside docklands. Jobs have been created, and incomes have risen.

New problems

The developments have, however, been very controversial. The LDDC has been opposed because it is not elected by local people, but it has been given powers taken from the local councils. Local residents formed groups to oppose developments. They are critical of the new jobs which are not suitable for the manual workers in the area and of the new houses. Many of these are too expensive for local people, so that a more affluent population has moved into the area. They have also been critical of the noise and disturbance caused by some of the new developments,

Fig. 4 New developments in dockland

such as newspaper printing and the airport for light aircraft. There has also been opposition by those who wished to develop amenities such as parks rather than industry and houses.

QUESTIONS

Reasons for change

1 Look at the photographs (Figs. 1 and 2) of the London docks as they have changed over the years. Describe the changes indicated by the photographs. [3]
2 Look at the photograph of Tilbury docks (Fig. 3) and explain how and why this differs from the other docks close to London. [5]
3 Examine the likely effects of the LDDC developments (as shown in Fig. 4) on local shopkeepers and residents. [6]
4 What are the main changes in the use of land which are taking place in your area? (You could use photographs and a survey and develop this as the basis of a project.) [6]

EXTENSION ACTIVITIES

1 **Investigate** in your own area the jobs which depend on activity in other industries.

   a) Which organisations provide services to large employers?
   b) Which organisations provide goods and services to residents?

2 a) **Hold a meeting** to discuss the developments in a docklands area. Some of the class should take the role of local councillors, residents' associations, environmental groups, senior citizens' and youth associations, sports clubs, the chamber of commerce and local industry.
   b) **Summarise** the conclusions of the meeting about the most appropriate development for the area.

UNEMPLOYMENT

In this unit we shall consider the questions of who are the unemployed and why they are out of work. Unit 6.8 is concerned with the effects of unemployment on the unemployed and their families.

Who are the unemployed?

The number of unemployed people in Britain is estimated mainly by counting the numbers registered with the Department of Employment as available for work and claiming benefits. Many people who would prefer to be in employment are not eligible for benefits and are therefore not counted, including the following groups:

- People who have not paid sufficient national insurance contributions to be eligible for unemployment benefit. This group includes women who would like to return to work after staying at home with children but are unable to find jobs.
- People seeking part-time work, or those who are very restricted in the hours or place where they can work.
- Men and women over the age of retirement.
- Students and pupils over sixteen on full-time courses.
- People on Manpower Services Commission schemes.
- People in part-time jobs who would prefer full-time work.
- Those who delay registering after losing their jobs.

It is uncertain exactly how large the percentage of people who are out of work is. The unemployed population is underestimated for the reasons given above. The increase in unemployment during the 1980s is also underestimated because of changes in the way in which unemployment is measured.

At the same time, however, there has been an increase in the size of the working population. This increase has included a large proportion of female part-time workers, partly because more women are now seeking work. (See also Unit 4.7 on employment inequality.) Many of these women are not eligible for benefits and do not appear as part of the unemployed population when there is no work available for them.

Unemployment is not evenly spread throughout the population. It is concentrated in the younger age groups, in some of the ethnic minority groups (particularly Afro-Caribbean males), in certain regions of the country (particularly the North), in the inner cities, and among unskilled and semi-skilled workers. (See also Unit 4.9 on race, inequality and employment.)

The changes in the way unemployment is measured illustrates a common problem in the use of statistics. It is difficult to make comparisons over time or between countries unless you know how the statistics were measured and what the likely inaccuracies are.

Why are they unemployed?

The term *unemployed* is used to describe a diverse assortment of people. Many people are out of work for a period, however short, at some time in their lives. Other experience frequent periods of unemployment between jobs. And there are those who are unemployed for longer periods of a year or more.

The following are the main causes of unemployment:

Seasonal

Unemployment reaches two peaks in each year. The first is in the months of January and February when many catering and outdoor workers (especially construction workers) are laid off. The second is in the summer and autumn, as students and school-leavers look for work.

Frictional

Even during periods such as the 1950s, when employers had difficulty recruiting enough labour, there were some people unemployed because they were in the process of changing jobs. This group is likely to be particularly large if there are major structural or technical changes in industry.

Structural

Workers are often not able to move easily between the declining and the expanding industries. The expansion in recent years has been mainly in services which have required skills, qualifications and personal qualities different from those needed in the declining occupations in mining and heavy industry. It may be difficult for an individual to acquire new skills because of the cost and availability of training and the drop in income during training. Some workers, therefore, become part of the long-term unemployed because of structural changes in industry. (See also Unit 6.4 on occupational changes.)

Regional

Jobs are declining in some parts of the country and expanding in areas such as the South-East and the counties south and west of London. It is difficult for people in the declining areas to move to the areas where there are jobs because of family and social ties, children's education and housing. Homes are more expensive in areas where there are jobs, and a move to a council house in such an area is not normally possible. (See also Unit 6.5 on regional changes.)

Technical

It is sometimes argued that increased automation will not cause unemployment for the following reaons: first, because the rising standard of living will create more demand and therefore more jobs; and second, because a country which becomes more efficient is able to compete successfully, and there will be more jobs producing goods for export. On the other hand, there may be large increases in unemployment because new technology reduces the number of employees needed to produce the same quantity of goods and services. (See also Unit 6.3 on new technology and working conditions.)

Level of demand

Britain has experienced rises and falls in the general level of unemployment since the eighteenth century; these fluctuations are sometimes described as the *business cycle*. This unemployment is caused by a fall in the general level of demand for goods and services. Recent unemployment in Britain has been partly caused by policies to reduce the rate of inflation. Policies which hold down inflation generally reduce the demand for goods. Less demand for goods, of course, means less demand for workers to produce them.

Residual

There are some people who are likely to be unemployed whatever the number of vacancies. These include some of the people who are better off on state benefits than they would be in work (the so-called *poverty trap*), as well as those who do not wish to work. (See also Unit 9.2 on the Welfare State and Unit 4.11 on poverty.)

The working population

The *working population* of the United Kingdom means the number of people either in work or available for work. In 1985 the figures were as shown in Fig. 1.

Fig. 1 The working population, 1985 (thousands)

Total working population	27,593
Males	16,443
Females	11,150
Unemployed	3,179
Males	2,197
Females	982
Employed labour force	24,414
Self-employed	2,623
HM Forces	325

From *Annual Abstract of Statistics* (HMSO, 1986), p. 107, table 6.1.

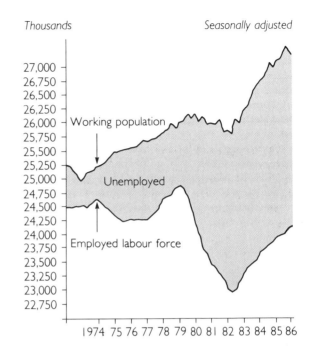

Fig. 2 The working population and employed labour force of Great Britain

Thousands *Seasonally adjusted*

Working population
Unemployed
Employed labour force

1974 75 76 77 78 79 80 81 82 83 84 85 86

From *Employment Gazette*, (HMSO, February, 1987.)

5 Account for the increasing number of people who are self-employed. (See also Unit 6.4 on occupational changes.) [5]
6 Unemployment increased in the 1980s. Discuss the reasons for this in groups, and then write your answer. [10]

EXTENSION ACTIVITIES

1 **Use government statistics** to find out what the most recent figure is for national unemployment. (There are lots of publications containing these statistics including *Employment Gazette, Monthly Digest of Statistics,* the *Economic Progress Reports* published by the Treasury and the Lloyds Bank *Economic Bulletins,* published monthly.) Did unemployment increase or decrease in the preceding five quarters?
2 **Draw a graph** to show the changes in unemployment over the last five quarters. Can you give any explanation for the changes shown on your graph?
3 **Use statistics** for the area in which you live to find out which groups in the population – analysed by age, sex, race and occupation or skill – show the highest rates of unemployment. Can you explain why these groups are more likely to be unemployed? (See also Units 4.7 on gender, inequality and work and 4.9 on race, inequality and employment.)

QUESTIONS

1 How many of the working population of the UK were not in employment in 1985? [1]
2 Draw a suitable chart to show the statistics given in Fig. 1. [5]
3 What information do Figs. 1 and 2 provide about changes in unemployment? [5]
4 Account for the differences between the male and female statistics for the unemployed population. [4]

EFFECTS OF UNEMPLOYMENT

The most obvious effect of unemployment is the waste of resources (Fig. 1). The unemployed population are not producing goods and services. Unemployment also costs the government large sums in unemployment, social security and other benefits, and it reduces the taxes which can be paid.

Statements are often made about unemployment, such as 'unemployment causes riots' or 'unemployment causes illness'. Such statements are hard to prove, but by examining the statistics we can see whether riots or illness appear to be more likely to affect the unemployed than those in work.

Fig. 1

Effects on health and families

There are difficulties in proving that unemployment is directly the cause of any problem. For example, the unemployed may be more likely to be ill than those in work, but is it the illness that reduces the chance of finding a job or the unemployment which causes the illness? Could it be that both illness and unemployment are caused by something else (such as the area where people live)? Could the unemployment cause some other problem, such as poverty, which is then the direct cause of the illness?

There is also the possibility that unemployment could affect various groups of people in different ways – for example, the young compared with the middle-aged. The effects on people now may differ from the 1930s. (See also Unit 1.5 on secondary sources.)

Many studies have attempted to answer some of the questions about the effects of unemployment on health and family life. They generally indicate that unemployment has some effect on suicides and psychological health, although the extent of these effects is uncertain.

Fig. 2

40-year old – unemployed for 5 years – commits suicide

Unemployment causes stress, say experts

Job loss led to marriage breakdown

Distress

Researchers at Sheffield University interviewed more than 1,100 seventeen-year-olds and found that anxiety, depression and psychological distress were higher than among those with jobs (although a quarter said that they liked the 'freedom of being unemployed'). Women exhibited higher levels of anxiety, depression and distress than men.

Cancer

Several studies, including one at the City University, London, which used the results of the 1971 census, found higher rates of lung cancer among unemployed than among employed men of the same social class and age. The wives of the unemployed men also suffered a similarly higher death rate.

Suicides

Researchers at the Royal Edinburgh Hospital examined the employment and medical records of men who had attempted suicide. They found that men who were unemployed were ten times more likely to commit suicide than men who were in work. There did not appear to be any other explanation for the attempted suicides; they did not depend on social class, or the area where the men lived, or physical and mental health.

Less height and more hospital

Studies have indicated increases in divorce rates, domestic violence, abortions, unwanted pregnancies and deaths associated with childbirth among the unemployed. The children of the unemployed tend on average to be shorter; this effect is greater in the case of the long-term unemployed (although there are obviously big variations in the height of children from both unemployed and employed parents). A Glasgow study has now found that children of unemployed parents are more likely to be admitted to hospital.

Effects on crime and disorder

There does not appear to be a simple connection between unemployment and crime rates. The type of crime which is most likely to be affected is *street crime* (burglaries, theft, muggings, assault), rather than fraud or tax evasion. Unemployment combines with other factors to cause crime. For example, young people are more likely to turn to street crime than the elderly are, and crime rates appear to be related to relative deprivation (poverty of the offenders compared with other people around them) rather than absolute deprivation.

Following the riots and disorder in Britain in 1981, some politicians and newspapers suggested that there is a connection between unemployment and riots. The evidence for this is mixed, because there have been periods of high unemployment and no disorder in parts of Britain. United States studies, too, have indicated that there is no consistent relationship between riots and deprivation.

Lord Scarman (a Lord of Appeal) considered the evidence regarding the causes of the 1981 riots and prepared a controversial report. He found a number of factors which had contributed to the cause of the disorders, including the role played by the police and the media and the disadvantages felt by racial groups in the inner cities. Part of Lord Scarman's analysis of the effects of unemployment is given below.

Unemployment is now generally regarded as an important problem which governments are expected to solve. Governments are also expected to control the rate at which prices rise, and the reasons for this concern with inflation are considered in Units 6.9 and 6.10.

The urban riots of the 1980s

'Whatever the special employment problems of black people, and of young black people in particular, unemployment remains nevertheless an evil that touches all the community. There can be no doubt that it was a major factor in the complex pattern of conditions which lies at the root of the disorders in Brixton and elsewhere. In a materialistic society, the relative (not by any means – given our social security system – absolute) deprivation it entails is keenly felt, and idleness gives time for resentment and envy to grow. When there is added the natural aggression of youth, and with the media ever-present to relay examples of violence, there arises a devastating and dangerous combination of factors tending to unrest and disorder. The solution, of course, depends on a successful outcome of current economic problems.'

From Lord Scarman, *The Scarman Report : The Brixton Disorders, 10–12 April 1981* (Pelican, 1982), p. 168.

The experience of unemployment

'Stephanie left college at the age of twenty-two. Over the six years since then she has had a variety of temporary jobs, interspersed with stretches of unemployment. Recollecting one of these periods without work, she vividly describes how unpleasant the experience was:

"I just deteriorated into a vegetable. It was awful. I couldn't string two words together. I couldn't hold a conversation with anybody. I didn't bother about what I looked like, where I went, or what time I got up in the morning. I was very, very unhappy with the way things were. I stopped reading, I stopped writing, I stopped being interested in anything. I didn't want to go anywhere. I just went downhill rapidly and got to the stage where I wasn't applying for jobs either – I didn't have that motivation there."

From Stephen Evans, 'The Story of Stephanie', *New Society*, 10 January 1986.

Stephanie later made a deliberate decision to change her routine, and she is working towards turning a hobby into a small business of her own. Some unemployed people do not follow Stephanie's pattern and although many eventually come to terms with unemployment, they have no optimism for their future. Adjustment to unemployment appears to be easier for young people such as Stephanie than for older workers.

QUESTIONS

Measuring effects

1 Prepare a table to list the effects of unemployment on a) the unemployed, b) their families and c) other people.
2 Using the evidence given in this unit, discuss whether the information proves that unemployment is responsible for physical and mental ill-health, crime or riots.
3 Discuss how you would feel about long-term unemployment if it happened to you.
4 Suggest how life for the unemployed could be improved.
5 Explain why unemployment is regarded as a problem for the government.

EXTENSION ACTIVITIES

1 **Interview** two people who are unemployed and describe their feelings about unemployment. If possible, interview them again after two months and examine any differences between the two interviews.
2 **Compare** the results of your interviews with those of three other people in your class.

   a) What conclusions can you draw from your interviews about the effects of unemployment?
   b) Explain any differences or similarities between the results of your interviews.
   c) Compare the feelings of the people in your sample with those of Stephanie.

3 **Visit** a centre for the unemployed or job club. Find out what the centre does to help the unemployed and how it is organised and financed.

INFLATION

Inflation means that prices in general are rising and that the increase in prices is continuous over a period of time, usually several months or even years.

We are all aware of inflation affecting the prices of the goods we buy and the incomes we receive. For example, in 1984, £3.73 was needed to buy the same goods which had cost £1 in 1974. Both wages and prices rise in a period of inflation, although there may be differences between them in the rate of increase.

The most commonly used measure of inflation is the *index of retail prices*, also called the *cost of living index*, which is compiled and published by the government.

The cost of living index

Retail prices are the prices paid by consumers in the shops and in their bills for services such as gas and electricity. Some items bought by consumers have far more importance than others in the family budget. We may all be more concerned about an increase in petrol prices or bus fares than about an increase in the price of, for example, shoelaces or peppermints.

The index therefore measures the increase in the cost of the average family 'shopping basket' of goods and services (Fig. 1). The contents of this average shopping basket are discovered by family expenditure surveys.

Fig. 1

The cost of living index is an average measure, and this may disguise the fact that some households are affected more than others by rises in the prices of basic items such as heating, bread, milk and potatoes. A separate index is produced by the government for pensioners, who spend a larger proportion of their income on food but less on clothes than working households. An independent organisation called the Low Pay Unit produces a 'low paid price index' which shows that the cost of living of the low paid increased by 64 per cent between 1979 and 1984, compared with the increase for all households of only 59 per cent.

Any index is used to measure change over a number of years. The first year (called the *base year*) of any series of figures is given the figure of 100, and changes are measured from this starting-point. For example, we may call the year 2000 a base year and give it the price index number of 100; if prices in 2001 rise by 10 per cent, the index will rise to 110.

QUESTIONS

Measuring inflation

1 Give the percentage increase or decrease for year 1 in each of the following price indices:

 a) Base year: 100; year 1: 110.
 b) Base year: 100; year 1: 97.
 c) Base year: 100; year 1: 125.

2 Which goods and services do you think would have a large effect on the cost of living for a low-income family with children aged 2, 6 and 15?

3 Which groups of the population would be most affected by an increase in the charges for gas and electricity? Why?

4 If wages increase more rapidly than the rate of inflation, would you expect the standard of living to rise or fall? (See also Unit 6.1 on the standard of living.)

Hyper-inflation

We have to distinguish between the rates of inflation which have been experienced in Britain in the twentieth century (which have not exceeded 30 per cent in any one year) and the very rapid rise in prices experienced elsewhere, such as in Germany during the years 1922–3 and in a number of Latin American countries today (e.g. Mexico and Bolivia).

Very rapid inflation, to the extent that people are reluctant to hold notes and coins at all, is known as *hyper-inflation*. If money is falling in value very rapidly, people become reluctant to hold money and rush to buy goods which will hold their value better. If prices are increasing steeply by the day, workers may demand payment daily or even twice daily, as many of them did in Germany, in order to rush out and buy goods. People will be reluctant to save money. In some Latin American countries, savings are commonly held in the form of United States dollars rather than the country's own currency.

Some people lose more than others as a result of hyper-inflation. The most vulnerable are those who have not been able to spend or transfer their savings to another currency, and those whose incomes do not increase as inflation increases.

The effects of hyper-inflation: Germany in 1923
In Fig. 2 you can see a grocer packing banknotes into a tea chest because the till will not hold them. This picture was taken in Germany when inflation had risen so far that money had to be carried in very large amounts in order to make small purchases.

The following account of the German inflation in 1923 illustrates the problems of hyper-inflation.

Fig. 2 Hyper-inflation in Germany in the 1920s made shopping very difficult

'There were stories of Americans in the greatest difficulties in Berlin because no one had enough marks to change a five dollar bill ... and of foreign students who bought up whole rows of houses out of their allowances.

There were stories of shoppers who found that thieves had stolen the baskets and suitcases in which they carried their money, leaving the money itself behind on the ground; and of life supported by selling every day or so a single tiny link from a long gold crucifix chain. There were stories (many of them as the summer wore on and as exchange rates altered several times a day) of restaurant meals which cost more when the bills came than when they were ordered. A 5,000 mark cup of coffee would cost 8,000 marks by the time it was drunk.

The reality behind such inflationary anecdotes, amusing in retrospect, was exceedingly grim. The agony was displayed as much by the shrunken-necked gentlemen to be seen in the streets, with their mended white collars and shiny suits saved from the war, as by the exhausted workmen queuing impatiently outside the pay windows with big shopping bags in which to rush their wages away to the shops. Badly off as wage-earners were, their standards were still at a level distinctly comparable with the past. Throughout Germany, Austria and Hungary the old standards of salary earners, pensioners and people living on savings had often dropped almost out of sight.'

From Adam Fergusson, *When Money Dies* (Kimber, 1975), p. 140.

By the autumn of 1923 the farmers were unwilling to send food to the towns in exchange for paper money, and there was widespread hunger, disorder and rioting. The government had to take drastic action. A new currency was issued, government spending was cut, and the inflation was brought under control.

QUESTIONS

Worthless money
Work in groups, each group representing a section of the population in a country where there is hyper-inflation.

Group A: the farmers.
Group B: the self-employed.
Group C: the pensioners and government employees.
Group D: the bankers.
Group E: the tourists and students from overseas.

5   Each group should prepare a report on the effects of the hyper-inflation on their section of the population. Each group may wish to prove that it is worse affected than other sections of the population and therefore deserves more help from the government.

6   One representative from each group should report to the government subcommittee (consisting of whole class).

7   Prepare a brief written report on the effects of the hyper-inflation for presentation to a government minister.

8   What would people expect the government to do about the problems of hyper-inflation?

EFFECTS OF INFLATION

There are a variety of views on how harmful inflation is and whether it is worth suffering higher unemployment in order to introduce policies to control inflation (Fig. 1). Although there are some harmful effects of inflation, there are also benefits for some people and organisations.

The effects of inflation include the following:

More inflation

If inflation has been experienced in the recent past there may be more inflation in the future. This is partly because trade union negotiators will base their expectations of future inflation on recent experience. Similarly, in the case of some suppliers of goods (such as chocolate bars, books and newspapers) prices are fixed infrequently. The increases in price must therefore take account of future increases in costs.

Wealth holding

Fear of inflation causes people to keep their wealth in goods which will hold their value in a time of inflation. Such goods include gold coins and jewellery, antiques, paintings and foreign currencies.

Saving

Inflation may cause savings to rise or to fall depending on whether or not people are trying to maintain the real value of their bank balances and savings.

Redistribution of income

As shown in the work on hyper-inflation in Unit 6.9, and in the questions below, inflation does not affect all people equally.

Planning

Business planning is made harder if inflation is not constant and predictable, because it becomes more difficult for organisations to estimate their costs and fix prices in advance. For example, many builders now insist on a term in the contract which states that they can raise their prices if costs rise. This makes planning harder for the local authorities, health authorities and other organisations which are committed to purchasing the buildings.

Exports and imports

If prices of British goods rise faster than those of our competitors overseas, people in Britain and the rest of the world will not wish to buy British goods. This causes the exchange rate to fall, so that, for example, fewer US dollars or West German marks can be bought for £1. We then have to pay more for our imported goods, and this causes costs to rise further.

Psychological effects

People may feel they are worse off because prices are rising, even though their incomes are rising equally. It is very hard to know whether complaints about inflation are deeply felt.

Fig. 1

QUESTIONS

1 A trade union negotiator may be faced with the following: two years ago inflation was 5 per cent, one year ago it was 10 per cent and this year it is expected to be approximately 18 per cent. What would you as a union negotiator guess that inflation might be next year?

2 If you were a producer of chocolates and intended to raise your prices next month, discuss all the factors you would need to consider before making a final decision about the size of the increase.

3 Would people become more reluctant to lend money to the government or to industry at a time of inflation? Give your reasons.

4 Imagine a situation where you wish to buy a car and cars are rising in price at 20 per cent a year. The rate of interest is only 10 per cent on savings or 21 per cent on bank loans. Discuss what you would do.

5 The following examples relate to a year when inflation was 20 per cent. Who were the most likely gainers and who were the losers in each case?

  a) Paul's pocket-money was increased from £2 to £2.25 during the year. (According to the regular surveys by Wall's Ice-Cream, children's pocket-money commonly fails to increase in line with inflation when prices are rising rapidly.)

  b) The workers employed by an expanding and profitable company with a large investment in machinery threatened a strike because their wages had not risen as fast as the rate of inflation. Shop workers are not well organised in trade unions but were also concerned about their falling standard of living.

  c) Sharon found that her daughter was no longer eligible for free school meals because the family's money incomes had risen by 17 per cent after tax.

6 Video Imports Ltd is a small company which has made an agreement to supply a large chain of shops with video players at a fixed price. The video players will be imported from South Korea, and the company must borrow money in order to buy them. What would be the likely effects of an increase in the rate of inflation on this company?

Claire's experience: inflation and the family

Mum: Why don't you go and see Emma instead of sitting there looking so bored?

Claire: She has gone to the cinema with some others from our class. I can't afford to go tonight.

Mum: But you've had your pocket-money. Surely you haven't spent it already?

Claire: Mum, the bus fares have gone up, and you expect me to buy my own tights, and I had to spend twice as much on David's birthday present this year to get him something worth having.

Mum: Well, my pay hasn't gone up and I've got to pay more for everything too. The union has put in for a rise, but I don't think they will get very much. We don't seem to be as strong or well organised as a lot of workers. The child benefit won't go up for a few months yet, and goodness knows when I'll get an increase in maintenance from your dad, now he's got another family to support. The amount I've got put away in the savings bank is hardly enough to cover one month's rent or an electricity bill.

The above dialogue illustrates one family's experience of inflation.

QUESTIONS

7 Explain why Claire's family is losing as a result of inflation.

8 What questions would you need to ask in order to find out whether the family were gaining in any way as a result of inflation?

9 Would inflation necessarily be worse for those on low incomes than for those on incomes which are above the average?

EXTENSION ACTIVITIES

1 **Obtain information** from any two political parties on their policies on inflation and unemployment.

2 **Compare** the parties' statements on unemployment and inflation. Which of the two problems is regarded by each of the parties as the greater problem at the present time? Give reasons for your answer.

3 **Interview** a sample of people to gain their recollection of the experience of periods of inflation in the 1970s. Were they gainers or losers? Why?

4 **Test the hypothesis** that inflation is unpopular:

  a) Devise a short questionnaire and discuss the choice of questions and the selection of your sample. (See also Unit 1.4 on surveys and sampling and Unit 1.1 on the questionnaire.)

  b) Obtain answers to your questions and combine your results. (You may use a computer program to sort and add your results, and to draw graphs to illustrate your analysis.)

  c) What conclusions can you draw?

  d) What were the limitations of your test?

  e) What faults did you identify in your questionnaire?

POWER AND AUTHORITY

This section is concerned with how decisions are made. Later sections will return to the problems of scarcity, inequality and unemployment and consider decision-making in relation to these problems.

Many decisions involve a consideration of power and authority. We all use the terms *power* and *authority* in a variety of ways. We may have different ideas about what it means to have power over someone else or to have the power to do something.

Power

What do you think is meant by *power*? Do you have power over other people? Are there people who exercise power over you?

The term *power* is used to refer to the ability of people to carry out their own will in spite of resistance. It is also often said that a person has power if he or she can deliberately make other people behave in any particular way.

Views of power

The following conversation expresses different views of power.

Neerose: The teachers have power to make us do our homework, because if we don't conform we get detentions.

Matthew: Perhaps we could just not turn up for detentions?

Neerose: We couldn't do that – but . . .

Peter: I always do maths because Miss Akhtar is OK, and you can't fool around with her.

Jane: You don't even know who is exercising power over you. Some people are able to convince you that you are doing what you want when you are really doing what *they* want.

Simon: The newspapers have power to influence the way we think and what we discuss. And education affects our way of seeing the world later.

Peter: Nobody makes me do anything I don't want to do.

Simon: But you may not always realise why you are doing something and who has influenced your decisions.

Lucy: I feel I've got lots of power when I can drive myself somewhere in my car, and that's not making anyone else do anything.

QUESTIONS

1 What are the different views of power expressed in the conversation above?

Example: the foreman's power

Fig. 1 Demolition workers in Oxford Street, London, in the 1920s

The following is a description by a retired demolition worker of his job as a young man in the years following the First World War (Fig. 1).

'My introduction to really hard work was at Peter Robinson's, the big department store in Oxford Street, on nights. Gawd, was it hard! I was one of a gang of four men loading the skips and occasionally it became necessary to use a 14-pound hammer to reduce large lumps of brick to liftable proportions. This sort of exercise caused large and painful blisters to form on my lady-like and soft hands. I began to slow down as the hours went by and at one point the foreman, Bill Worsley, stopped to admonish me:

"Come on, young Stumps, you'll have to do better than that if you want to keep the job."

I was trembling with exhaustion when we knocked off for sandwiches and cups of tea (supplied by the "teaboy" at a penny a mug). While we were sitting around on upturned baskets, baulks of timber, or whatever was convenient, Dad asked me how I was getting on. Now my father was not a big man – about 5 foot 2 inches, I would say. "Ginger" was his name when he was younger and had more hair, but now most of the men who were regular housebreakers knew him as "Stumps". When he was drunk or spoiling for a fight, he roared. Short, tough and muscular, nobody took liberties with him and he was respected for his abilities as a topman. (He was like a cat when he was up aloft. He would trip across a forty-foot gap, if a four-inch girder or timber spanned it, without hesitation, if it saved going down a ladder and up the other side.) When I told him what Bill Worsley had said, he got up and went in search of him. I worked under Bill on several jobs after that and never did he complain about my work again.'

From John Welch, 'Demolition Labourer', in *Working Lives: 1905 to 1945* (Hackney WEA with Centreprise Publishing Project, undated), p. 32.

2 What powers did the foreman have over the young worker described above? [4]
3 Describe and explain the reactions of 'young Stumps' to the foreman's warning. [4]
4 The passage implies that the father was able to stop the foreman from complaining again about the young man's work. How and why might the father have been able to do this? [6]
5 Compare the power of a foreman or forewoman over his or her workers with the power of a teacher over pupils. [6]

Authority

People and laws may be obeyed for reasons other than the fear of economic or physical penalties. When we accept the rule of others or of the law, it is usually because we accept their *authority*. This means that we accept that they have a *legitimate right* to our obedience. Some people may refuse to accept that authority if it seriously conflicts with their own moral or religious principles. However, for the most part we accept the authority of a wide range of people and institutions over our daily lives.

Types of authority

The German sociologist Max Weber identified three types of claim which could be made by rulers to justify their domination over others. Later writers have discussed these as types of authority, as given below.

The first type of authority is *legal*. We accept the authority because it is based on law. Without such legal order many of our daily activities would be impossible. The government makes laws to regulate many aspects of life. These laws are generally accepted because they provide a framework within which individuals can carry out their own activities. Laws or 'rules' having similar authority can also be made by other organisations – for example, clubs, schools, factories and trade unions.

The second type of authority is *traditional*. We accept the authority of others because we, and possibly generations of others, have always done so.

The third type of authority is *charismatic*. Authority may be accepted on an emotional basis, perhaps because we respect the abilities, knowledge and judgement of someone else, or because someone is highly admired as a leader. This is where we accept orders because of the special personality of the leader. Examples of charismatic authority include the case of people following the Prophets, Jesus and Mohammad.

Our reasons for accepting authority are often complex and include elements of more than one of the types given above. If you examine, for example, the authority of the teacher in the classroom you will find that it does not fall easily into any one type of authority; any of the three types of authority may be claimed on behalf of teachers in the classroom.

Example: the lifeguard's authority

In the following example (Fig. 2) and questions you are asked to consider the authority of swimming-pool attendants and teachers, but you may also be able to discuss the authority of parents, judges and magistrates, and your managers in a part-time job.

Fig. 2 Authority at the swimming pool

6 One of the group of children in Fig. 2 has been successfully leading the others in fooling around in the water. What would be the possible sources of that leader's authority? [4]
7 The swimming-pool lifeguard would have powers to take action against anyone not observing the rules. What would these actions be likely to include? [4]
8 The lifeguard may also have some authority because of his or her position and abilities. Discuss what type of authority this could be. [6]
9 A teacher takes a group of children swimming, and there is a lifeguard also present. Compare the sources of the lifeguard's authority with those of the teacher. (Refer to the three types of authority described above.) [6]

THE USE OF POWER

Coercion

Coercion involves making people do things against their will. Coercion may be based on the use of economic or physical force or threats to use such force.

Coercion was used, for example, in the occupation of many countries in Europe by the Germans and the Japanese during the Second World War, and in the controls exercised over African people by European colonial powers in the nineteenth and twentieth centuries. It is used today in the exercise of police power and the economic power of the white people in South Africa to control the black people.

A common example of an individual using coercion would be the school bully who forces other children to carry out his or her wishes with threats of physical violence. In some cases control is exercised through the use of a combination of authority and coercion.

QUESTIONS

1   Read the following interview between Bill, a skinhead gang leader, and his social worker, and then answer the questions which follow.

Q. 'When did you become leader of the gang?'
A. 'Nine months ago.'
Q. 'How did you become leader?'
A. 'I beat up Harry [previous leader]. Now the rest of the gang do what I tell them.'
Q. 'So, if your friends don't do as they're told, you beat them up?'
A. 'No! We decide together what to do. It's only when someone gets heavy [aggressive] that I have to sort him out – or he leaves the gang. I like to be fair, though. I'm not a bully. Some leave the gang because they chicken out.'
Q. 'What sort of things do the gang do?'
A. 'Well, we go fighting, nicking and smashing things. The best thing is being chased by the police.'

   a)   Many people would consider that the activities of the gang challenge 'authority'. Why do you think this is so?
   b)   Does Bill have power, or authority, or both, over the gang? Give reasons for your answer.

(Based on the specimen paper of the Southern Examining Group.)

Coercion or authority?

Fig. 1

Fig. 2

QUESTIONS

2   Look at the photographs in Figs. 1 and 2. In each case discuss the following questions in groups. Give reasons for your answers and be prepared to discuss your answers with the rest of the class.

   a)   Are the people shown in the photographs most likely to be influencing decisions through physical or economic coercion, or through their authority?
   b)   What are the sources of their authority likely to be?

Economic power

We have considered the Marxist view of power in Unit 4.3 on occupations and social class. Karl Marx wrote about the economic power of the owners of the factories, the land and the banks and financial institutions. For Marx, economic power was based on the ownership of *the means of production* (capital). This economic power, in relatively few hands, according to Marx, also provided political power for the owners of capital.

Economic power has been analysed by many writers since the time of Marx, and various types of economic power have been studied. Examples of the use of economic power are given below.

Examples of economic power

Local authority refuses to buy from local firm

The County Council has again demonstrated its policy of purchasing only from companies which operate policies of non-discrimination on grounds of race or sex. This County Council is one of the largest local authority purchasers in the country. The latest firm to be hit by this is a local business. The loss of the contract is a big blow to the company and could mean the loss of over forty jobs in the next few weeks.

Fig. 3

Telephone charges up again

The national telephone company has increased its charges for domestic calls. Consumer organisations have complained about the increase, which will add to the cost of living for millions of people. A group of angry consumers presented a sackful of complaints to the government minister yesterday. Their leader, Bill Posters, pointed out that the telephone company is a monopoly and most people have no choice but to pay the charges or to be very isolated, especially in rural areas.

Fig. 4

QUESTIONS

3   The newspaper article in Fig. 3 provides an example of the power of customers to influence sellers of goods. Why might the producers take notice of the purchasing policy of this local authority?

4   In Fig. 4 the newspaper article gives an example of a company which has *monopoly power*. This means there is no competition and the company is therefore able to raise its prices without fearing a loss of business. Why are telephone companies so powerful compared with many other companies? Can you find three other examples of organisations with monopoly power?

QUESTIONS

Everyday products and monopoly power

5   Work in groups. Each group should choose one 'supermarket' type of product (e.g. detergents, toothpaste or margarine). Then discuss how to share out the work, which consists of the following:

a) Choose five or more brand names which exist for this product. (Try to avoid supermarkets' own brands because it is difficult to find out which company makes them.)

b) Find out which company makes at least four of these brands. This information is often on the label.

c) Who owns these companies? Use *Who Owns Whom* (Dunne and Bradstreet, 1986) for this; copies are found in most reference libraries. (The company which owns others is called the *parent company*.)

d) Which other companies are owned by this parent company (also in *Who Owns Whom*). What other products do these companies make?

e) If possible, find out in which country the parent company is based and where the products are produced.

f) Present your answer as a chart, either on paper or on an overhead-projector slide so that an oral presentation can be made to the whole class.

EXTENSION ACTIVITIES

Parents are often uncertain about how to care for a first baby.

1   **Interview** (in pairs if possible) a parent with a young child to find out how people obtain advice about caring for infants, to what extent they feel they must accept that advice and the reasons why they accept it.

2   **Write a report** which includes answers to the following questions:

a) Who are the various people who might give advice on the care of babies?

b) What authority do these advisers have?

c) What do you think are the possible sources of that authority?

REASONS FOR POLITICAL DECISIONS

Power and decision-making within families were considered in Unit 2.5 on the egalitarian family. This unit will compare how decisions can be made both within the family and in the wider society.

A family's decisions

Jane: I don't want to go out with my parents this Sunday, but Mum says I have to.

Richard: We have to visit my uncle because he's in hospital. I don't mind really, but it means missing the football with my friends.

Jane: Mum always thinks she can tell me what to do, and I'm never allowed any choice.

Richard: We might go on holiday this year but we can't decide where. My brother says he should help to decide because he is paying for part of it. My sister says she should join in because she is over eighteen, even though she isn't working. Dad doesn't mind so long as it's Majorca, and Mum says anywhere *but* Majorca. Nobody asks me, because they think I'm just a kid.

Jane: Couldn't you have a vote on it?

Richard: That's no good, because if it was Majorca, Mum wouldn't be pleased, and if it's Blackpool again, Dad will be furious. And my brother wants to go somewhere with plenty of angling.

Jane: At least you all discuss it. We're just told what to do.

QUESTIONS

1 Discuss the reasons why Jane, in the above conversation, feels unable to influence decisions in her family. Do you think there is anything she might do to influence decisions?

2 When Richard says he has to go and see his uncle, does he necessarily mean that his parents will make him go, or could his statement have other meanings?

3 Richard's family are having difficulty in deciding where to go for their holidays. Working in groups, examine the power of each member of his family to influence decisions. What are the alternative ways of making the decision about holidays? How do you think the decision should be made? Choose a spokesperson to report back to the class.

Political decisions

We live in societies composed of many cultures and many different interests, traditions and groups. Politics is a way of establishing a system of order acceptable to these various individuals and groups in society. It involves open and public actions in attempting to persuade others to agree to any particular point of view. Political activities take place through a variety of institutions such as political parties and trade unions.

Political decisions are made on a wide range of issues. These include the organisation of the country's economy, defence, the type of education system to be provided, the standard of health care and the type of housing for people to live in.

Political decisions are not limited to the national level, however. On the international level, some decisions involve the settlement of difference between countries. And on the regional or community level, political decisions centre on local issues and involve local people in attempting to reach an agreement about matters which concern only themselves. People may not always realise that they are involved in political decision-making.

How decisions are made

Some decisions involve conflicts of interest. I may like a particular chair in the staff room, but that chair may also be the favourite chair of another member of staff. We are hardly likely to fight over the issue, but ways have to be found of making decisions where two people or groups of people are opposed in their views or interests.

In some cases, decisions can be made because all of the people involved recognise that they have a common interest. They are therefore willing to make some compromises. For example, in Britain during recent years trade unions have sometimes agreed to limit their demands for higher wages in order to control the rate of inflation. (See also Unit 7.7 on unions and employers.)

Political decisions in Britain are made within a variety of institutions such as trade unions, employers' associations, local councils and Parliament. Individuals may attempt to influence the decisions of governments in many different ways including directly contacting their MP or local councillor, or joining a group of people who also feel strongly on the same issue. These ways of taking action are discussed in Unit 7.4.

Political involvement

Fig. I

4   Give five ways in which the people in Fig. I are affected by political decisions.

1   **Choose** an issue in your local area about which you feel strongly. It may be a development which directly affects the area, such as a new hypermarket, a new road or the demolition of a building; or an issue which is particularly relevant to your area, such as fox hunting.
    Discuss what you could do to influence the decisions of the government or the local authority on this issue.

2   **Give your assessment** of the proposal by a youth organisation to establish a disco close to your school. (You could organise a role-play to prepare the arguments for and against this.) Who would be affected by this decision? What would be their arguments? How might the people concerned try to influence the decision?

INDIVIDUAL AND GROUP ACTION

People may attempt to influence government policies about new developments in industry or government spending or taxes. They may also try to change existing laws. Fig. 1 is concerned with some of the measures which individuals and groups might take to try to change the law.

QUESTIONS

1 What percentage of the people interviewed (Fig. 1) have considered a law to be unjust or harmful, assuming all of the sample answered this question? [1]
2 Of the action actually taken, signing a petition was the most common. However, it was not considered to be the most effective action by the majority of respondents.
   a) Explain why it is so popular. b) Why is it considered to be less effective than other actions? [6]
3 Is there any other action, not listed on the table, which people might have taken? [2]
4 Who is your MP, and how would you contact him or her? [2]
5 a) Are there any laws which you consider to be unjust or harmful? b) If so, what could you do about these laws? c) What action do you think would be most effective? Give your reasons. [9]

Group action

Politics involves allowing the various groups in society to speak freely, listening to them and finding some common ground as far as is possible.

> Politics arises from accepting the fact of the simultaneous existence of different groups, hence different interests and different traditions, within a territorial unit under a common rule . . . Politics represents at least some tolerance of differing truths, some recognition that government is possible, indeed best conducted, amid the open canvassing of rival interests.

From Bernard Crick, *In Defence of Politics* (Pelican, 1964), p. 18.

According to Professor Crick, politics are the public actions of free individuals. Tyranny and oligarchy are alternatives to politics. *Tyranny* is the rule of one person in his or her own interests; *oligarchy* means rule by a few or a small group in their own interests.

Fig. 1 Responses to the prospect of an unjust or harmful law

	Have taken %	Would take %	Considered most effective %
Personal action:			
Contact MP	3	46	34
Speak to influential person	1	10	4
Contact government department	1	7	5
Contact radio, TV or newspaper	1	14	23
Collective action:			
Sign petition	9	54	11
Raise issue in an organisation I belong to	2	9	2
Go on protest or demonstration	2	8	5
Form a group of like-minded people	1	6	4
None of these	19	14	9

Percentage who have never considered a law unjust or harmful = 69

From Roger Jowell and Colin Airey, *British Social Attitudes: The 1984 Report* (Gower, 1984), p. 21.

The nuclear power debate

From the *Daily Telegraph*, 13 March 1986

'Green' groups plan Sizewell battle

By John Shaw

Anti-nuclear and "Green" groups announced last night a predictably strong reaction to the announcement by Mr Walker, Energy Secretary, of government approval for Sizewell B nuclear power station.

The Campaign for Nuclear Disarmament and Friends of the Earth said they planned to hold a joint demonstration in London on April 25, a year after the Chernobyl disaster, to demonstrate support for what both organisations called "a nuclear-free Britain."

Atom power vital for UK, says union chief

By Keith Harper, Labour Editor

The Labour and Liberal parties were last night accused by Mr John Lyons, leader of the Engineers' and Managers' Association, of setting out to speed the de-industrialisation of Britain by closing down the nuclear power industry.

Mr Lyons, who heads a strongly pro-nuclear trade union, said that phasing out nuclear power would deny British industry the chance to participate in the worldwide development of a vital energy source. But it would continue whatever "narrow-minded" politicians thought.

From the *Guardian*, 14 October 1986

SAFETY JOLT FOR A-PLANT BOSSES

The Sellafield nuclear complex in Cumbria was ordered yesterday to make improvements within 12 months or face being shut down.

The order was delivered by the Health and Safety Executive, which sent nuclear inspectors to Sellafield after a spate of incidents earlier this year.

The Director General of the HSE, John Rimington, said the improvements must be made within a year.

He warned: "If we do not get what we want we are quite prepared to stop reprocessing temporarily until we have."

Mr Rimington added that the inspector's report was intended as a "major jolt" to Sellafield bosses.

Eddy Ryder, chief inspector at the Nuclear Installations Inspectorate, said the safety investigation had NOT discovered anything new that would affect the risk to the public.

Sellafield and radiation doses to workers were not as low as they should be.

Mr Rimington told a news conference in London that British Nuclear Fuels' main policies were right. "But," he said, "the application of these priorities has reduced the attention paid to potentially hazardous parts of the older plant.

"Some of these do not yet come up to the scrupulously high standard we demand of the nuclear industry and there are matters which must be put right."

British Nuclear Fuels said it would "respond positively" to the report's findings.

Leaks

But, he said, there had been too many small leaks at

From the *Daily Mirror*, 12 December 1986

Fig. 2

QUESTIONS

Look at Fig. 2 and answer the following:

6 Why are there different views about whether Britain should produce nuclear power?
7 What evidence is there for and against the view that Britain is a country where political debate can be conducted?
8 What different groups and organisations are involved in the politics of the debate over nuclear power? (You may have additional information about the nuclear power debate, for example from newspapers and television.)

EXTENSION ACTIVITIES

1 **Obtain information** from newspapers, radio and television and the people involved, about any issue on which there is political debate at present.
2 **Identify** the differences in views between the various groups involved.
3 **Find out** how these groups are attempting to influence the local authority, the government or international organisations.
4 What are the advantages of a system where groups, organisations and in some cases individuals are able to publicise their views and try to obtain support for them?

PRESSURE GROUPS

Unit 7.4 considered the actions which individuals and groups might take to influence governments. This unit is concerned with organised groups which attempt to influence government policies (Fig. 1). They may influence central or local government, or international organisations such as the European Community.

Types of pressure group

Sectional interest groups

Some pressure groups seek *to defend their members' interests*. Such organisations include tenants' associations (which seek to prevent unfair rent increases or to improve the standards of service in property repairs), trade unions and employers' associations.

Cause groups

Other groups seek *to promote a cause*. Examples include the Child Poverty Action Group (which seeks to reduce family poverty), Shelter (the campaign for the homeless) and Friends of the Earth (which is concerned with environmental issues). Some charities are also pressure groups. They seek to deal directly with a problem, e.g. through giving aid and development assistance to poor countries, while at the same time seeking to influence governments to tackle the cause of the problem. Such charities include Oxfam and War on Want, which are international relief organisations as well as pressure groups.

Multi-function groups

Some pressure groups combine several functions, both to support a cause and to defend an interest. Examples include trade unions, which seek to promote their members' interests with the government, although their main function is to bargain with employers and to provide services of various kinds for members. Trade unions may also support other causes which are not directly connected with the self-interest of their members, such as the rights of black people in South Africa.

Specialist groups

In Britain the system of government is highly centralised. Pressure groups, therefore, operate by trying to influence party policy, and by establishing contact with the central government so that they are consulted when there are any issues which concern their members.

Much effective pressure group activity is unseen by the public. Government departments may find the process of consultation useful because it provides a way of securing agreement for government policy and therefore reduces criticism. It also provides a two-way channel for receiving and giving out information, and in some cases pressure

Fig. 1 Student campaign calls for increase in level of student grants

groups sort and filter complaints from the public. Pressure groups also have special knowledge or experience which is useful to the government, as in the case of the Royal National Institute for the Blind, or the National Farmers' Union.

The Civil Service maintains close links with some pressure groups which are able to provide specialist advice or expertise. In some cases representatives of pressure groups sit on advisory committees with civil servants.

Professional groups

Some pressure groups regulate the qualifications and behaviour of their members as well as acting to promote their members' interests. Examples of this kind of group include professional organisations such as the Law Society (to which solicitors belong) and the British Medical Association (for doctors).

Ad hoc groups

Pressure groups are sometimes *ad hoc* groups, set up for a particular purpose, such as preventing a development in a specific area. Examples include local campaign groups to prevent the closure of a school, and the recent campaigns of local groups of people to prevent toxic nuclear waste being buried on sites near their communities.

Campaigning groups

Other groups are *permanent* or long-lasting. They may support a range of related issues and campaign in several different ways. For example, the Child Poverty Action Group is concerned with a range of issues related to poverty; and Friends of the Earth organises different campaigns on a variety of environmental issues including acid rain, damage to the environment through the use of pesticides, the destruction of tropical rain forests, the dumping of waste into the sea and the killing of whales. Another example is the National Campaign for Civil Liberties, which is discussed in Unit 7.6.

Methods used by pressure groups

The methods used by pressure groups to secure their aims include those shown in Fig. 2.

Representations to committees or Royal Commissions which have been established to advise the government on policy.

Informal contacts with civil servants and MPs to attempt to influence policies.

Sponsoring or even employing MPs. Some MPs are sponsored by trade unions or are employed as directors or consultants by a variety of organisations. This is regarded as acceptable by Parliament, provided MPs register their interests so that the information is publicly available.

PARTY CONFERENCE

The **research departments** of pressure groups provide MPs with information and specialist knowledge and even prepare Bills for sympathetic MPs to present to Parliament.

OUT   IN

Public campaigns are run by pressure groups. Such campaigns may consist of articles in newspapers and magazines, public meetings, petitions, lectures and debates, demonstrations, protest marches, strikes and even breaking the law by such activities as trespassing on private property (as in the case of some protests against nuclear bases), or releasing animals kept for some research purposes.

EXTENSION ACTIVITIES

1 **Choose** any pressure group which interests you.
2 **Find out** the following:

   a) What the aims of that pressure group are and what methods it uses.
   b) Does it seek to influence central or local government, or both?
   c) Is it an *ad hoc* or a permanent group?
   d) How effective does the group appear to be in achieving its aims?

3 **Compare** the pressure group you have chosen with other groups involved with the same or similar issues. Note any differences in the organisation and in the methods used by the two or more groups.

PRESSURE GROUPS AND INDIVIDUAL RIGHTS

Some pressure groups are concerned with the protection of individual rights, such as the rights of freedom of assembly and the rights associated with citizenship. Such groups include the National Council for Civil Liberties (NCCL) and the Campaign Against Racism and Fascism (CARF), both of which are described below.

The NCCL

The National Council for Civil Liberties was founded in 1934. Its founder, Ronald Kidd, was concerned about the behaviour of the police agents he had seen in demonstrations; people were encouraged to advance against a line of police officers blocking a road, and the demonstrators were then arrested.

In its early days the NCCL attracted the support of such well-known writers as E. M. Forster, A. P. Herbert and H. G. Wells. In the 1930s it was particularly concerned with the fight against fascism, but over the period of more than fifty years since the NCCL's foundation it has been concerned with many aspects of civil liberties such as film censorship, the treatment of travellers (gypsies), the treatment of prisoners and the rights of women, ethnic minorities and homosexuals. In some cases the work of the NCCL overlaps with that of other pressure groups. For example, in the case of prisoners there is some overlap with the work of the Howard League for Penal Reform or, in the case of race relations, the Campaign Against Racism and Fascism.

The NCCL has always depended heavily on volunteers who carry out many functions, including acting as observers at demonstrations – they observe and record events and act as independent witnesses. In 1963 the NCCL established a research and educational organisation concerned with civil liberties called the Cobden Trust. This has produced research publications in such areas as immigration law, the legal system in Northern Ireland and legal aid.

The case of Rosemary's baby

The NCCL takes up individual cases and in doing so achieves changes in the law or in policies. It was involved in the efforts to change the rules regarding the rights of British women to bring their husbands and children to live in Britain, as in the following case.

It was not only husbands who were left stranded by the fact that women could not convey their nationality to others. In the late seventies, NCCL received a number of enquiries from women afraid that their children would be born stateless. One such was Rosemary, a British woman working in Stockholm. She was not married to the American father of her child, which meant that the baby could not take his citizenship, and had no right to British citizenship since this could not be inherited from the mother.

A campaign organised by NCCL, the Equal Opportunities Commission and a number of MPs culminated in a Private Member's Bill put forward by Jill Knight MP, to amend the law and so allow children to take their mother's nationality. Faced with this all-party onslaught, the Home Secretary, Merlyn Rees, announced on 7 February 1979 that he would henceforth normally use his discretionary power to register as a British citizen the child of a British woman born in the UK.

There were further changes to the law regarding nationality in the British Nationality Act of 1981, but this Act added a further twist to the problem by depriving children born in the UK of the automatic entitlement to British citizenship.

Adapted from Mark Lilly, *The National Council for Civil Liberties: The First Fifty Years* (Macmillan, 1984), p. 145.

Deportation of the Khan family: CARF in action

The newspapers commonly feature families who are resisting deportation and wish to remain in Britain as immigrants (Fig. 1). In some cases such families are helped by local and national pressure groups, and they may use the procedures available to challenge administrative decisions.

One example of such a case was that of the Khan family. Mrs Khan had lived in England for several years and married a man who was in England as a temporary visitor. The couple had children and had started a small business, a shop, when, in 1981, Mr Khan was threatened with deportation. He apparently had no rights to remain in the country. A woman would have gained such rights through marriage.

The Khans contacted their MP and the Joint Council for the Welfare of Immigrants for help. Their first appeal was rejected by a government adjudicator. The MP was informed that there were no grounds for Mr Khan to remain in Britain.

The local pressure group, the Redbridge Campaign Against Racism and Fascism (RCARF), also became involved in the case. The organisation of a campaign by existing pressure groups provided various advantages including the fact that the groups already had networks of contacts. A campaign was organised in which thousands of signatures were collected in support of the Khans. The MP presented this in his meeting with the minister to discuss the case. Public meetings were organised and

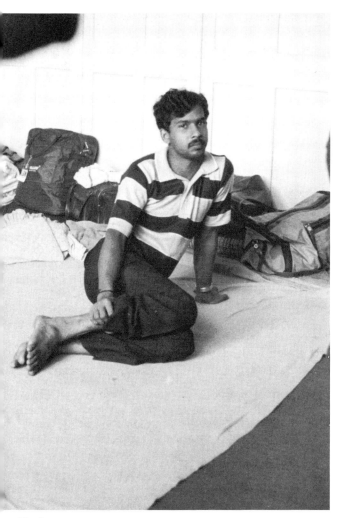

Fig. 1

attended by large numbers of people from not only the Muslim population but also from the Sikh and Hindu communities, Jewish groups, the churches and the trades council (the organisation of local trade unions). The local newspaper was sympathetic to the case and publicised these developments.

The MP was able to speak on the case in an adjournment debate. These debates are held at the end of the day in Parliament and a lottery determines which MPs will have the right to speak. The Khans' MP won the lottery and was able to raise their case and to ask questions of the minister responsible. This delayed Mr Khan's deportation for some months, because he could not be deported while the case was under consideration by a minister.

RCARF took the opportunity of the delay to publicise the case at the Conservative party conference in the autumn on behalf of the Khans.

The pressure groups also used a solicitor to pursue the possibility of appeals through the tribunal system. The appeal against deportation went before an adjudicator, who could consider not only the procedures followed by the officials but all the circumstances of the case including the humanitarian arguments. The Khans again lost their case. The next stage was to take the case to the Immigration

Appeal Tribunal, and this tribunal referred the case back to the adjudicator. This is a way of saying that the adjudicator should reconsider the case.

The case was also taken to the European Commission and was waiting with other cases to be considered by the European Court. The European Community was involved because British law in this example obviously treated men and women very differently and therefore did not follow European law. The wives of British citizens had the right to live in Britain wherever their husbands were born; for husbands, as we have seen, the law was totally different.

In February 1983, partly as a result of cases before the European Commission which indicated that British law did not conform to the law of the European Community, the rules were changed so that the husband or wife of a British citizen, wherever that citizen was born, would have the right to live in Britain. Although there was still a technicality to be resolved regarding Mrs Khan's citizenship, the Khans now had the right to remain in Britain.

The pressure groups in this case had been successful, although many hours of work by volunteers were involved. It is doubtful whether they were responsible for changing the law, although they may have contributed to the pressure to change it. They succeeded, however, in delaying Mr Khan's deportation until the change in the law took place so that he was able to remain in Britain with his family.

QUESTIONS

Campaigning on rights

1 Hold a meeting, with one person taking each of the following roles: the Home Secretary, an MP, the secretary of a pressure group, a person threatened with deportation, assistants or friends for each of the above. Present the arguments which you think would be likely to be used by each of these people. The Home Secretary should reach a decision and give the reasons for this decision.

2 Use the two examples featured in this unit to answer the following questions:

   a) What methods were used by the pressure groups in these examples?

   b) Discuss why the NCCL and RCARF were successful in the campaigns described above.

   c) The cases raise important issues of equal treatment of the sexes and racial equality. What are the issues?

3 From your experience, or from newspaper and radio/television reports, discuss other cases of individuals or groups seeking to challenge administrative decisions – for example, on immigration, housing, planning or social security benefits.

4 Answer the following question (from the Northern Examining Association specimen paper): 'Pressure groups are the means whereby anyone in Britain can have their say and influence decisions made about life in Britain.' Discuss this statement and include examples in your answer.

UNIONS AND EMPLOYERS

Trade unions

Section 7 has been concerned with the use of power to influence decisions. Trade unions are organisations of employees which exercise power in the workplace. They have also been able to influence government policies. Although they now provide a wide range of services for their members, their main function is to protect and improve pay and conditions. (Conditions include hours of work, overtime pay, holidays and other matters relating to employment such as health and safety.)

In the workplace

Trade unions 'bargain' with employers about pay and conditions. Unions acting on behalf of a group of workers have more power than individual workers. For example, a whole work-force in a factory, or a group of workers with the same skills, may stop production in order to gain their demands (Fig. 1). Workers are thus more powerful when they bargain together (this is called *collective bargaining*) than when they bargain individually.

Unions may bargain with groups of employers or *employers' associations*. Increasingly in recent years they have bargained separately with individual employers, sometimes at the level of the individual factory or workplace.

Fig. 1

In government

Trade unions may also seek to achieve their aims by acting as pressure groups. They may seek to influence legislation (for example, to control working hours or Sunday working in shops). In the 1970s legislation was introduced which improved the rights of individual workers (such as laws concerning equal pay, sex and race discrimination, and redundancy). In return, the unions gave their support to agreements with the Labour government to restrain wages and prices in order to hold down inflation.

For many years the unions have had very close ties with the Labour Party, although some unions also support MPs from other parties. The unions have been involved in politics in order to obtain legislation which allows them to bargain with employers and to take industrial action. Unions have also, on occasion, supported legislation to improve conditions of working and living for the weakest groups who have least power to bargain. Unions have also provided a means for their members to take a part in policy-making, especially through the Labour Party.

Some unions also join with employers or their associations to try to exert pressure on the government to introduce policies favourable to their industry. Examples of such policies include import duties on textiles for the textile workers and employers, and campaigns for lower duties on cigarettes by the tobacco workers and employers.

Many unions have *political funds* which are used for pressure group activities and to support a political party (usually Labour). Since 1984 the unions have been required to hold regular ballots of their members if they wish to continue to hold political funds and to take a *political levy* from their members. Most unions (including all of the larger unions) have voted in favour of such funds. Unit 8.2 on political parties considers the financing of the parties including the funds provided for the Conservatives by business interests.

QUESTIONS

Political activity

1 Why are trade unions more likely to provide funds for the Labour Party than for the Conservative Party?
2 Give two reasons why unions may seek to influence governments.
3 Why may employers seek to influence governments?
4 What method do trade unions and employers use to influence the government? (See also Unit 7.5 on pressure groups.)
5 Compare the power of the following:

   a) Women sewing garments in their own homes for an employer who sells the goods to the shops or to wholesalers.
   b) Teachers' unions.
   c) Workers in the water industry.

Example of an industrial dispute

Pat Putissem is a supervisor in the Packing Department of a manufacturing company. She is new to the job and anxious to make a good impression on the managers. The seven workers in the Production Department are working on an urgent order which must be completed and sent out today. Pat's group in the following discussions will include other supervisors.

The workers have problems as follows:

Myra has been refused permission to leave early to collect her child from the child minder's. She must do this because of particular problems on this day only.

Phil has been asked to move some waste material from an adjacent room but he is concerned that it might contain asbestos.

Mark has been told he must work overtime but he wants to leave on time because it is his daughter's second birthday party.

Amjid is thinking of leaving immediately because Pat spoke to him in terms which he considered to be insulting and racist.

Kim is the shop steward and intends to support the interests of the union members.

Lou is the assistant supervisor and wants to make a good impression on Pat without upsetting the rest of the department.

Jo and friends are keen to work as many hours as possible for extra money.

QUESTIONS

6 Get into groups, each group representing one of the above.
7 In your groups, decide on the action you would take in your own case and in support of other workers or supervisors.
8 Each of the groups representing Myra, Phil, Mark, Amjid and Jo should meet with Kim or any other member of Kim's group to decide on the action to be taken in each case.
9 Pat, Lou and the other supervisors and managers should discuss their action in each case.
10 Each group of workers should meet with a supervisor or assistant supervisor and discuss the problems.
11 You will probably need at least two meetings before you can reach a final agreement on each case.

EXTENSION ACTIVITIES

1 **Choose** one trade union or employers' association and **find out** what the aims of that organisation are. You could write to obtain more detailed information from the union, or invite a union official to speak to your class.
2 **Answer** the following questions by asking for and obtaining suitable information about the union or association you have chosen in activity 1:

a) Has the union or association attempted to influence the government recently? If so, what were its aims as a pressure group and how did it seek to achieve them?

b) Does the union or association agree with some aspects of government policy and attempt to support them?
c) Which party does it support and how does it support it?
d) Has it been involved in any industrial dispute? If so, why, and what was the result?

3 You may know of industrial action (such as a strike or a ban on overtime work) which has taken place recently or is currently taking place.

a) **Read** the newspaper reports of the industrial action.
b) **Talk** to people about the action. You may be able to interview some of the people involved.
c) **Discuss** *why* the action is taking place, *what power* the workers have (explaining the reasons for your answer) and *whether* there are any reasons why they might not succeed in achieving their aims in the dispute.
d) **Compare** this analysis with your work on trade unions and technical change – extension activity 1 in Unit 6.3.

4 **Watch television and read newspaper reports** about the TUC (Trades Union Congress) or CBI (Confederation of British Industry) annual conference. Make notes, and answer the following:

a) What are these organisations? You can find the answer in books on industrial relations or trade unions in your library (use the catalogue), or in reference books such as J. Eaton and C. Gill, *The Trade Union Directory* (Pluto, 1983), or Jack Jones and Max Morris, *A–Z of Trade Unionism and Industrial Relations* (Heinemann, 1982).
b) What issues were discussed at the annual conference?
c) How were decisions made?
d) What policies were they hoping to get the government to support?
e) What plans for the organisation were discussed?
f) Give two examples of issues on which there were strong differences of opinion among the members.
g) Which members appeared to have most power?
h) Explain why they appeared to be especially powerful.

5 **Find out** about the industrial relations in one workplace. It could be a department of a local authority, a factory or a large shop or store. You could interview someone who works in the organisation, or invite someone to speak to your class and answer questions. Try to answer the following:

a) What unions are there in this workplace?
b) What committees exist for unions and management to discuss and negotiate matters concerning pay or working conditions?
c) Refer back to Units 7.1 and 7.2 and comment on the power and authority of the union workplace representatives (the shop stewards).

REPRESENTATIVES AND ELITES

Previous units have considered some of the groups which influence decision-making. A question which is often raised in relation to politics is whether there are certain groups which from generation to generation dominate all others. Such groups, if sufficiently united, could be regarded as a *ruling élite* (Fig. 1).

Fig. 1

It is possible to consider as an élite the leaders or owners of organisations such as big businesses, the newspapers, trade unions, some pressure groups and the armed forces. Such organisations may influence government policies. Some people argue that there is not an élite but lots of conflicting groups and organisations which compete for influence. Others argue that there may be some people who continually act in ways that benefit each other and are so powerful that they can be regarded as an élite (Fig. 2).

We can view an élite as a class of people connected by wealth, kinship, education or social background. For example, many positions of power are held by people who attended public schools and Oxford or Cambridge University, as illustrated by the examples below. However, a person's political views and actions are not entirely predictable even when we have evidence of their social background. There is therefore conflicting evidence on the use of political power by the most powerful social élites.

Élites and the Civil Service

The Civil Service consists of permanent government employees. The staff who are employed in the most senior administrative posts exercise considerable influence over policy-making in central government. Civil servants exercise influence through the information and advice they give to ministers, and through the discretion they exercise in carrying out policies. The advice which civil servants give to ministers is confidential, and ministers must answer in public for the operation of their departments. There is therefore considerable secrecy surrounding the operations of the Civil Service.

In Britain, unlike many other countries, civil servants remain in their posts in spite of changes in government, although in recent years some Prime Ministers have appointed their own teams of temporary policy advisers. Civil servants therefore remain in their posts longer than most ministers, and are able to exert influence over long periods of time.

Recruitment to the Civil Service

Fig. 2 Statistics from Civil Service Commission final selection board, 1985

Number of external candidates passing the three stages of selection		
Sex	Men	50
	Women	16
University	Oxford or Cambridge	42
	Other	24
Degree subject	Arts	37
	Social science	18
	Science/technology	11

From the Civil Service Commission, *Annual Report, 1985* (HMSO, 1986), p. 44.

(The Civil Service Commission selects the people who are expected to be the 'high-flyers' in the Civil Service.)

QUESTIONS

1 How many successful candidates passed the final stage of selection? [1]

2 What proportion of successful candidates were women? [1]

3 Would you expect there to be more women selected? Give your reasons. [4]

4 Is there anything in the table to suggest that these recruits were not typical of the population as a whole? [5]

5 What could be the effects on policy-making of a Civil Service which consists of an élite group recruited mainly from one social class and educational background? [9]

Social and educational background

❝Our top institutions are dominated by people from privileged social backgrounds, educated in the main at public schools and Oxbridge [Oxford and Cambridge]. Only about 5 per cent of the population go to public schools, for example, but 40 per cent of all MPs did, as well as 60 per cent of principal judges, 86 per cent of army officers and 85 per cent of Anglican❞ bishops.

From Michael Williams, *Society Today* (Macmillan, 1986), p. 168; a useful source for further information and analysis of élites and other topics.

QUESTIONS

6 Can you give any reasons why a relatively large proportion of people in positions of power were educated in public schools?

7 Does this passage provide evidence that there is a powerful élite in Britain today? Give reasons for your answer.

Representation of women

As mentioned above, information about a person's social background and interests does not necessarily provide accurate information about his or her political views. However, the fact that some groups are consistently under-represented in political life has been seen as a cause for concern.

Women have been consistently under-represented in Parliament compared with men. There have been very few women ministers, and the Cabinet has rarely included more than one woman. Although the first Labour Cabinet minister (Margaret Bonfield) was appointed in 1929, the Conservatives did not appoint a woman as a Cabinet minister until 1955. Serious questions have been raised about how far women's interests are represented when so few women are in Parliament.

Women in power

❝Margaret Thatcher is certainly the most prominent woman in British politics today. In the 1970–4 Conservative government Thatcher served as Minister of Education and Science for almost four years. The public image that she projected during this period was far from popular ... She supported the principle of meritocracy against the open-enrolment school policy of the Labour government. In another unpopular move, she raised the price of school lunches and eliminated the distribution of free milk to school children. In some ways Thatcher appears to be typical of the classic Conservative politician: middle-class, Oxford educated, a member of the meritocracy, an upholder of traditional values. She stands for law and order, individual enterprise and traditional moral values.

From February 1974 until her election as party leader she served in the Shadow Cabinet and was the spokesperson on Treasury and economic affairs. On 12 February 1975 Thatcher was elected head of the Conservative Party, becoming the first woman to lead a major British political party. Thatcher's emergence on the British political scene was surprising; she acknowledged that she did not think that the Conservatives would be ready for a woman leader in her lifetime.

On 3 May 1979 Margaret Thatcher and the Conservative Party won a decisive victory in Britain's general election. Thatcher thereby became the first woman Prime Minister in European history ... Following her victory, Thatcher appointed an all-male Cabinet of twenty-two members. She did, however, appoint two women Ministers of State (without Cabinet rank) ...

It is doubtful that Thatcher would do more to advance the cause of women in politics than would a male Labour Prime Minister. When asked her opinion of the women's liberation movement, she responded, "What's it ever done for me?" Historically, the Conservatives have placed fewer women in positions of influence and power. In fact Thatcher's voting record in the House of Commons over the past twenty years has been consistently right-wing Conservative, especially on social reform issues. For example, she has voted in favour of restoring the death penalty and has opposed❞ abortion law reforms.

From Donna S. Sanzone, 'Women in Positions of Political Leadership in Britain, France and West Germany', in J. Siltanen and M. Stanworth (eds.), *Women and the Public Sphere* (Hutchinson, 1984), p. 166.

QUESTIONS

8 What evidence is there in the above extract that Mrs Thatcher belongs to an élite group in terms of her background and education?

9 Mrs Thatcher was grammar-school rather than public-school educated. Examine the extent to which she is typical of the Conservative politician. In order to do this, you will need to look at the backgrounds of some present Conservative politicians, and if possible some former Conservative Prime Ministers. (There are several useful directories which you could use, including *Who's Who* (A & C. Black, 1987) and David Butler and Gareth Butler, *British Political Facts 1900–1985* (Macmillan, 1986), in public libraries.)

10 What are the main issues on which the interests of women are likely to be different from those of men?

THE MAKING OF LAW

Section 7 was concerned with how decisions are made. In Section 8 we shall consider particular aspects of decision-making in Britain, including the system of elections, the political parties and the making of laws.

The need for rules

In any society there are rules, and we have all experienced the existence of rules in clubs, societies and schools. The rules of a society may be agreed by the members or by a committee of the members, and may be written in a rule book and perhaps expressed in the form of a written constitution. (See also Unit 10.1 on the individual and society.)

QUESTIONS

School rules

1 List three rules in your school which are written down and three which are well known but unwritten.
2 Give examples of the following different types of rule:
a) rules about who makes decisions, b) rules about how pupils should behave towards each other, c) rules about settling disputes.
3 Have all these rules been agreed by a committee, or declared by a senior teacher, or are some of them accepted as customs which people have been expected to follow for many years?

Shipwrecked!

Fig. 1

Imagine that your class is shipwrecked on an island which is warm in the daytime but very cold at night. There are no other inhabitants. You have ninety assorted cans of food and drink, a hut which will hold five people and an abundant supply of wood. But water has to be carried three miles, and six of the class are injured. The teacher is severely injured and unable to make any decisions. In this situation, rules would be essential.

QUESTIONS

4 What sort of thing might happen to the shipwrecked class if no rules were agreed on?
5 Working in groups of five or six, make six rules which would ensure that the maximum number of people survived, assuming you will be rescued within a week.
6 Exchange your rules with another group. How would you behave to maximise your personal chances of survival without breaking the rules?
7 Discuss whether the rules you devised were adequate to ensure the survival of the maximum number, and what types of activity would have to be covered by rules.

Statute laws and common law

There are rules and principles which are accepted and enforced as the laws of the country. Some of these are *statute laws* (legislation) and some are part of the *common law*.

Statute laws have been passed by both Houses of Parliament and signed by the monarch. The common law has been developed through custom and judgments in courts. It is often assumed, wrongly, that the common law is entirely unwritten. In fact, many court judgments are recorded and read by lawyers in order to find out exactly what the law is on any particular point.

Many rules which originated in common law have now been included in statutes. But among the important areas of common law which remain are many of the rules relating to contracts. (Contracts are agreements between two or more people which may be enforced in a court of law.)

Sometimes there is doubt as to what the law means in a particular situation. This applies to both the common law and statutes. Judges interpret the law, and a record is made of their *judgments* when they conclude a case. These judgments are statements of their decisions and of the reasons for them. Some judgments on the meaning of the law then become *precedents* for future cases; judges and barristers refer to the precedents to give authority to their decisions and arguments.

Legislation

Statutes are Acts of Parliament passed by the Houses of Parliament in several stages. Most of the Bills which successfully become law are introduced initially by the government. This means that they are approved by the Cabinet and are usually prepared in a government department. Some Bills are introduced by individual Members of Parliament but very few of these obtain sufficient parliamentary time to become law.

Bills have to pass through similar stages in both the House of Commons and the House of Lords. There are thus several stages in the passing of legislation where it may be changed. Groups of people who feel strongly about a particular Bill can contact their MPs or the newspapers to try to influence the form the law will finally take.

The extent to which the public can effectively prevent legislation is very limited, although amendments are made following pressure and advice from various groups in society. For most Bills, MPs are expected to vote with their parties. The *party whips* are the MPs who have the duty of communicating between the party leadership and the other MPs and making sure party members vote the way the leadership wants them to. The term *three-line whip* is used to describe the requirement that all MPs must vote with their party. Occasionally *free votes* are allowed where MPs may choose without pressure from their party how to vote on an issue; but such votes are usually only on matters where there is no firm party policy, such as abortion or homosexuality.

On the whole, MPs are under pressure to vote according to the party line. By voting against the policies of their party they may reduce their chances of being appointed to the Cabinet, and may make themselves unpopular with their colleagues in the party and with party supporters in the constituency.

The obligations of the MP: an example

Mary and John Smith were what is known as *floating voters*. They sometimes voted for one party, sometimes for another. In the last general election they both had great difficulty in deciding which way to vote. There is one issue on which they feel very strongly, however, and that is animal rights. They therefore voted for Chris Jones because of a proposal in Chris's party's manifesto to limit animal vivisection. They felt so strongly about this single issue that they even joined Chris Jones's party.

Chris Jones is generally a loyal member of the party and does not normally vote against policy. However, Chris represents a constituency where there is a branch of a multinational pharmaceutical company which claims that experiments on animals are essential for its research.

Chris is concerned about the effects of the Bill on research in Britain. It could also lose the MP a lot of votes. Chris has voted against the Bill and is a member of the House of Commons committee which is now discussing possible amendments.

Leslie Gould is the chairperson of Chris's constituency

party and is concerned that this issue is causing so much controversy in the party. Mary and John Smith have persuaded their branch of the party to put forward a motion to the constituency calling for Chris to resign.

A panel discussion is to be held, with Leslie Gould in the chair and Chris Jones answering questions. The Smiths and the regional director of the local pharmaceutical company, Robin Muller, have decided to join the discussion in order to present their points of view. Robin Muller is a member of the same party and supports it on most issues except vivisection: Robin also voted for the party at the last election.

QUESTIONS

8 Work in groups to prepare your statements and arguments for the discussion, with each group taking the role of one of the following:

Group 1: Mary or John Smith.
Group 2: Chris Jones.
Group 3: Robin Muller.

(Chris Jones, Robin Muller and Leslie Gould could be male or female.) Each group should choose one spokesperson and one supporter.

9 Select your chairperson, Leslie Gould, and hold the discussion.

10 Write your report for the local newspaper, stating what happened at the discussion and the main arguments which were presented.

11 Write an editorial for the local paper on the behaviour of Chris Jones. The editorial should be related to the news but it must present your views. It should be supported by a balanced argument about what Chris Jones has done. It should examine the extent to which MPs should be expected to vote with their party, or in the interests of their constituencies, or according to their own conscience.

EXTENSION ACTIVITIES

1 **Choose** one Bill that is going or has gone through Parliament. **Find Out** a) why it was introduced and b) what were the views of the political parties and other commentators (such as journalists and pressure groups with a special interest in the Bill).

2 **Read** about a case recently reported in the newspapers which clarifies a part of the law (such as rights to obtain abortions or surrogate motherhood or equal pay laws). It may be controversial and may provide an interpretation of the law which many people had not expected.

a) Why is it controversial?
b) What will be the effects of the judgment?
c) Discuss whether the example you have chosen is likely to lead to any change in statute law.

POLITICAL PARTIES

Party policies

Post-war agreement

The period from the end of the Second World War in 1945 until 1970 was a time when the major parties broadly agreed on issues such as providing benefits for the unemployed and pensions for the elderly, and on the need for collaboration between employers, unions and government in order to achieve benefits for all.

During this period both Labour and Conservative governments made agreements with unions and employers to limit increases in wages and prices. Both consulted the employers' organisations and the trade unions on policies for industry.

Benefits

There were differences of view between the parties on the level of benefits which should be provided. Labour has generally supported greater provision of benefits through the Welfare State. Conservatives have been more in favour of reducing the level of taxation.

Equality of opportunity

Labour has favoured policies to promote equality of opportunity. In the period 1964 to 1970 the Labour government expanded the provision of higher education through polytechnics and by the foundation of the Open University. During the 1960s and 1970s Labour in both national and local government supported the replacement of the selective grammar-school system by comprehensive schools in order to provide greater equality of opportunity in education. (See also Unit 3.2).

Race relations

There have been differences of view on the best type of immigration control, although both Labour and Conservative parties have retained controls over immigration since the 1960s. Labour has introduced legislation to make sex and race discrimination illegal and has been in favour of more action by the state to prevent discrimination.

Nationalisation

A further difference between the parties has been nationalisation. Although Labour supported the nationalisation of industry and the Conservatives opposed it, Labour governments after 1964 carried out only a very limited programme of nationalisation (in the steel industry), and the Conservatives denationalised steel (they sold some of it to private enterprise) and nationalised Rolls-Royce. Privatisation increased during the periods of Conservative government following 1979. (See also Unit 9.3 on the question of ownership.)

Defence

There are also differences between the parties on defence, particularly on whether to retain nuclear weapons and the balance between nuclear and conventional weapons.

Party politics

Since 1979 the Labour and Conservative parties have moved further apart in their views on major issues. The Conservatives have firmly established themselves as the party which supports the development of free markets; this includes efforts to reduce wage costs and to cut taxes, and attempts to reduce government spending. Labour has supported income redistribution in favour of the less well off, and state management of the economy.

The Conservative policies of reducing state intervention in the planning of business activities (sometimes described as *laissez-faire*) are said to be *right-wing* policies. The Labour policies of greater state planning and direction of the economy, and income redistribution in favour of the less well off, are referred to as *left-wing*. These terms can be used to describe differences within parties as well as differences between them.

Fig. 1 Campaigning in an election

Party finance

The Conservative Party receives funds from large companies (particularly banks and insurance companies). Labour receives funds from trade unions. The Conservative Party is by far the largest in terms of membership and the richest of the parties. There are also informal links between the interests of financial institutions and the Conservative Party through the directorships, which Conservative MPs hold (and have held) in the City of London.

The other parties

The *Liberal Party* in recent years has stressed the importance of changing the system of election in favour of *proportional representation*. This would mean that the number of seats each party gained in Parliament would be directly related to the number of votes that party received at the election. They have also emphasised local issues. (See also Unit 8.4 on elections.)

The *Social Democratic Party* (SDP) is the newest of the four major parties. It was formally declared to be a separate party in 1981 by a group of Labour MPs (including Dr David Owen) who had disagreed with Labour Party policy in two major areas. One was withdrawal from the European Community, and the other was the changes in the constitution of the Labour Party which removed the automatic selection of Labour MPs as election candidates for the same constituency. For the 1983 and 1987 general elections the Liberals and the SDP joined forces and were known as the *Alliance*. In 1988 Liberals and members of the SDP joined and became known as the Social and Liberal Democratic Party.

A fifth national party, the *Green Party*, had 133 candidates and gained 89,000 votes in the 1987 general election. Founded in 1972 as the Ecology Party, the party changed its name in 1984 and is part of the world-wide movement concerned with the environment.

QUESTIONS

Selection meetings
Hold selection meetings to choose election candidates for the Conservative Party, the Labour Party, either the Social and Liberal Democratic Party or the Social Democratic Party and – if you like – the Green Party. Work in groups as follows.

1 Three selection committees should make notes on what they require from their candidates.
2 Meanwhile, there should be four candidates before each selection committee. Helped by their supporters, they should prepare statements of their policies and personal characteristics (not necessarily true for this exercise – assume imaginary personalities).
3 What characteristics and policies were you looking for in your candidate? The chairperson of each selection committee should report back to the rest of the class the decision that was made, and the reasons. The rest of the class may criticise the decision.
4 Discuss the differences between the parties in the policies and other characteristics which they were seeking in their candidates.

Election manifestoes
Obtain copies of the most recent election manifestos of the main political parties, and if possible the election publicity produced by the candidates for your constituency.

5 What do you consider to be the most significant differences between the parties?
6 Which of the manifestos do you most agree with, and why?
7 Have any policies which were in any of the manifestos yet been introduced?

Party-political issues
8 Find out what the policies of each of the major parties is on any two of the following issues: a) education of 11- to 16-year-olds, b) grants for students, c) sales of council houses, d) nuclear weapons, e) the National Health Service.
9 Choose two parties for each issue and examine the main differences between them.

EXTENSION ACTIVITIES

1 **Work in groups** of four. **Choose newspapers:** each group member should choose two newspapers so that you cover eight papers between you. One tabloid newspaper with large print and plenty of pictures, such as the *Daily Mirror* or *Daily Express*, and one 'quality' paper such as the *Guardian, Independent* or *Sunday Times*. Try to work out which party the paper mainly supports. Give reasons for your answer.
2 **Draw up a table** (one for each group) to show the newspapers and the parties they support, with very brief statements of evidence.
3 **Choose one issue** on which the parties disagree.
   a) **Compare** the way this is reported in four different newspapers.
   b) **Identify** evidence of support for one of the parties by each newspaper.
   c) **Compare** the television reporting of the same issue.
   d) **Identify** any differences of view *within* each of the parties.
4 **Choose any issue** which either of the Houses of Parliament has discussed in the last few weeks. Explain which departments of the government and which Cabinet ministers and opposition spokespersons were involved, what the views of the political parties were and (briefly) what you see as the main cause of the disagreement between the parties.
5 If there is an election during your course, **note and describe** the methods used by the party leadership and the local candidates to persuade people to vote for them. Which were the most effective in catching your eye and drawing attention to the party?

VOTING BEHAVIOUR

Why we vote

Jack: I vote for the person, not the party. I think that if you have a good candidate, that is the most important thing.

Claire: But if you do that, you might be voting for a whole lot of policies you disagree with. I vote for the party myself.

Sarah: I agree with Claire. But if you don't like the candidate there doesn't seem much you can do except become active in the local branch to try to influence who they select.

Nicos: I have changed the party I support because I disagree with their policies on cutting government service.

Ravi: I gave up attending meetings and joining in party activities – I had no time. But I'm still a member and pay my annual subscription. I think the party leader is more important than the local candidate or even any particular policy.

Paul: Well, I think they should have more women and more black candidates, and then we might have more female and black people on the council and in Parliament.

QUESTIONS

Discuss the following, giving reasons for your answers.

1　Would your vote be influenced by the sex or colour of the candidate?

2　What would you vote for at elections?

3　Is there any difference between the way you would vote in local and in national elections?

4　What do you think influences the votes of other people? (Perhaps you could devise your own survey to find out what influences the way people use their votes.)

Influences on voting

There are many factors which affect the way people vote and whether they take the trouble to vote. In Britain *by-elections* are held when an MP (or local councillor) dies or resigns, and these elections affect only one constituency (or ward). They would therefore normally have very little effect on the ability of the government (or local council) to continue running the country (or local authority), and voting in by-elections may show patterns which differ from general elections.

General elections must be held at least once every five years, and all constituencies elect their MPs at the same time (Fig. 1). People may vote for the party which serves their interests best, but on the other hand one vote makes

Fig. I People voting in a general election

very little difference and it is probable that more general ideas affect people's voting. Many people identify with a party which they feel represents their view of the world.

The factors which influence party identification have been analysed using surveys to find out about the characteristics of voters or supporters of political parties. The characteristics which have been studied include sex and race, social and family background, income and social class, occupation, housing, religion, education and neighbourhood and regional differences. Some examples of the results of surveys are given below. Housing tenure and class affected the support for Labour compared with the Conservatives, and there appears to be some relationship between education and the support for the Alliance (the Liberals and the Social Democratic Party).

Income

Fig. 2 Party identification by household income (1985)

	Less than £5,000 %	£5,000 to £7,999 %	£8,000 to £11,999 %	£12,000 and over %
Conservative	30	33	45	49
Alliance	11	16	14	17
Labour	47	37	32	24
Non-aligned	8	9	4	7

From Roger Jowell and Sharon Witherspoon, *British Social Attitudes: The 1985 Report* (Gower, 1985), p. 7.

QUESTIONS

Answer the following questions in groups of two or three, helping each other where necessary.

5　What is meant in Fig. 2 by a) the Alliance and b) 'non-aligned'? [2]

6　Which income group showed the largest percentage support for the Conservatives, and which for Labour? [3]

7　Can you explain the reasons for the party identifications which you described in your answer to question 6? [6]

8 Is any party overwhelmingly dependent on one income group? [3]
9 What other information would you need in order to find out how many people identified with Labour and how many with the Conservatives? [6]

Social class
Social class does not just depend on level of income, and the effects of class on voting behaviour have been analysed by a variety of writers using different definitions of social class. The analysis in Fig. 3 is based on a survey of voters in the 1983 election. (See also Unit 4.3 on occupations and social class.)

QUESTIONS

10 What percentage of the sample of routine non-manual workers supported the Alliance in Fig. 3? [1]
11 How, on the basis of Fig. 3, would you predict the following would vote: a) doctors and b) a van driver working as an employee? How certain could you be of these predictions? [5]
12 Which is the class which gives most support to the Conservatives and which is strongest in its support for Labour? [1]
13 Approximately how many (in number, not percentage) of the sample of foremen/women and technicians supported the Alliance? [2]
14 The average income of the petty-bourgeoisie in the sample was less than that of any other group. The income of the salariat was highest. Compare this result with the relationship between income and party identification given in Fig. 2. [5]
15 In recent years the classes numbered 1, 2 and 3 in Fig. 3 have been increasing, whereas 4 and 5 have been declining. a) What are the possible effects of these developments on the Labour Party? b) What other factors would also have to be considered? [5]

Section 8 *Political Decisions in Britain*

Housing
The type of housing tenure is clearly associated with voting behaviour, as shown in Fig. 4, which is again based on the 1983 election.

Fig. 4 Housing and vote

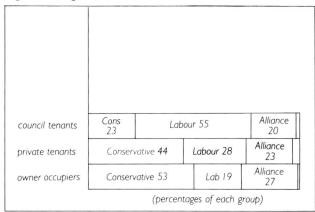

(percentages of each group)

QUESTIONS

16 Describe the relationship between party support and housing tenure shown in Fig. 4. [4]
17 In recent years many council tenants have bought their homes, and the number of owner-occupiers has increased. What effects might this development have on voting in general elections? [3]
18 What other information would you need in order to decide whether this development *does* affect voting patterns in general elections? [3]
19 Support for the Alliance does not appear to be strongly related to housing tenure compared with the other two parties' support. The same survey showed that support for the Alliance was related to education, and there was well-known regional variations in support for the Liberal Party. What kind of test would you conduct to find out whether there was any association between support for the Alliance and education levels? Give details (in about 500 words) of how you would design the survey. [20]

Fig. 3 The political distinctiveness of the classes

	Conservative	Labour	Alliance	Other	Sample size
	(percentages of each class)				
1 *Salariat* (e.g. managers, administrators, professionals)	54	14	31	1	867
2 *Routine non-manual* (e.g. clerks, salesworkers, secretaries)	46	25	27	2	749
3 *Petty-bourgeoisie* (e.g. farmers, self-employed workers)	71	12	17	0	245
4 *Foremen/women and technicians*	48	26	25	1	220
5 *Working class* (skilled and unskilled manual workers in industry and farming)	30	49	20	1	992

(Further analysis showed differences within some of these classes. For example, managers in the salariat group were more likely to be Conservative than teachers or nurses.)

From Anthony Heath, Roger Jowell and John Curtice, *How Britain Votes* (Pergamon, 1985), p. 20.

ELECTIONS

The character of the party

In Unit 8.3 we looked at why people identify with a party. Although this is important, the way people vote is affected by other factors. There are variations in how people vote which cannot be explained by changes in income, social class, housing, education or the areas where they live. We therefore have to look at party leadership, values and policies for additional explanations of voting, and these will be considered in this unit.

The Moore family: a case study

Fig. I

Jim and Margaret Moore live in a council house on an estate in Stockton-on-Tees (Fig. 1). Jim is a skilled electrician employed in a chemical factory. Margaret works as a clerk in a building society. They live on an estate where there is a high rate of unemployment. Jim is a member of a trade union and has served on the committee of his local branch. He believes that strong unions are essential if skilled workers are to maintain their levels of pay compared with other workers. He is concerned about the large number of unemployed youths who are hanging around the estate all day and is worried that he, like many of his friends, might be made redundant.

Margaret thinks inflation was brought under control by the Conservative government in the period 1979 to 1987, but she too is worried about unemployment and the fall in the number of council houses available. Most of the people she works with are Conservative or Alliance supporters, and her parents were Liberals. Margaret would like to see more of her daughter, Julie, who lives in Hertfordshire. Julie is a teacher, and has been pleased with the shares she has bought in the nationalised industries which the Conservatives sold, such as British Gas; but she disagrees with their proposals on education and teachers' pay.

The Moores' son, John, runs his own business as an electrician and is buying a house on a new estate at Thornaby near Stockton. His wife is a director in a small family bus and coach company. John thinks his father does not understand the importance of providing rewards to encourage people to work hard and start new businesses. Jim tries to avoid political discussions with John and his wife. He thinks they do not understand the problems of the unemployed, and he would like to see more money spent on the health service. He is bored by his son's talk about taxes and scroungers.

Electoral stability and floating voters

'Overall swings in British elections are usually slight, and tradition speaks of a stable electorate. But opinion polling between elections reveals wide variations in the lead one party has over the other. These have grown wider since the 1950s, suggesting a yet more volatile electorate (that is, more likely to change rapidly), less inclined to vote with its upbringing or its class interest.

Individual voters are even more volatile. In 1970, 40 per cent claimed to feel "very strongly" identified with one of the two major parties; in 1979 the figure was only 20 per cent.

This suggests that the familiar rise of (Liberal/Alliance) protest votes between elections, and collapse at them, may be lessening. The "protest" voter may stay protesting when there is some prospect his or her vote could make a real difference to who holds power. But it still leaves 20 to 25 per cent of switched votes at each election – let alone others who think of switching but do not, the 25 per cent who normally do not vote and the 8 to 9 per cent of new voters. In normal times much of this potential volatility will cancel out. But crisis or extreme change could offer an exceptional leader or party far more catchable votes than the traditional picture of electoral stability suggests.'

Adapted from Economist Publications, *Political Britain Today* (1984), p. 4.

QUESTIONS

1 What is meant by a *floating voter* and *protest votes*? [3]
2 What percentage of the electorate normally do not vote? [1]
3 How would the various members of the Moore family above, be most likely to vote? Give reasons for your answers. [7]
4 Would the voting you have described in your answers to question 3 be inevitable or is there some uncertainty about how each of them would vote? [6]
5 Give three reasons why people sometimes switch their voting from one party to another. [3]

The electoral system

The British electoral system is known as a *first-past-the-post* system (Fig. 2). This means that in any constituency the person elected will be the one with the most votes. The votes for any other candidates are 'lost' votes – they do not count towards any other candidate for that party anywhere else in the country.

Fig. 2

This system leads to strong government. One party usually has a majority of the seats in the House of Commons, and a second party is recognised as the official Opposition with the second largest number of seats. Each Member of Parliament has a constituency which has elected him or her, and the MP represents the interests of the people in that area. However, in this system it is possible for a party to win the election without gaining the support of the majority of the electorate – this has been the case in most elections. Minority parties are under-represented, as shown in the table below. A party can gain a large number of votes throughout the country without gaining a single seat in Parliament. It is difficult to know what is the full extent of the support for the minority parties because sometimes people vote *tactically*; this means that they vote for a party which they think might stand some chance of success in their constituency in order to keep out the party they like least. For example, Labour supporters in a Conservative area might vote Alliance if they felt that the Alliance might gain the seat whereas Labour stood no chance at all.

Alternatives to the British system are found in the various types of *proportional representation* which exist in Europe. These systems give seats in Parliament in proportion to the number of votes cast for each party. For example, if a party gets half the votes in the country it gets roughly half the MPs.

QUESTIONS

Look at Fig. 3 and answer the following questions:

6   How many seats are there in the House of Commons? [2]
7   How large is the Conservative majority over all other parties? [2]
8   Compare the number of seats gained by each party with the number of votes received by the party. [4]
9   Which parties are under-represented in Parliament and which are over-represented compared with the votes they received? [4]
10 The first-past-the-post system has some advantages and some disadvantages. List as many of each as you can. [8]

Fig. 3 British general election results, June 1987

	Votes	Percentage of vote	Number of seats (MPs)
Conservative	13,763,134	42.3	375
Labour	10,033,633	30.8	229
Alliance (Liberal/SDP)	7,339,912	22.6	22
Nationalists	540,462	1.7	6
Others	859,111	2.6	18
Turn-out (75.4 per cent of the electorate)	30,671,137		

From the *Guardian*, 13 June 1987.

WHERE POLITICAL DECISIONS ARE MADE

Central government

The British system of government has developed gradually over a period of at least nine hundred years since England was united under one ruler. The thrones of England and Scotland were united when King James of Scotland became King of England in 1603. Wales had been conquered by the English in the fourteenth century. Ireland was united with Britain from 1800 to 1922; and although the Republic of Ireland is now a separate country, Northern Ireland is governed as part of the United Kingdom.

Britain differs from many other countries in that the power to make political decisions is concentrated in the government at Westminster. Other countries, such as the United States of America, Canada and West Germany, are federations (collections) of a number of states or provinces, and the powers of the central government are limited.

Head of state

Britain also differs from many other countries in that the head of state is a monarch rather than a president, as in the United States and France. In the USA the President is a political figure who has and uses powers to introduce or veto new laws. There are big variations in the powers of the president in different countries, however. Many presidents are elected for a limited term (four years in the case of the US President).

A constitutional monarch, such as Queen Elizabeth, is not elected but inherits her position because she is the daughter (or in other cases, of course, the son) of the monarch. The Queen does not normally take an active role in government, although she may advise and warn the Prime Minister in private meetings which take place regularly.

Canada: example of a federal system

The Canadian system of government is in many ways similar to the British. The Queen is recognised as the head of state, and there is a Parliament (Fig. 1) with many traditions which are shared with Britain. This is true of many of the countries which have had strong historic ties with Britain, such as India and Australia.

The Canadian system is also similar to the British system because the powers of the various institutions, and the rules for elections and the making of laws, are determined partly by customs and traditions (called *conventions*) and partly by Acts of Parliament.

Although the Canadian system of government is similar to the British system, there are separate provinces which have powers to impose income taxes and to make laws concerning a wide range of activities (including trade unions and social security). In some cases responsibilities are shared between the federal (central) government and the provinces – for example, concerning immigration and agriculture. There is also a further tier of local or *municipal* government in Canada, but the powers of the municipal government can be changed by the governments in the provinces.

Devolution

The British system of government is centralised in one place: Westminster. When we look at powers to make laws and raise taxes, we are looking mainly at central government.

In the United Kingdom, local authorities have some powers, but these powers can be modified or taken away by the central government in Westminster. One example of this was the abolition of the Greater London Council and

Fig. 1 The Canadian federal Parliament in Ottawa

the metropolitan counties by the Conservative government in 1986. The devolution of power to Scotland and Wales has been discussed, but proposals for this were rejected by a *referendum* (a vote by the people on this single issue) in Wales and failed to gain an adequate majority in Scotland. Devolution is still an issue, however, for many people in Wales and Scotland, who consider that there are important differences of culture and interest between the Welsh or the Scots and the English.

The debate about Welsh independence

The following views on the arguments for and against greater independence for Wales are taken from an article by David Selbourne in *New Society* of 25 April 1985. Selbourne interviewed several members of the Labour Party and Plaid Cymru (the Welsh Nationalist Party) in Meirionnydd, North Wales.

Owen Edwards of the local Labour Party was asked whether Plaid Cymru was attracting increasing radical support. He answered:

> First of all, the only true radical party in Wales is the Labour Party. Second, there is no economic foundation for an independent Wales, Welsh embassies abroad, devolution, Welsh language or whatnot. With 48 million English people paying rates and taxes we can always call on the English to subsidise our deficiencies. Third, two-thirds of the Welsh population live in South Wales, not here. They're mostly English-speaking.

A Plaid Cymru member, on the other hand, described Wales as 'one of the small, exploited and peripheral nations', which is treated merely as 'part and parcel of an English-based system'. When asked how Welsh politics differed from English politics, he replied:

> An ordinary Englishman and an ordinary Welshman are two human beings. But there is definitely something different between us … Most of the difference is the language. You can't translate feelings. Every question you've asked me I've had to translate my answers from Welsh into English.
>
> We have to be a bilingual nation. We've been tied to England for centuries, but there's no point in breaking with England. Our dream is of a Plaid Cymru ruling the whole of Wales, with the right to govern, and with a Welsh government in a Welsh nation. At the moment we are dormant. Wales, the Welsh nation of people, is politically drowsy or sleeping.

In the same article, a Plaid Cymru leader was quoted as saying:

> The stage we are at is linking ourselves to Welsh socialist traditions, and pushing forward the notion that the Welsh people … must take control of their own affairs in the community and the workplace.

QUESTIONS

1 Explain what is meant by a federal system of government.
2 Compare the advantages of the system in Canada with the advantages of the more centralised system in Britain.
3 What are the arguments for and against an independent Welsh nation?
4 What are the advantages in providing some services such as defence and foreign relations through a central government rather than through provincial or local government?
5 The last quotatio . om the Plaid Cymru leader, above, does not refer to an independent Wales but to greater powers for the Welsh to control their own affairs. What activities in particular might best be controlled within Wales, by and for the Welsh?
6 Consider whether the arguments for and against the devolution of power to a government in Wales also apply to *one* of the following: Scotland, Northern Ireland, Northern England, a major city such as London or Birmingham, or the county in which you live.

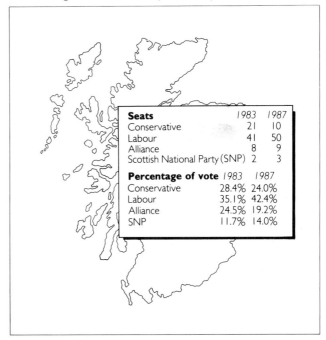

Seats	1983	1987
Conservative	21	10
Labour	41	50
Alliance	8	9
Scottish National Party (SNP)	2	3

Percentage of vote	1983	1987
Conservative	28.4%	24.0%
Labour	35.1%	42.4%
Alliance	24.5%	19.2%
SNP	11.7%	14.0%

Fig. 2 Party power in Scotland (parliamentary elections)

EXTENSION ACTIVITIES

1 **Make a survey**. If you live in an area where there are holiday homes, you could conduct your own research project to find out what the views of local people are on these homes. Are the views of local people likely to differ from those in the majority of Britain?
2 **Discuss** the arguments for and against the view that Scotland is governed by a party which it has not elected, and it should therefore have greater independence. (Consider Fig. 2, use other information in this unit and look again at Unit 8.4 on elections.)

LOCAL DECISIONS

Unit 8.5 considered some of the advantages in the devolution of control over the type and quality of services which are provided. Variations in services can reflect differences in the incomes and needs in different areas and differences in the preferences of the voters from different areas.

Local authorities in Britain are responsible for large areas of public spending and for the provision of services such as education, housing, rubbish collection, local roads, libraries, social workers and home helps (Fig. 1).

Fig. 1

Finance for local services in Britain is obtained from central government grants and local taxes (such as rates and community charges), and by borrowing. The powers of local government were restricted in the 1980s by the Conservative government, which imposed financial penalties on authorities which increase the rates above the level that Westminster considered necessary.

Local taxes

The *community charge* is a local tax which is collected from each adult in the population. It has been criticised because the same amount is collected from almost everybody regardless of income level. It has also been claimed that this charge may discourage people from registering as electors if they cannot afford to pay the community charge.

Rates are a type of taxation on business property, such as factories and offices. Rates on houses are to be abolished, but rates will continue to be paid by businesses, which take no direct part in electing the local councillors but benefit from some of the services provided. Although there has been criticism of this form of taxation, rates are cheap and easy to collect.

Alternative local taxes which have been considered include local sales taxes and income taxes.

1 Find out from discussions with your family, and from any information published by your local authority, how your local authority finances its spending.
2 Compare two alternative ways of financing local government spending, to be agreed with your teacher. State which method of finance you think is best and give reasons for your answer.

How local government works

The structure of local government

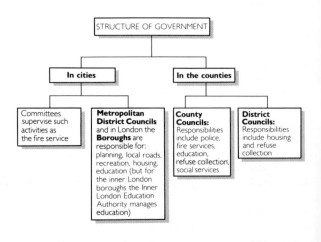

Fig. 2

Employment in local government

Of the 21.8 million people employed in Britain in September 1987, more than 2 million were employed in local authorities. This includes over 1 million employed as lecturers, teachers and other workers in the education service, over 273,000 in social services, and a police service (including traffic wardens) of more than 186,000 (statistics from *Monthly Digest of Statistics*, February 1988).

3 Draw a diagram to illustrate the above statistics. [7]
4 Comment on the importance of local authority employment as a part of total employment. [6]
5 Comment on the relative importance of the different departments of local authority work [7]

Education and local government

One of the major spending areas of local government is education. Local authorities are required to provide compulsory and free education from the age of 5 to 16. Schools must provide the national curriculum laid down by the government in Westminster. Education must also meet the standards required by Her Majesty's Inspectors (HMIs), who are employed by the Department of Education and Science. However, local authorities decide on the types of schools provided. For example, the decision whether to have single-sex or co-educational schools is a local decision, and some local areas have retained the selection of pupils for grammar schools. Local authorities also have the power to decide whether to provide nursery education and how much to provide; and there are local variations in the average size of classes and the amount of money spent on buildings and equipment. The local authority decides whether to provide schools for 11- to 16-year-olds and separate sixth-form colleges, or combined schools for the 11- to 18-year-old pupils. Many authorities have had to reorganise and to close schools because of the fall in the number of children born during the 1970s.

The reorganisation of schools is a subject on which people often feel strongly. Local and national pressure groups are commonly involved in campaigns to influence local authorities' decisions. Proposals for the reorganisation of schools may be overruled by the Secretary of State for Education. The pressure groups therefore aim their campaigns at both the local and national decision-makers and at public opinion in the local area. The pressure groups usually include the teachers' unions and the parents' associations, churches and other religious and cultural organisations, where these are affected, and national associations concerned with education such as the Campaign for the Advancement of State Education (CASE). Some campaigns of this type are managed by a co-ordinating committee which brings together the activities of political parties and pressure groups with similar views.

QUESTIONS

1 What are the arguments for and against the local control of education?
2 Find out about the effects of changes in the birth rate on the schools in your area.
3 Examine the way in which your local authority has dealt with this problem, and the activities of any pressure groups in response to changes in the organisation of education in your area.

EXTENSION ACTIVITIES

1 **Visit** a council meeting or a meeting of a local government committee. Find out about how decisions are made in your local authority and about local political controversies. What are the differences between the parties on local issues?

2 **Interview** a councillor or invite one to speak to your class. Ask them the following questions:
   a) What kinds of problem do people bring to their councillors?
   b) What can the councillor do about these problems?
   c) What are the functions of a councillor in the control of local activities?
   d) What problems does the councillor have in carrying out these functions?

3 **Compare** the role of a councillor with that of an MP.

4 **Describe** what *your* aims and policies would be as a local councillor. You could express these aims in a short statement suitable for an election campaign leaflet.

5 **Hold a mock local election** within your class or school. Decide whether to fight it on local or national issues.

6 **Find out** what committees and what departments there are in your local authority. Keep a diary of the local authority services you use over two weeks, the departments responsible for them and the charges if any.

7 **Investigate** the work of an agency which is supported by your local authority – for example, the local Community Relations Council or the Citizen's Advice Bureau. Find out what the aims of the organisation are, how it is financed, what its problems are, how decisions are made and what powers the local organisers have to make decisions. If possible, observe in person one or more of the activities of the organisation.

8 **Find out** about the *decentralisation* of local sevices. Some local authorities have decentralised some of their services so that social workers, housing officers and other staff are available in neighbourhood centres on estates. If there is a centre of this kind in your area, find out what services it provides to tenants and what powers it has to make decisions affecting people on the estates. Find out what advantages there are in neighbourhood centres compared with departments in the town hall. You could do this by asking the workers in the centres themselves and by asking a sample of the local residents. Are there any disadvantages?

GOVERNMENT INTERVENTION

Government intervention in all aspects of our lives, from how we build our houses to how much money we take home from our wages, has increased throughout the twentieth century.

The government has gradually, particularly since the Second World War, assumed responsibility for controlling the level of unemployment. Any increase in unemployment leads to criticism of the government in power, and government success or failure in controlling unemployment is debated in the election campaigns. Inflation has also become an election issue, and from time to time the exchange rate and balance of payments have been regarded as important problems which the government of the day has been expected to solve.

Government and the level of income

Spending in the economy takes several different forms. If I buy a new coat which is made in Britain, there is an addition to spending which will add (a little) to incomes and employment in the British textile trade. If the government spends money on new schools, or employing more teachers, or rebuilding sewers and roads, there will be an increase in spending which will add to the jobs available. Businesses may spend on investment: new microcomputers, or new buildings and machinery. This spending also adds to the total demand in the economy. If we export goods we also add to the demand for goods and to jobs.

We can see, then, that the total demand for goods in the economy (and therefore total incomes) is the result of adding together the following:

consumer spending + government spending + investment + exports.

Incomes may be used in a variety of ways. We use some of our incomes to buy consumer goods and services; we pay taxes to the government; we may save some of our income; and we may buy imported goods. We can see, then, that total income in the economy is the result of adding together:

consumer spending + government taxation + saving + imports.

Government spending and taxes are therefore very important in their effects on the demand for goods.

In Fig. 1 you can see that an increase in government spending adds to incomes. As an example, if the government spends money on paying teachers more, the teachers will go out and spend their incomes (e.g. new cars). If they buy goods produced in Britain (such as British cars), there will be an increase in jobs and incomes for other workers (e.g. car workers).

If the government takes more away in taxes, there will be a fall in the level of demand for goods and services. This could lead to less jobs and lower incomes.

Taxes and government spending are not necessarily equal in any one year. The government may choose to borrow rather than to raise enough income through taxation.

Demand for goods can thus be increased by the government through reducing taxes or increasing spending. This is usually done through the government's statements of planned spending and taxation (revenue) at least once a year (usually in early spring); this is known as *the Budget*.

One of the problems facing governments in recent years has been *inflation* (see also Unit 6.9). Increasing demand may reduce unemployment, but higher demand for goods can lead to higher prices. Some of the unemployed would remain unemployed even if demand increased (see also Unit 6.7 on unemployment) and we should be faced with rising prices.

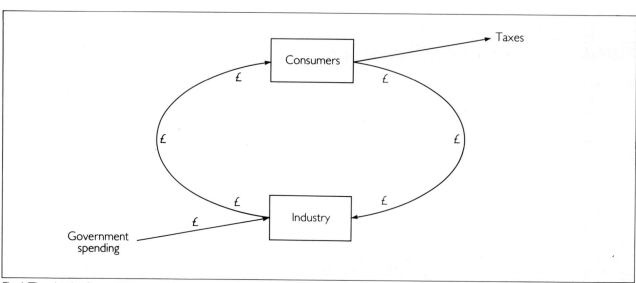

Fig. 1 The circular flow of income

Planning by government

Governments may plan their spending in different sectors of the economy, such as building, engineering and agriculture. They may also plan the amount which will be spent in total and the amount which will be allocated to investment. There has been very little planning by governments in Britain in peacetime. In general, the government plays a much greater role in planning economic activity in communist countries – e.g. those of Eastern Europe – than in the capitalist countries of the West.

Capitalist, communist and mixed economies

There are several distinctions which may be drawn between a *capitalist* or free-enterprise economy and a *socialist* (communist) or planned economy. The first is in the planning and the direction of resources by the state as described above. A second difference is in the role played by prices and profits. In a capitalist country profits play an important role in encouraging businesses to produce more of the goods demanded by consumers. But in a communist country the state directs resources and controls prices.

Finally, the ownership of the resources: in a communist country the resources are generally owned by the state, although there are exceptions (particularly in Yugoslavia, where the workers own their factories in the form of worker co-operatives). In capitalist countries, resources are mainly privately owned.

Most economies, including those of Western Europe, are *mixed*. This means that they include quite large elements of state ownership and state control as well as a large private sector.

Public goods

Public goods are those goods which benefit everybody and where it is not possible to exclude anyone from the benefits. Decisions by governments, unlike those of the private sector, can take account of social costs and social benefit. (See also Unit 5.7 on the environment.)

Examples of public goods include the following:

- *Defence* – we all gain from the defence of the country. It is not possible to exclude some people and therefore it is not possible for each of us to provide this service for ourself, privately and independently. Defence is provided by the state in all countries.
- *Sanitation and refuse disposal* – we all gain if our neighbours dispose of their rubbish in a way which does not damage the environment. Good sanitation and refuse disposal are important. They make the environment more pleasant and attractive, and prevent epidemics of diseases which were found in Europe in previous centuries.
- *Street lighting* – we all gain if streets are well lit. This too is therefore a service which must be paid for out of taxation.

In most cases public goods are paid for out of taxation. Either they are provided directly by the state, or the government may employ a business organisation to provide the service.

Some goods provide a mixture of private and social benefits. The education of specialists such as engineers and scientists is one example. We may all gain in the future if the country has more well-qualified engineers or scientists. A university or polytechnic degree may allow the graduate to earn more than people who have not gained a degree. The benefits of education in universities and polytechnics are therefore both private benefits (raising the income of the individual and perhaps giving the pleasure of studying and of university life) and social benefits.

EXTENSION ACTIVITIES

Study the government's Budget this year. Answer the following questions in not more than 1,000 words in total, quoting your sources of information.

1   Who introduces the Budget into the House of Commons?
2   According to the reports you have read or heard, will taxation increase by more or less than government spending?
3   What are the expected effects on:

   a) Unemployment and inflation?
   b) The low paid and those on higher incomes?
   c) Pensioners and people receiving social security benefits?
   d) Services provided by the public sector?

4   Which taxes will be increased and which (if any) reduced?
5   What criticisms were made by the opposition parties in the House of Commons?
6   What were the reactions of pressure groups?
7   What would you have changed in the Budget? Give your reasons.

THE WELFARE STATE

The role of the government

During the twentieth century, the government has gradually taken on the responsibilities for the relief of poverty and the provision of a minimum standard of education and health. This provision by the government, especially since 1945, is often referred to as the *Welfare State*.

The introduction of the Welfare State was influenced by a government report (the *Beveridge Report*) published in 1942. It was based on ideas of the elimination of poverty and the provision of basic necessities. It has been argued, however, that the Welfare State was introduced and retained by the government as a means of securing the political support of working-class people.

The National Health Service and the system of supplementary benefits introduced by the Labour government following the Second World War have continued in existence under both Conservative and Labour governments, although in the 1980s attempts have been made to cut public spending on them.

Problems of the Welfare State

Some of the strengths and the problems of the Welfare State at the present time can be traced to its origins and the ideas which influenced its foundation, as we shall see below.

Benefits in kind

State benefits were introduced to provide for the poorest members of the population who were unable to work because of age or ill health. The benefits were not entirely in the form of cash but included benefits *in kind* (goods and services) provided directly by the state, particularly education and health care.

The provision of benefits in kind rather than cash has been regarded as part of a paternalistic approach by government. The term *paternalistic* describes the government acting in a role similar to that of a parent – that is, introducing measures to benefit people who might not otherwise act in their own best interests. Such measures include the provision of free school meals rather than an increased cash benefit to poorer families.

Incentives to work and the poverty trap

The Beveridge Report introduced plans for the provision of benefits to prevent anyone falling below minimum living standards. The schemes introduced in Britain aimed to retain the incentive to work, except in the case of married women. It was assumed that households consisted of male bread-winners and dependent wives and children. This assumption has led to some anomalies (pecularities) in today's social security system. The system provides benefits for people who are unemployed, provided they are not married to, or co-habiting with, a working person. Many women are therefore excluded from benefits, and wives of unemployed men sometimes find that their husbands' benefits are reduced if they work.

The system of social security in Britain has thus not been entirely successful in supporting the incentive to work. Some people with children and the opportunity to earn only a low wage are made better off by not working and by claiming social security, free school meals and other benefits. These people are therefore 'trapped' at the very low social security level of income – this is sometimes referred to as the *poverty trap*. Even so, many people work for low wages, either because they are not eligible for benefits, or because of the unpleasantness of the claims process and the fraud investigations and their own wish to have a job and earn a wage.

Unclaimed benefits

A further problem in the current system of social security is the fact that many benefits are not claimed. David Donnison, who was chairperson of the Supplementary Benefits Commission from 1975 until it was dissolved in 1980, described one such case:

> Whenever you begin to grow convinced that everyone in "real" need claims the benefits to which they are entitled, you run across someone who doesn't. A spiky little widow in Islington, for example: the state had owed her money for years – nearly £4 a week when we found her – because she kept herself to herself and didn't want to be bothered by officials. Provided we do our best to help people to claim their right, we must recognise that they also have a right to do without us. We had come to see her because she had been struggling for nine months to pay off an electricity bill a few shillings at a time, which had dragged her living standards still further down. Coaxing her to accept a supplementary pension was like persuading a fierce and frightened animal to take food. She eventually agreed when we said that we could settle the rest of the electricity bill right away. The taxpayers had owed her much more than that for a long time. She seemed to have no family or friends, but got by with the help of a day centre where she was given hot meals.

From David Donnison, *The Politics of Poverty* (Martin Robertson, 1982). p.2.

1 Discuss the possible reasons why the widow described above was reluctant to claim benefits.
2 What evidence is there that the widow was living in poverty? Could there be any alternative explanation for her problems?
3 Why do some people work for wages which are below the level of state benefits?

The cost of the welfare state

The costs of the Welfare State have increased as the numbers of people in long-term unemployment, single parenthood and old age have risen, and as more services have been demanded (e.g. in connection with children and families with problems). The range of services includes services to help people remain in their own homes, such as meals on wheels and home helps, as well as the services of social workers, homes for the elderly and the payment of benefits. Social services are now one of the largest items of government spending.

The costs of the health service have risen as new, expensive drugs and equipment are developed to treat and often cure illnesses which were formerly considered to be fatal. The rising costs of health care have been a problem for successive governments.

QUESTIONS

4 The graph in Fig. 1 indicates an increase in the number of people claiming certain benefits. How would you account for this increase?
5 What other information, apart from the picture and graphs, would you need to assess whether poverty has increased?
6 For the following you will need to use a reference library.

   a) Find out the average amount received in earnings and the average amount received in one type of benefit over a three-year period. Illustrate these statistics on a graph or chart.
   b) Comment on any changes in the relative poverty of those dependent on benefits.
      (You may, if you wish, choose just one type of benefit, but your answer should clearly indicate which benefit(s) you have included for which years, and the sources of your information.)

EXTENSION ACTIVITIES

1 **Design** a poster to encourage people to claim their benefits.
2 **Discuss** the arguments for and against a comprehensive system of free health care.
3 **Hold a class debate** on the issue that prescription charges should be abolished.

Fig. 1 Number of people claiming benefit.

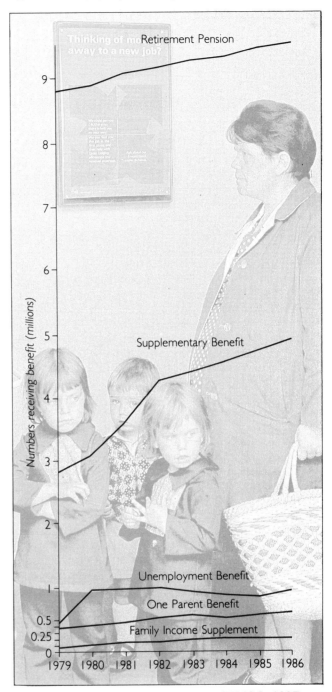

Adapted from Social Security Statistics (HMSO, 1987) table 50, pages 278-281.

4 **Find out** the details of any single state benefit – for example, family credit, one-parent benefit or free school meals. (Leaflets are generally available at social security offices.) Find out what the conditions are for claiming benefit and how to apply for the benefit. Which households benefit, and which low-income households are excluded?
5 **Examine** the purpose and effects of the benefit you chose to investigate in extension activity 4.

THE QUESTION OF OWNERSHIP

A party-political issue

One issue which faces the major political parties in both central and local government is the debate about which industries and services should be owned directly by the public sector, and which should be run by the private sector (such as companies and partnerships).

Privatisation or nationalisation

Privatisation is the selling of state-owned assets to the private sector. In general, the growth of privatisation is favoured by those who wish to reduce the role of the government in the economy. Reducing the role of government is seen to be a means of encouraging free enterprise – this means the running of industry and provision of services by organisations which aim to make profits. The Conservative government in the period after 1979 adopted a policy of selling state-owned organisations. The industries which were privatised include British Telecom, British Gas, British Aerospace, National Freight, Jaguar Cars and Rolls-Royce.

Nationalisation is the taking over of private-sector assets by the state. It is more likely to be favoured by those who support a socialist economy (sometimes referred to as a *planned economy*) with greater state ownership, the provision of services by the state and government controls or influence over planning and the distribution of income. There has been opposition to the privatisation of industry on the grounds that the government is losing future earnings from profitable industries (such as telecommunications), and consumers may have to pay higher prices because of the monopoly power of these industries.

Industries have been nationalised by Conservative as well as Labour governments, particularly Rolls-Royce and Upper Clyde Shipbuilders in the 1970s (during Mr Heath's period as Prime Minister). Generally, Labour has favoured more nationalisation, although it has not always been given a high priority in Labour's programme. The post-war Labour government in the 1940s nationalised some industries which were very important to the rest of the economy including coal, steel, rail and road services and the Bank of England. In recent years Labour Party policy has emphasised government support for investment in industry and social ownership rather than nationalisation.

The views of the parties

Conservative

‘The overwhelming majority of employees have become shareholders in the newly privatised companies. They want their companies to succeed. Their companies have been released from the detailed controls of Whitehall and given more freedom to manage their own affairs. And they have been exposed to the full commercial disciplines of the customer. Even former monopolies now face increased competition.’

From *The Next Moves Forward*, the Conservative Party manifesto, 1987.

Labour

‘Social ownership of basic utilities like gas and water is vital to ensure that every individual has access to their use and that the companies contribute to Britain's industrial recovery, for instance, by buying British. We shall start by using the existing 49 per cent holding in British Telecom to ensure proper influence in their decisions.’

From *Britain Will Win*, the Labour Party manifesto, 1987.

Alliance

‘We will continue to judge whether industries should be in the public or private sector on objective criteria related to competition and efficiency. We opposed the privatisation of British Gas and British Telecom – although we would not reverse it but instead concentrate on improving consumer choice and protection. We supported the privatisation of Rolls-Royce. We would not privatise water authorities and the Central Electricity Generating Board on grounds of public policy relating to safety standards and care for the environment.’

From *Britain United*, the SDP/Liberal Alliance manifesto, 1987.

QUESTIONS

1 Which of the above do you agree with, and why?
2 Choose one industry or service (except for water) which has been involved in plans for privatisation or nationalisation. Do you think that this industry or service should be in private ownership or public ownership? Give reasons for your answer.

Fig. 1

There are some advantages in the private provision of services. Many industrial organisations in recent years have brought in specialist organisations to provide their catering and other services because this can reduce their management costs and the cost of employing people at times when there is not enough work for them. Specialist caterers and laundry and cleaning organisations bring their own technical knowledge and management experience. For the government, a further advantage is that the wages which are paid can be just sufficient to attract labour in that part of the country, hence there can be lower wage rates in the areas of high unemployment.

On the other hand, there are disadvantages and risks including the effects on standards of work and on employees. Trade unions object to the use of private contractors because in many cases these contractors pay wages well below the rates which the unions have negotiated, and offer less holiday pay and poorer conditions to the workers. They may also be under such pressure to cut costs that the standards of service and even of hygiene and safety fall. Also, there are often aspects of a job which are not fully noted in the description of the work done, as in the case of hospital cleaners who might carry messages to the nursing staff. In some jobs, the quality of the service can be maintained only by much supervision, and the authorities may underestimate the amount of management time involved in supervising the private contractors.

Ownership of water

Environmental pressure groups are concerned about the effects of privatisation on the non-profitable services of the water authorities, such as pollution control, land drainage, river and lake management, sea defences, bathing beaches and sewage treatment (Fig. 1). Water was one of the most controversial privatisation proposals of the Conservative government elected in 1987.

QUESTIONS

3   Discuss the reasons why a privatised water company might be unwilling or unable to continue loss-making services (such as cleaning rivers). Consider the possible ways in which the government could persuade or require a privatised company to provide these services, and what the problems of enforcement would be.

4   Find out what the views of at least two parties and one pressure group are on this issue, and what the arguments are for and against private ownership of the organisation supplying water.

Privatisation of services

In the case of local government and hospital services, the authorities have been encouraged by central government to use the private sector for the provision of some services including hospital laundry, cleaning and catering, local authority building and maintenance, refuse disposal and even school meals.

EXTENSION ACTIVITIES

1   **Debate** the motion 'The school meals service should be provided by private contractors'.

2   **Interview** an employee in an industry or service where privatisation has been proposed or introduced.

   a) What were the effects, if any, on the management and organisation of the industries, and what are the views of your interviewee about the possible effects on his or her working conditions?

   b) What are the possible problems and the advantages of the privatisation of this organisation?

3   a) **Conduct a public opinion survey** to find out what people's views are about whether there should be a reduction or increase in public ownership, and which party your respondents support. For example, are Conservatives more likely to support a reduction in public ownership and Labour supporters less likely to support this? Are there some Conservatives who do not support privatisation and Labour supporters who do not support nationalisation?

   b) **Analyse** and comment on your results in extension activity 3a.

   c) **Compare** your small sample results with the larger survey in Roger Jowell and Sharon Witherspoon, *British Social Attitudes: The 1985 Report* (Gower, 1985, or later editions).

INTERNATIONAL TRADE

Britain depends on selling goods and services overseas to buy materials, food and consumer goods from other countries. Without such imports, the standard of living would be lower.

Competition

In recent years, especially in the first few years of the 1980s, Britain found it more difficult to export goods because of the growth of *competition*. Gradually, during the period since the Second World War, countries of the British Commonwealth (such as India, Nigeria and Ghana), which had been captive markets for Britain, became free to buy goods from any country they wished, and other countries developed their industries.

Competition in manufactured goods has been growing throughout the twentieth century. In recent years Britain has found it progressively more difficult to compete with countries where the costs of employing labour are much lower. At the same time, electronic goods are now exported from the Far East at a price and with a design quality which other countries find hard to match.

QUESTIONS

A price comparison
Choose one product (perhaps something you hope to receive for your next birthday or for Christmas, or to buy with your earnings).

1 Find out where that product is made and if possible where the company has its head office. (For example, some goods are made in Britain by Japanese companies.)
2 What is the main competition? (Look at the competing products in the catalogues or shops.)
3 Where are the competing products made?
4 If there is a British product, how does it compare in price and quality with the imported goods?

Imports and exports

Figs. 1 and 2 are based on figures from the *Monthly Digest of Statistics*, February 1987 (HMSO), and show the value of imports and exports in 1986. These imports and exports are sometimes referred to as *visible trade*. Between 1980 and 1985 exports of manufactured goods increased by 50 per cent, but imports increased by 100 per cent.

Payments for services, such as tourism, are called *invisibles*. Invisible trade also includes shipping and air services, interest and profits which are paid overseas or received from other countries, and the earnings of the

banking and financial institutions in the City of London. The earnings from invisible exports are usually larger than the earnings from exported goods.

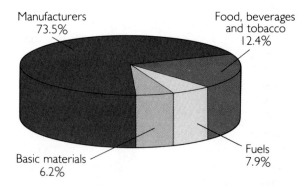

Fig. 1 Value of imports to Britain, 1986

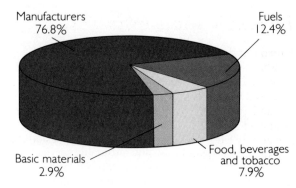

Fig. 2 Value of exports by Britain, 1986

QUESTIONS

Paying for imports
5 Using the information given on imports and exports, and the diagrams, discuss the view that the manufacturing of goods is no longer important to British trade.
6 Britain usually imports more goods than it exports. How does it pay for these imports?

Exchange rates

The *exchange rate* is the price at which currencies may be bought and sold. For example, if the exchange rate of the £ for the dollar is $1.5, this means that I can receive $1.5 for every £1.

If the exchange rate of the £ rises to $2 to each £, British people have to give up less £s for imported American books or wheat, or a holiday in Florida. When the £ rises, we say that it has become stronger; when it falls we describe it as weakening. A stronger £ is very nice for those wanting to buy goods from other countries or foreign currencies for their holidays, but it makes it harder for British companies to export goods to other countries.

You can find out what the exchange rate is by looking at the notice-boards in most banks and some travel agents, or in the financial pages of many newspapers.

Pesetas

7 Write down the current exchange rates of the Spanish peseta against the £. Note the exchange rate again a week later and see whether it has risen or fallen.

8 A school visit to Spain could be concerned about changes in exchange rates. If the organisers think that the £ will fall compared with the Spanish peseta, will they require more money or less to pay for the expenses of the visit? Alternatively, will they buy pesetas sooner if they think the £ will fall, or later?

9 A company is hoping to export goods to Spain. If the £ falls in value, they should be able to sell the goods for a lower price in Spain and get more Spanish customers. Explain why this is so.

The textile industry: a case study

The textile industry has declined in Britain. Textiles and the clothing industry now account for only a small part of our national output, whereas wool, and later silk and cotton, used to be major industries, especially in the North of England, in the East Midlands (Nottingham and Leicester) and East London.

The account in Fig. 3 shows the effects of a rise in the £ on one small Lancashire company.

Textiles

10 Work in groups of four, with two pupils representing management and two representing unions. The management have to explain to the workers what the company's problems are and what action they propose to take. The union representatives may object, ask questions or propose alternative actions.

11 Work in groups consisting of representatives from the company's management, the unions involved and the local chamber of commerce, to draft a letter to the MP for Blackburn (Labour) to demand government action to help companies in this kind of difficulty. What do you think the government should and might do? (Alternatively, arrange a meeting, with two students in each group taking the roles of local MPs, each from a different party.)

12 If you live in a textile-producing area, interview someone who is or was employed in the industry and find out which companies have declined or closed down. What use is now being made of the buildings?

13 The decline of a manufacturing company and the loss of jobs means that less income is available to be spent in local shops and on local services. Examine the effects of the decline of this company on the local community. If possible refer to examples of declining industries (not necessarily textiles) in your area.

Fig. 3

Textiles firm sacks 30 workers
Strong £ forces job cuts

By JEFF HANSON, Industrial correspondent

A TEXTILES company which had an orders boom while the pound was weak has had to make 30 redundancies due to a drop in export sales.

Blackburn company Prospect-Reesdale, formerly the Prospect Manufacturing Company, has scrapped the night shift at its Walter Street Mill, but says the remaining 100 jobs at the firm are safe.

Managing director Mr Andrew Noble said the company was a victim of the strength of sterling, with buying power of customers in major export markets like South East Asia and Australasia reduced by a third.

"The net result is that we are no longer competitive," he said. The 30 workers concerned received the unexpected news just before the Easter holiday.

Mr Noble said that the company had excellent contacts in the countries where orders had fallen off and if the exchange rate moved in the company's favour it could soon be back in business there.

Curtains

"Sooner or later the politicians are going to have to get round a table and sort something out, because rapid fluctuations in exchange rates make planning a business and output levels very difficult," he said.

Prospect-Reesdale were one of few textiles companies to boost their workforce during the recession. One of the reasons for this was a decision to produce ready-made curtains from raw yarn.

Said Mr Noble: "As far as we can see this move helps to secure the position for the majority. I am sure we will be operating a third shift again at some point, but the problem is not going to be resolved quickly. We cannot keep people on because without the orders we do not have the resources to keep them indefinitely."

"All the people who work here have been doing a tremendous job and it is galling to have to take this action," he added.

From the *Lancashire Evening Telegraph*, 3 April 1986.

INTERNATIONAL DECISIONS

Governments frequently have to take account of the effects of their decisions on other countries, and on some issues decisions are made at an international level.

We have looked at several examples of international rules and decision-making, including the co-operation necessary to reduce acid rain and other types of pollution (see Units 5.7 and 5.8). We have also referred to the European Community, particularly in its powers to make rules which must be followed by member states (see Unit 7.6 on pressure groups and individual rights).

In this unit we shall look at some international decisions affecting trade, and in particular we shall examine the European Community.

Import controls

Controls may be imposed by the government on imports of goods into the country. This *protection* can take the form of import duties (taxes) on goods at the ports, or restrictions on the quantities of goods coming into Britain from any country.

The policy of putting duties on imported goods is in many ways an attractive one for governments. By limiting imports we may preserve jobs in this country. We can also prevent other countries from selling goods at low prices in order to gain extra markets for their goods (they may raise the prices later after gaining part of the UK market). Import controls can be used to protect new industries which might have difficulty in competing until they have grown in size.

On the other hand, there are many objections to import controls. Taxes or restrictions on imported goods raise the cost of living for all of us; consumers benefit by reductions in taxes on imported food, clothes or other goods.

People in developing countries also gain if import duties are reduced in the wealthier countries of the world. If developing countries can export their clothing to us, they can use the currency they gain to import food, or machinery which will help their economy to grow. (See also Unit 6.2 on economic growth.)

In a world without import duties, countries would be able to specialise in those goods which they can produce at comparatively low cost. (See also unit 5.2 on opportunity cost.) For example, some countries can produce wheat by making only a small sacrifice in manufacturing output. These would be able to specialise in the production of wheat and import televisions, while other countries import food and export consumer goods.

Import duties are sometimes increased to retaliate against another country's actions. If Britain raises import duties against textiles from a country, we are likely to find that the country in question raises import duties against British goods, or cancels agreements to buy British goods.

GATT

There is an international organisation which aims to reduce import duties. Ninety-two countries of the world (including most of Europe and the Americas but excluding the Soviet Union and China) are members of the *General Agreement on Tariffs and Trade* (GATT). These countries negotiate to reduce import duties and together make rules about import restrictions. Until recently, GATT was concerned mainly with manufactured goods but it is now also concerned with services and agriculture.

The European Community

The European Community (the EC, previously known as the European Economic Community, or EEC) consists of the following countries: Britain, France, West Germany, Italy, Belgium, the Netherlands, Denmark, Ireland, Luxemburg, plus the recent additions of Greece, Spain and Portugal.

One of the main original aims of the European Community was to create a *customs union*. This means that there would be no import duties between member countries. At the same time, each of the member states would impose the same import duties against the rest of the world.

The Community's policies now cover many issues, such as the grants to the regions with the highest unemployment and the rights of individuals to move to any member country. But the Community's policies are also concerned with the rights of individuals as citizens and as employees, and with other issues such as the quality of food and nuclear safety.

The EC is run by a *Council of Ministers*. These are ministers from the various member states, and the ministers who attend each session vary depending on the topics for discussion. There is also a *Commission*, which consists of full-time members responsible for policy-making.

There are two other institutions involved in policy-making: the *European Parliament* and the *Economic and Social Committee*. The Parliament is now directly elected by the voters of the member states – there are usually separate elections for the Members of the European Parliament (MEPs). The Economic and Social Committee consists of representatives from various pressure groups (such as trade unions and employers' associations) throughout Europe.

Laws covering a wide range of issues, from nationality rights to pollution and food additives, are made by the EC and must be observed in the member states. These laws are made as follows:

Fig. I

1 The Commission investigates proposals and drafts legislation.

↓

2 The European Parliament and the Economic and Social Committee are consulted.

↓

3 The Council of Ministers accepts or rejects the proposal.

↓

4 The Commission is then responsible for enforcing the law. Any law-breakers may be taken before the European Court of Justice, which consists of independent judges from the member states.

Food and farming

The *Common Agriculture Policy* of the European Community aims to encourage farmers and to help the home production of food (Fig. 2). Farmers are producers with special problems and they have formed important pressure groups in Europe. Food prices tend to fluctuate in an unpredictable way if the government does not intervene. If farmers go out of business because of low prices, consumers suffer in future years because there will be less food.

The EC imposes taxes on food imported from countries outside the Community. This affects Britain more than the rest of Europe because we have a very small proportion of our population working in agriculture and we used to import more food from other countries such as the USA and New Zealand.

Fig. 2 Food production in France

The Community also keeps food prices high by buying stocks of surplus food and putting these stocks into stores for future use, or selling them cheaply overseas. The Community has been successful in increasing productivity in agriculture, and this success has contributed to the problem of surpluses (Fig. 3). It does not necessarily help poor countries if wealthy countries sell them cheap food – we can drive their farmers out of business so that they face future hunger and poverty in rural areas.

Fig. 3 Tomatoes being destroyed

The destruction of food is unpopular, and there are serious problems now in both Europe and North America about what to do with the mountains of grain, and in Europe the *wine lakes* and *butter mountains* which have built up. In some cases grain and dried milk can be used for famine relief, but the European Community is embarrased by its own surpluses, and by the cost of maintaining these surpluses, and has tried to reduce agricultural production.

QUESTIONS

Surplus food

1 Why does the European Community have stocks of surplus food?
2 What can the EC do with the surplus food?
3 What are the arguments in favour of Europe importing more food from developing countries?
4 Is it never a good idea to give food to poorer countries?
5 Why does the production of food receive such special treatment by the European Community?
6 Examine the views of any pressure group or political party on the Common Agricultural Policy.

EXTENSION ACTIVITIES

1 **Choose and discuss** any issue other than agriculture. Briefly describe the policy of the EC. How does this policy affect Britain?
2 **Make a survey.** If you live in a rural area, obtain the views of a sample of farmers about the problems and benefits of the Common Agricultural Policy.

INTERNATIONAL INFLUENCES

Economic power

We have considered the idea of economic power in previous pages. We have also considered the influences on government economic policies. This unit looks at some of the international influences on the policies of countries and organisations. (See particularly Unit 7.2 on the use of power.)

There are difficulties in comparing the standard of living in developing countries (see Unit 6.1 on the standard of living). We have to take account of the differences in the way in which the statistics are measured and in their accuracy. For example, in many developing countries people grow their own food and build their own houses, and this does not appear in the statistics. But even so there are undoubted differences between the incomes of the more affluent northern countries (including Europe and North America) and the poorer countries of the Southern Hemisphere (Latin America, Africa and much of Asia).

OPEC

Some of the less affluent countries of the world increased their economic power in 1973 by agreeing together to raise the price of their main export – oil. These countries were members of the *Organisation of Petroleum Exporting Countries* (OPEC) and included Saudi Arabia, Kuwait, Libya, Iraq, Iran and Nigeria. Saudi Arabia is particularly rich in oil and influential in OPEC.

Since the 1970s other countries, including Britain and Norway, have developed their own oil exploration and development. OPEC has experienced difficulty in getting all of its members to agree to control the output of oil in order to keep the price high.

In spite of the problems of OPEC in the 1980s, and their lack of agreement on production of oil, some of the member countries (particularly Saudi Arabia) have remained wealthy and important markets for British goods and services.

Commodities

Many of the poorest countries of the world gain their income from exporting foodstuffs such as coffee, cocoa, sugarcane and tea, raw materials like rubber and minerals such as tin, copper and zinc. These unprocessed foods and materials are generally referred to as *commodities*. Some of these producer countries have attempted to agree to raise prices but with less success than OPEC.

Problems of development

The world demand for raw materials has fallen since the early 1970s and therefore prices have fallen, reducing the incomes of the poorest countries. They have also become poorer because of population growth and wars, and because they have borrowed large sums of money from banks in the developed world and the rates of interest on this debt have increased. In some cases such loans have been spent on expensive consumer goods for the most powerful élite in the country. In other cases loans were used to improve the standard of living of the people immediately, or to buy arms. However, some of the loans to developing countries have been invested to produce goods in the future, but it has become harder to sell those goods as incomes have fallen. Some people say that the international trading system works in such a way that the rich countries get richer and the poor get poorer. (See also Unit 7.8 on representatives and elites and Unit 6.2 on economic growth.)

There are a variety of ways of helping the poorest countries of the world. First, we can increase our imports from these countries, and this will provide them with incomes to develop their economies and buy goods from abroad. A second type of help takes the form of loans to the developing countries. Some loans are made by individual governments, but others are made through an international organisation to which many countries contribute, known as the *World Bank* (also called the International Bank for Reconstruction and Development). A third possibility is to give aid, either directly by governments or through international organisations and development agencies.

Some international aid is *tied* so that it must be spent on particular items from the country providing the aid. When Britain provides aid in this way it obviously helps British exports and therefore provides jobs in Britain. It is often not the most useful form of aid for the developing country.

Some writers have argued that, because the world's

Fig. 1 Small farmers using fibre reinforced irrigation channels, with technical assistance from a western aid agency.

resources are limited and economic growth often leads to damage to the environment, all of us in the developed world must return to a simpler life-style. It has been said that the types of project which should be encouraged in developing countries are small-scale development projects (such as providing wells, and improvements in the recycling of waste) to help rural communities (Fig. 1). These views are particularly associated with pressure groups concerned about the environment.

QUESTIONS

Power and development

1 Why did OPEC have the power to raise prices?
2 Why have the poorer countries of the world been unable to increase their standard of living?
3 How could the richer countries of the world help the poorer countries?
4 What does Britain gain by providing aid to developing countries?
5 Can you suggest any ways in which people in Britain could return to a simpler life-style?

Multinationals

Multinational companies are very large companies which have operations (factories, warehouses and offices) in several different countries. They include large United States companies such as Exxon (which owns Esso), General Motors (which owns Vauxhall), Ford and IBM. Some British companies are multinationals, including BP, and the joint British–Dutch enterprises of Shell and Unilever. Most of the larger oil companies and banks are now multinationals, and some of the growing multinationals in recent years have been Japanese companies such as Hitachi and Sony.

The larger multinationals have incomes which are greater than those of many countries in the world. They have immense power to move their wealth from one country to another if they are unhappy about any political or economic developments. They can search the world for the cheapest raw materials and labour, and for new markets.

Multinationals have been accused of giving less consideration to safety in other countries than they would in their own country. It has been alleged that this was so in the case of an explosion at a chemical factory owned by an American company operating in India, which led to considerable loss of life and injuries. There has also been criticism of their marketing techniques, particularly the marketing of dried milk for babies in developing countries. In some of these countries the mothers did not have access to water which was sufficiently clean for mixing artificial baby milk and would have been better advised to breast-feed. Pharmaceutical companies have also been criticised for the over-pricing and testing of drugs in developing countries.

In spite of these and other criticisms, governments have often welcomed foreign companies into their country because these companies provide management skills, jobs and, in some cases, investment (Fig. 2).

Fig. 2 A team meeting area in a Japanese company in Britain

EXTENSION ACTIVITIES

1 **Investigate** a multinational company. Find out what it produces and where. Answer as many of the following questions as possible.

   a) Has the company been involved in any political issues, such as leaving South Africa?
   b) Has the company increased or reduced its employment of people in Britain in recent years?
   c) Has it been discussed in the newspapers because of its policies or effects on any country?
   d) Has it had any effect on people's tastes or ways of eating and living?

2 **Work in groups** to form the boards of directors of a chain of supermarkets which sells South African goods and a chain of cinemas with branches in South Africa.

   a) Decide what action you would take in view of the political situation in South Africa.
   b) The secretary of each board should make a record of and report back to the class on the decisions made and the arguments which were put forward for and against these decisions.

3 **Find out** about any international organisation – for example, the United Nations, the North Atlantic Treaty Organisation (NATO) or an international agency or pressure group such as Greenpeace, War on Want, the International Red Cross, the World Wildlife Fund or Band-Aid. (See also Unit 4.11 on Poverty.)

   a) Find out what its aims are, and how it seeks to achieve them.
   b) Is it a pressure group which seeks to influence governments and international organisations? (Give examples of its activities.)
   c) Does it have any power or authority?
   d) What are its effects?

THE INDIVIDUAL AND SOCIETY

Society and human nature

In Britain there are 55 million people, each an individual. There are also many different groups – racial and ethnic groups, social classes, occupational groups, income groups, political and religious groups. All these individuals and groups do not always agree; in fact, some might say that it is a sign of life in a society that arguments and disputes arise. However, we are not in a constant state of civil war or revolution, and in spite of the diversity our society is fairly stable. If you think about it, this is a remarkable situation – so much difference, but there is still order.

For hundreds of years there has been disagreement about the basic quality of human nature. Some people have argued that human beings are basically selfish, and that they have to be forced to co-operate with each other – through, for example, strong laws and effective policing. On the other hand, some have said that human beings are basically reasonable creatures, who will co-operate when they see the need for it. The truth probably lies somewhere in between the two theories.

If people are to live together in a society, they need to agree on a basic set of rules to go by. And those among them who try to break the rules need to be prevented from doing so or persuaded to accept them. There are various ways by which society ensures that its rules are followed, and through the process of *socialisation* (see Sections 2 and 3), via the family, the school, religious bodies and other agencies, most people come to accept that both the rules and the way they are enforced are mostly fair and reasonable.

Social control

Society has ways of making us follow its rules. This is called *social control*. There are two types of social control: *formal* social control, which consists of special agents appointed to make us keep the rules, such as the police or the army; and *informal* methods of social control, which work through ideas and behaviour.

Formal social control

Fig. 2 The Army

Fig. I The Police

Fig. 3 Traffic warden

6   If you walked around with your finger up your nose or your hand held high in the air, how would you know that you were breaking the informal rules of your school or college? Make a list of the ways people might put pressure on you to stop, i.e. conform.

Norms

Informal social controls are less easy than formal controls to define and detect. The most important are *norms*. These are approved patterns of behaviour which we are taught by the family, the school or other agencies. If we break a norm we are not formally punished, but people show their disapproval.

If you behaved oddly, perhaps in the way described in the last question, you would see people frowning at you, being sarcastic, laughing at you. These are all ways we make each other conform.

Sociologists have divided norms into two types. *Mores* are norms which are considered very important and they are often concerned with moral behaviour; for example, not to hurt people or break a promise. Some mores are considered so important they have been made into laws. The other type of norms are *customs*. These are traditional ways of behaving, such as shaking hands or sending birthday-cards.

QUESTIONS

1   What is the name of the set of rules all these agents enforce?   [1]
2   Name the agents of formal social control shown in Figs. 1, 2 and 3.   [3]
3   Give three reasons why we obey the agent shown in Fig. 1.   [3]
4   Which of these agents is the least popular? Give reasons for your choice.   [5]
5   What functions do these agents perform in our society? Why so some people not accept them?   [8]

Informal social control

The formal agencies of social control have to act only when informal methods break down. Most of us, for most of the time, follow the rules of society. The reason why we do this is that we are controlled, or persuaded, by informal methods. Often we do not realise that we are being controlled in this way.

EXTENSION ACTIVITIES

1   **Write explanations**, using examples of your own, of what is meant by norms, mores and customs.
2   **Compare** formal and informal methods of social control.
3   **Discuss** whether we should encourage people or discourage people from being different.
4   **Devise an experiment** to test informal social control. For example, behave or dress in a peculiar way. Make a note of the reactions of different people, what they say to you and how they act. Also be aware of your own feelings, whether you feel embarrassed, and how you feel when you have stopped breaking the norms of your group.
5   **Investigate** one of the agents of formal control: the police, the army or the courts. Think of the best method for your study and explain why you have chosen it. Describe the methods of control the agency uses – both formal and informal. Try to arrange to visit and talk to members of your chosen agency. Ask them how they feel about enforcing society's rules, who are the easiest people to control and who are the hardest. Record your own feelings about the agency.

SOCIAL CONTROL AND SOCIAL CHANGE

Agencies of socialisation and social control

Many of the organisations in our society that we have looked at, such as the family and the school, are agencies of *socialisation*. A further aspect of their role is *social control*. In fact, it is hard to say where socialisation ends and social control begins. For example, schools both try to teach people to understand the reasons for society's rules and at the same time enforce their own rules.

Fig. 1 shows society's main agencies of socialisation and social control. Some of them, for example the mass media, are more agents of socialisation than of control; they form opinions but have little power to control people directly. Other agencies, such as the army and the legal system, are much more agencies of control than of socialisation.

Social change

A society is a living thing, because it is made up of living people. All living things grow, change and adapt. A society that never changed would become extinct, like the dinosaurs.

Our society has changed greatly over the centuries, and change has been especially fast during the twentieth century. One reason has been the need to adapt to the different needs of individuals and groups.

The process of change is not always easy. It usually comes about through disagreements between different groups in the society, one group arguing for one way of doing things and another arguing for a different way. In a democratic society like Britain, the majority of the population are usually able to decide on the outcome of such disputes – although this is not always a very straightforward process.

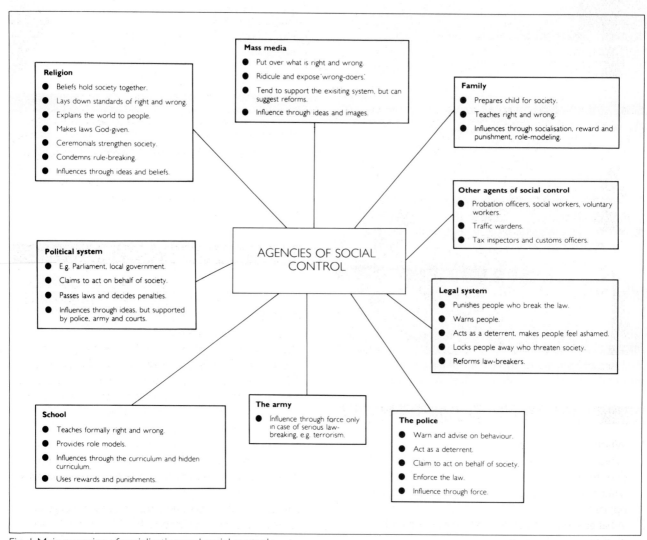

Fig. 1 Main agencies of socialisation and social control

Fig. 2 Women peace demonstrators at Greenham Common

Fig. 3 Archbishop Desmond Tutu

QUESTIONS

1 Which are the two social groups shown in Fig. 2? [2]
2 Which is the agency of social control shown in Fig. 3? How does the practice of religion by the man in Fig. 3 seem to differ from that suggested for religion in the diagram opposite? [2]
3 What government policies do the people in each photograph disagree with? [2]
4 Give four methods used by both of these groups to get the law changed. [4]
5 If you wanted to change a rule in your school, how would you go about it? [4]
6 How do you feel about the aims and methods of either of the groups shown in the photographs? [6]

EXTENSION ACTIVITIES

1 **Write** about any two agencies of social control and the methods they use to prevent people from breaking rules.
2 **Compare** the police and the school as agents of socialisation and social control.
3 **Make a study** of one type of law-breaking, e.g. soccer hooliganism, vandalism or drugs. Find out the extent of the problem both nationally and locally. What actions are being taken to prevent it? Look at research studies on it. Look at how it is dealt with in the media.
4 **Investigate** the influence of religion today. Draw up a questionnaire and carry out a small survey to find out how important an influence religion is on people's lives. Attend a religious service and analyse how it encourages co-operative behaviour.
5 **Discuss** the following statement: 'Too much change in society is as dangerous as too little.' Give examples and reasons for your views.

APPROACHES TO CRIME AND DEVIANCE

Deviance, delinquency and law-breaking

Minor differences in how people behave are often not commented on. But if we do something that is very different from other people we may be called funny, queer, eccentric or even *deviant*. There can be no clear definition of what is deviant, since this is a matter for the opinion of a particular group or society. It is not always the behaviour itself that is deviant, but more a question of where and when it takes place and what other people think about it.

Many students confuse deviancy with *delinquency*. Delinquency is just one type of deviant behaviour: behaviour by young people which breaks the law. The age at which young law-breakers are considered delinquents rather than adult criminals has changed over time. At present, offenders younger than eighteen are treated in a special way by the courts.

Most of us break the law in little ways – throwing down litter on the pavements, for example. The problem arises among the minority of the population who break the law in ways that are a serious danger to the rest of us. A number of different explanations of criminal behaviour have been suggested.

Explanations for crime

One of the earliest theories, which has now been discredited, is that criminals were born 'different' from other people. Signs of this abnormality were said to include large heads, ugly faces and slanting eyes. This view sounds silly to us now, especially because, as we have seen, so much human behaviour is learned, not born with us.

Environmental explanations

Another approach has been to suggest that criminal behaviour is largely a result of the environment where people live. In general, there is a close connection between city or community size and the crime rate; the larger the town or city, the higher the crime rate. The reasons seem to be that low-income people who live in large cities are usually crowded together in poor-quality housing with poor facilities, e.g. inadequate parks and open spaces. In these environments, social problems multiply, resulting in much more crime than elsewhere.

QUESTIONS

1 In which kind of community are people likely to be safest from the risk of crime? [2]
2 Is the total crime rate worse for medium-size towns than for England and Wales overall? Is the *serious* crime rate worse for medium-size towns than for England and Wales overall? [2]
3 In your own words, describe how the crime rate seems to be related to city or community size. [4]

Fig. 1 Crime rates and population size, England and Wales, 1965

Community size	Total crimes per 1,000 population	Serious crimes per 1,000 population*
London	3,378	1,565
Large cities (pop. more than 400,000)	3,327	1,365
Large towns (pop. 200,000–400,000)	3,333	867
Medium-size towns (pop. 100,000–200,000)	2,795	741
Small towns (pop. up to 100,000)	2,544	584
Rural areas	1,747	510
England and Wales average	2,374	788

* Includes crimes of violence and robbery.

From F.H. McClintock and N.H. Avison, *Crime in England and Wales* (Heinemann, 1968).

4 The figures in Fig. 1 are from more than twenty years ago. From what you have read in the newspapers or seen on television, would you say that crime rates have fallen, stayed about the same, risen a little or risen a great deal? Can you suggest reasons for any change? [4]

5 Give four reasons for the pattern described in your answer to question 4. [4]

Subcultural explanations

Related to environmental explanations of crime are *sub-cultural* ones. Sociologists say that another reason for crime being most common among working-class groups (in addition to poor environment) is that working-class people develop ideas and values different from those of the rest of the population. Such subcultural values as being tough or 'smart' may lead working-class people into conflict with the law. However, it is probable that without an environment that was worse than that enjoyed by the rest of society, such people would not feel the need to develop a subculture.

The deviance approach

This approach looks at how the law is applied to people by the police and other agents. Certain behaviour may be acceptable in some cases and not in others, where the people involved may be classified as *deviant*. This suggests that the law is not always applied justly or fairly. For example, for many years prostitutes walking the streets looking for customers have been arrested by the police, whereas men who cruise in cars looking for prostitutes have not been accused of law-breaking. Another example of society's 'double standards' is shown in Figs. 2 and 3.

Fig. 3

QUESTIONS

6 Describe what is happening in each photograph and which laws are being broken. [9]

7 Who do you think is more likely to be arrested and charged: the people in Fig. 2 or those in Fig. 3? Why? [4]

8 How do police officers such as those shown in the photographs, get their ideas on who is likely to be a criminal? [4]

9 Describe an incident with the police which you have seen or been involved in. Explain what happened, using the deviance approach. [8]

EXTENSION ACTIVITIES

Find out and write an account of one explanation of criminal behaviour.

2 **Debate** these two issues:

a) What should be done to reduce the crime rate?

b) Which of the present laws would you get rid of and why?

3 **Describe** how you would change the environment of the inner cities to reduce the amount of urban crime.

4 **Make a study** of the police. Why are they obeyed? What does society expect of them? What powers do they have? Do we expect too much from them? Interview two policemen and policewomen about how they carry out their duties. What do they think are the main causes of crime and the best possible solutions?

Fig. 2

CLASS, CRIME AND GENDER

We are all aware that crimes are committed by all sections of the population – poor and rich, men and women, black and white. But the crime rates for different groups vary. In this unit we look at two of these differences, those between social classes and between sexes.

Social class and crime

QUESTIONS

1 Which occupational group has the highest delinquency rate and which the lowest? [2]
2 How useful is it to list all crimes together in this way? [2]
3 Divide the occupations into middle class and working class and work out the delinquency rate for each class. [3 each]
4 What relationship do your answers to question 3 show between delinquency and social class? [3]

5 Look at the date of this research. How useful is it for sociologists thinking about crime today? [2]
6 Do you think the findings would be the same today? Give reasons for your answer. [5]

Explanations of class patterns of crime

Why is the crime rate higher among the working class than the middle class?

Fig. 1 has shown that a greater percentage of working-class youths are convicted of crime than youths from other social classes. The theories and explanations of crime which were outlined in Unit 4.13 can be used to explain this.

QUESTIONS

7 Look back at Unit 4.13 and then complete the following table by thinking how each theory may be more applicable to the working class. The last theory listed in the table was not covered in Unit 4.13, so you will have to try to work this one out by yourself.

Fig. 1 Percentage delinquency rate of boys grouped by father's occupation

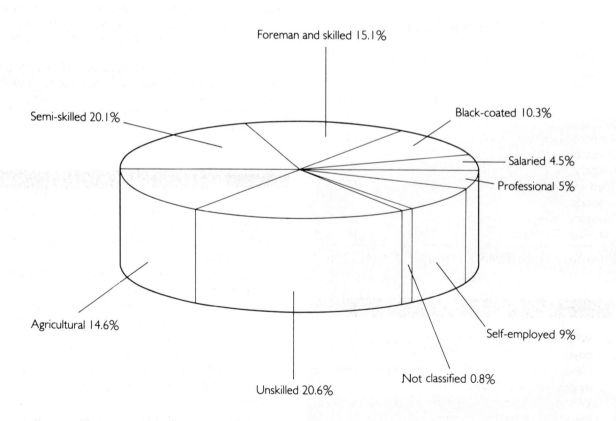

Foreman and skilled 15.1%

Black-coated 10.3%

Semi-skilled 20.1%

Salaried 4.5%

Professional 5%

Agricultural 14.6%

Self-employed 9%

Not classified 0.8%

Unskilled 20.6%

Adapted from J.W. Douglas *et al.*, 'Delinquency and Social Class', *British Journal of Criminology*, vol. 6, no. 3, (Oxford University Press, 1966), p. 294.

| | Explanations | Why the working class |

Environmental
(certain areas of towns and cities encourage crime)

Subcultures
(some groups in society have different values which can lead to crime)

Deviance approach
(the laws are applied in different ways to different groups)

Statistical
(lack of adequate knowledge about the distribution of crime)

Middle-class delinquency

Although delinquency rates are lower among middle-class youngsters, they still commit some crime. The theories we have outlined so far are not very good for explaining this. However, one theory by an American sociologist, Albert Cohen, in his book *Delinquent Boys*, suggested that middle-class delinquency happened because these youths had time on their hands when the standards required to get into college were reduced in the 1960s. Instead of having to study very hard, they could get in with less effort, so they began to form middle-class youth groups. The groups were interested in motor bikes, cars, parties, drinking and drugs, and these led them into trouble.

Gender and crime

Fig. 2 Percentage of young people aged 17–21 found guilty of, or cautioned for, indictable offences (1984)

	Males %	Females %
Violence against the person	29	22
Sexual offences	19	14
Burglary	31	27
Theft and handling stolen goods	23	15
Fraud and forgery	21	25
Motoring offences	23	14

From *Social Trends* (HMSO, 1986), p. 188, table 12.9.

QUESTIONS

8 Which offence was committed more by girls than by boys? [1]
9 Name one offence which you think is mainly committed by girls which is not listed here. [2]
10 Why are males more likely to be charged with violence against the person than females? [4]
11 Why are more males than females convicted of motoring offences? [4]
12 Explain the differences between the sexes in fraud and forgery offences. [4]
13 Fig. 2 combines people who are cautioned and those who are found guilty. Why are females more likely to be cautioned and let off than males? [5]

Problems with the figures on female crime

We can never find out the full number of criminals in society because a great deal of crime is unsolved and some is not reported. However, we do know that the amount of female crime is underestimated. Some crime, such as child cruelty and neglect, or poisoning, does not come to light. In other cases, men are unwilling to report that they have been robbed by a woman because it makes them look foolish.

In some crimes, such as fighting and drunkenness, which involve men and women, the latter are less likely to be arrested. On the other hand, figures for female prostitution seem higher than for males, because the police do not charge male prostitutes with this offence.

EXTENSION ACTIVITIES

1 **Choose** any crime which is committed mainly by males or mainly by females and explain why this is so.
2 **Write** an explanation for why boys are apparently more delinquent than girls.
3 **Discuss** whether prisons and reform schools should be single-sex institutions or mixed.
4 **Investigate** the 'short, sharp shock' system of punishment for young offenders. Explain what it was and why it was set up. Find how successful it has been. (You might find some useful information for this activity in *New Society*.)
5 **Prepare and carry out** a survey to compare the attitudes of boys and girls to the police. Prepare a short questionnaire, choose a suitable sample and then process your results. You could also choose samples from different age groups. Display your results in a suitable way.

INDEX